A Birder's
GUIDE TO JAPAN

By Jane Washburn Robinson

Ibis Publishing Company
Santa Monica, California 90401

Ibis Publishing Company
712 Wilshire Boulevard, Suite 1008
Santa Monica, CA 90401

ISBN No. 0-934797-02-1

To Robin

CONTENTS

PREFACE

They didn't identify themselves, so it is even unclear whether the higher powers responsible were Occidental or Oriental, but it does seem clear that my involvement with birding in Japan was destined. Shortly after I learned that I was moving to Japan, I met Ben King at the American Museum of Natural History in New York. He gave me the name of the prominent Japanese ornithologist, Mr. Masashi Yoshii of the Yamashina Institute for Ornithology. Ben cautioned that I should not trouble Yoshii-san with questions about birding in Japan, but I could telephone him, if I made it brief, to ask where I could go for information. I placed the card he wrote for me in my wallet without even noting the city in which the Yamashina Institute was located. But I knew where to find the card when I needed it.

Shortly thereafter, I made a preliminary trip to Japan to find a place to live. I spent ten days looking at 74 totally unacceptable places. It was hot, and I was discouraged and quite unhappy with Japan and everything Japanese. I saw number 75, the first one worthy of consideration, on my twenty-fifth wedding anniversary. To make matters worse, my husband had been taken by his company on a two-week grand tour of Japan, and I was neither invited nor allowed to go (the Japanese way). Somehow, it had never occurred to me that I would spend this anniversary alone in Tokyo.

The apartment which looked promising was under construction. I wanted to look at it again without the company of the people who were showing me around. If I could find it, I could get inside. So, with the day's list of places to see exhausted quite early, I set out alone on the subway to find a building in Tokyo at an unknown address.

Passengers getting off the Ginza subway line at Shibuya Station (one of the largest in Japan) find themselves on the third floor of a department store. I knew I was in a department store, but to one who could read no Japanese, the way out was far from obvious. Neither one flight up nor one flight down will do the trick.

I eventually found my way outside by, as fate would have it, the proper exit. I checked the configuration of roads coming into the station against my map, determined I was on the side of the station I should be, chose a road, and took off. I had walked without hesitation for about two blocks, still with at least 8,000 people in view without turning my head, when a man stepped out in front of me and said, "Pardon me, madam, are you lost?"

I certainly had been lost, but I didn't feel lost then and was surprised that I appeared to him to be lost. I replied, "No, thank you, I think I know where I am, but it was kind of you to ask," and started off.

"But where are you going?" said he. Well, how was I supposed to answer that? There was no way I could tell him where I was going without telling him a great deal more than I felt prepared to discuss with a strange man on the street. So I stood there looking blank.

"Are you going to the Philippine Embassy?"

"No."

"Are you going to church?"

"No."

"Then where are you going?"

By then I had figured out a response. I pointed to my map and said, "I am going to that neighborhood. Is it in this direction?"

"Yes."

"Good. Then I am not lost. Thank you very much."

"I will go with you and make sure you get to the right place."

There followed a five-minute discussion before I finally managed to convince this man that I appreciated his concern, but his help was not required. Undoubtedly, I left him thinking he had encountered a most peculiar woman.

Within fifteen minutes, I found the apartment. I spent a good deal of time examining, measuring, and trying to imagine what it would look like when finished. Then I set out to investigate the neighborhood. Tokyo is not like any city I knew, so I didn't know how to make a judgment. I began searching for someone I could talk to who could discuss the good and bad points of the area, but of course I could find no one who spoke English.

After a couple of hours, I gave up and headed back to Shibuya Station. I had gone no more than a block and a half from the apartment when I saw the same man walking toward me.

"Ah, it is you again."

"Yes," I replied, this time more eager to talk. "Do you live in this neighborhood?"

"No, but I work here at the Yamashina Institute for Ornithology." In response to my gasp he added, "Do you know it?"

I began to explain about having been given the name of someone there by Ben King. While I was rummaging in my purse to find my wallet, this man was telling me that he, too, knew Ben King. I handed him the card, his face drained of color, and he said, "But, I am Yoshii."

With that, he invited me to come to his office and have some tea. His invitation was immediately accepted, and there it all began. I knew at that moment my life in Japan was going to turn out very well. In a city where twelve million people live and another twelve million come every day to work, our meeting, not once but twice, cannot have been simply an accident.

From then my luck changed. The next day I found the apartment which became our home, and everything fell into place. One thing led to another. Before long I was asked by the Wild Bird Society of Japan to edit the *Field Guide to the Birds of Japan*. As soon as that book was published, the WBSJ asked me to write a bird-finding guide to Japan. That kept me occupied until we left Japan, sadly, three years later.

These tasks gave me exposure to Japanese people and aspects of Japanese culture seldom available to a foreigner. I traveled to obscure places from one end of Japan to the other, meeting the local birders and encountering the local people, many of whom had never met a foreigner before. I enjoyed the birding, but getting to know these people and their country has enriched my life. I am grateful.

Any book of this nature requires the help of a great many people, but this one required extraordinary effort on the part of those who set out to assist me. I had to gather all this information in a language I was trying to learn while I was doing the work, and I had to get it by asking, rather than reading. Learning to read Japanese well is the occupation of a lifetime.

I am deeply appreciative of all the Japanese who were patient and kind enough to struggle to communicate with me. It had to be difficult for them to figure out what I was trying to say and to phrase their responses in a way simple enough for me to understand. And the Japanese who spoke English were surely overcome by the deluge of questions I posed to them.

I want to thank Noritaka Ichida and Koichiro Sonobe and the other members of the staff of the Wild Bird Society of Japan who got me started on this project. They gave me a basic introduction to the best birding areas in the country, told me the most likely places for finding difficult birds, and arranged for me to meet members of the society throughout Japan. In addition, members of the staff often invited me to accompany them on trips and helped me gather information. I particularly want to thank those who took the time to find checklists and detailed maps for the areas I was considering and who cheerfully answered my questions and helped me solve many problems.

I am most indebted to the ornithologists and birdwatchers of Japan who taught me about their own areas. Many spent considerable time taking me or directing me to all the best places and giving me information about the birds which can be expected in each season.

It is difficult to express adequately my appreciation of those people who entertained me in their homes and those who, when they learned that I was coming to their area, invited me to stay overnight in their homes. The Japanese people were exceptionally thoughtful and generous, and saw to it that I had a wide variety of cultural experiences while I was gathering information for this book. I am particularly grateful to those who, despite our differences and the difficulties of communication, have offered true friendship.

Everyone who had a part in this book cannot be named here. In fact, I never learned the names of some of the birders I met in the field who made significant contributions. But I remember and wish to thank each person who was kind enough to speak to me and help in any way.

I owe very special thanks first to Yoshii-san for being the instrument of the gods and for the many kindnesses he and his wife have shown me, to Ben King for starting it all off, and, in fact, to Stuart Keith for sending me to Ben in the first place, and to Hideaki Anzai, Gen Eguchi, Kazunori Fujimoto, Hiroshi Furukawa, Shinichi Hanawa, Tsuneo Hayashida, Akira Hoshino, Yuichi Hoshino, Mitsuru Hyakutake, Chieko Katsura, Momoki Kawabe, Tadao Kawasaki, Reiki Kobayashi, Yoshihisa Kubota, Takeyoshi Matsuo, Hiromu Ohara, Misako Ohara, Takako Saito, Kimio Satoh, Masao Satoh, Katsuaki Shibahara, Tadashi Shimada, Hisashi Sugawa, Takeshi Sugimoto, Tsutomu Suzuki, Nobuaki Tabata, Fukiko Tagawa, Koichi Tagawa, Masaru Takada, the late Shinji Takano, Tsuyako Takano, Yoshitaka Takatsuki, Munenari Takeda, Michihiro Tazawa, Yozo Tsukamoto, Mamoru Tsuneda, Shunji Usui, Shin Yoshida, and Tomie Yoshikane.

Doug McWhirter not only guided me around Okinawa, but he also did much of my work there for me, making all the mileage measurements, drawing maps showing exactly where we had been, and sharing with me the material he had prepared on Okinawa birds. Subsequently, in phone conversations between Tokyo and Okinawa, Doug was the source of valuable advice and moral support. It was a great help to have such a knowledgeable fellow countryman available with whom I could communicate effortlessly when I encountered a problem.

There were three people without whom I could not have done this book. They are Keiko Kawai, Kanae Miura, and Michiko Mori.

My principal teachers, Keiko Kawai and Kanae Miura, made the study of the Japanese language a joy instead of the struggle it might have been. Because they are extraordinarily skilled, they were able very quickly to teach me enough of the language so I could travel alone and gather information. I appreciate the extra work they took on in order to tailor my lessons to prepare me for specific tasks I had to perform. They often went to great lengths to help me. The culmination was a trip to my apartment on the last moving day to write all the *kanji* in this book while sitting on the floor using packing boxes for desks.

But perhaps even more important than language skills, they taught me how to function in the Japanese society, explaining our cultural differences and how the Japanese people I encountered would expect me to behave. Although I failed continually to do things in true Japanese fashion, I owe my acceptance by many of the people I met to their patient teaching. These two were the ones I always turned to for advice when I found myself in unusual or difficult situations arising from misunderstandings or differences in value systems. They were always sympathetic and helpful. They both are treasured friends.

Michiko Mori has assisted me in endless ways for more than three years. Her aid has been invaluable. She has made countless telephone calls for me, gathering information, making arrangements, and checking facts. She did all the formal translations that I required and spent many hours reading articles in Japanese and telling me what was in them. Often, she helped me with things just because it made my work easier, and I always turned to Mori-san when I needed something I could not do for myself or get any other way. She never failed to accomplish the task. Throughout it all, Mori-san responded to my requests willingly and cheerfully, and provided what was needed with extraordinary efficiency.

The Japan National Travel Organization has provided a great deal of information and support. I particularly want to thank Takashi Nagaoka, Manager, Public Relations, for his interest in this project and for his advice and assistance; Mrs. Suamatsu of the Tokyo Tourist Information Center (TIC) for finding answers to long lists of questions regarding accommodations and transportation in parts of Japan no foreign tourist had ever inquired about before; and all the members of the staff who have given aid.

Above all, I thank my husband for his constant and immeasurable help and encouragement.

INTRODUCTION

The purpose of this book is to make the birds of Japan accessible at last to birdwatchers of the world who are unable to read or understand the Japanese language. It is intended to be used in conjunction with the *Field Guide to the Birds of Japan*, published in 1982 by the Wild Bird Society of Japan (WBSJ). That book, for the first time, provided a complete identification guide in English to all the species known to occur in Japan, but a visitor must know a great deal more than which birds to expect and how to identify them.

Japan may be the most difficult country in the world to travel in alone without knowledge of the language. Finding out where to find birds in Japan and then how to get to these places has been an almost insurmountable problem for foreign visitors.

I have selected what I consider to be the best birding areas in Japan, along with places where scarce or highly local species may be found. I consulted ornithologists, expert birders, and the staff of the WBSJ to get recommendations of places to consider for inclusion in this book. I then gathered all the published checklists which could be located and translated them to get further information about good birding areas. I visited more than 150 of these birding spots and made my own assessment of their importance and interest to visiting birders. The site guides give the information you will need in order to choose the places of most interest to you. Residents will want to become acquainted with the local birders and learn of other good places, but short-time visitors to Japan in any season will find more places recommended here than there will be time to visit.

To minimize confusion, the bird names in this book are identical to those in the field guide. Mention is made, however, of some differences of opinion regarding species between Japanese ornithologists and other authorities.

No checklists showing distribution and abundance are included because it is impossible to ensure accuracy. Japanese birders, as a whole, have not yet concerned themselves with keeping, compiling, and publishing detailed records. The checklists vary widely in their completeness and accuracy. Although some are excellent, many give absolutely no indication of abundance or the season when the bird occurs. The only checklists available for many areas cover sightings over extremely short periods of time.

Even knowing where to go to find the birds you want to see is not enough. Being able to determine the best way to travel, make the necessary arrangements, find the way, and take care of yourself while there is of equal importance. This book gives directions in such detail that, without any knowledge of the Japanese language, you should be able to get exactly where you mean to go. To do any serious birding in Japan, you will find yourself immersed in the local culture and forced to deal with Japanese food and restaurants, Japanese-style accommodations, beds, baths, and toilets, and Japanese people with whom you will have no words in common. I have included the practical information which I discovered a birder needs to know (but can't find out easily) in order to function in Japan.

This book is not intended to be a hotel or restaurant guide, but it does give information about places to stay near good birding areas and advice on what to do about food. The prices indicated will give you a way of estimating what you must pay. When you plan your trip, if you can determine the current cost of some things, it should be safe to assume that everything has increased by a similar percentage. Actually, in the last few years, with the exception of transportation costs, prices have remained fairly constant. Exchange rates, however, have fluctuated widely. Schedules are included only to give a rough idea of what you can expect in the number of services per day and the length of time required for a journey. Always check for the latest schedule.

The information here will help you understand what to expect so you will not be surprised or disappointed, and it will enable you to make intelligent decisions about where and when to go and the best way for you to travel. The difficulties are made clear, along with ways to overcome them. While you can use this book to travel independently in Japan, it will be equally useful if it helps you to realize that is not for you. Some people will prefer to go with a group and let someone else be responsible. I hope your birding in Japan is a complete success and you won't have to say, "If I had only known, I would have done it differently."

Foreign residents and visitors to Japan who have no particular interest in birdwatching, but who want to explore on their own far away from the tourist beat, will find much here that is useful. The site guides describe many places of natural beauty or cultural interest which anyone would enjoy. And even non-birders will appreciate the spectacle and beauty of such things as concentrations of cranes and sea-eagles. The directions to these places, along with the information on how to get along Japanese style, will open up many new possibilities for those who want to experience the real Japan.

BIRDWATCHING IN JAPAN

Birdwatching in Japan is considerably different from birdwatching in most countries. Not only do the local birders have somewhat different goals, but also the procedure for finding birds is different due to the population density.

Japan extends almost 3,000 kilometers from the northern tip of Hokkaido, near Sakhalin, to the island of Iriomote in the south, next to Taiwan. The latitude is about the same as from Bangor, Maine, to Havana, Cuba. From the southern islands to the high mountains, there are many life zones and an enormous variety of vegetation. More than 525 species of birds have been officially recorded in Japan, including at least 11 endemic species (depending on how you count). Many are difficult for birders to see elsewhere because travel is either limited or prohibited in much of the rest of their range. Nevertheless, a visitor to Japan who follows the route of the average tourist will be able to see only a handful of the birds of Japan.

After looking around the Tokyo area, you may be convinced that the entire country is concrete. Even the banks of many waterways (all of them in the cities) are clad in concrete. And you often see six-foot-high concrete tetrapods, like gigantic jacks, lining the shores and the mouths of rivers. To a newcomer, it seems to be impossible to get away from the urban ugliness. It is possible, but one is unlikely to do it by accident. There is spectacular scenery and fine birding habitat left in Japan, but you must know where to look.

Japan is not like many countries where you can make your way out of the cities, find some promising habitat, and expect to see birds. Except in parts of Hokkaido and on some of the small islands away from the four main islands, it is almost always fruitless to wander about at random searching for birds. And it is never worth driving all the way to your destination solely to look for birds along the way. You will seldom see birds of any interest while traveling between one birding spot and another.

The good habitat is seriously limited. The total area of Japan is roughly 87% that of California, but the population is about half that of the United States. With over 80% of the land so mountainous it is unsuitable for either cultivation or human habitation, Japan has little accessible territory which is not densely populated. It is necessary, therefore, to plan a birdwatching trip carefully and head for spots where the birds are known to be. Even then, you will not see birds in the numbers often found in other countries. People accustomed to vast expanses of undeveloped areas are often surprised to see how small some of Japan's most famous and productive birding spots actually are.

The site guides will tell you how to get to the best birding spots, where to find the species which regularly occur in Japan, and where to look for those which occasionally make an appearance. But you must also know where not to go. Japan is a country where few tourists, either foreign or Japanese, wander about on their own. Most foreigners think the language problem is insurmountable, so they choose to travel in groups. Why the Japanese do it is beyond the scope of this book, but believe me, they do it.

Somehow, certain places have been selected as appropriate destinations for sightseers, while others of equal attractiveness and possibly more interest have not. At one of these chosen spots, you will see little, if anything, besides countless tour buses, throngs of people, and more souvenir shops than you can believe. Occasionally, if the area in question is big enough, birdwatching is still possible because the buses don't stay long and the passengers don't stray far. As is true throughout the world, if you hike some distance from the roads, you leave the crowds behind. (This does not apply during the summer vacation when groups set out to go camping, hiking, or mountain climbing. And, of course, stay out of areas where people go for seasonal sports such as skiing.)

Famous scenic spots and places popular with tourists (Japanese and foreign) are best avoided, with some exceptions. You must not be deceived about national parks. Japanese tourists go to some of them in droves, so the crowds, as well as the facilities which are added to take care of them, do much to destroy the natural beauty and the reason for going in the first place.

The attitude of the Japanese government toward national parks differs from what many of us would expect. There are three classes of national parks in Japan. Only in one class is development totally prohibited. In another class, the only requirement is that any construction or development be reported.

In parks belonging to the third class, permission must be received before anything can be built. Some say this is hard to obtain, but it happens all the time and appears to be of little concern. Approval was given recently to reclaim part of a bay which is included in a national park (set aside originally because of its great scenic beauty) in order to construct a governmental crude oil storage center. Don't expect to find untouched wilderness areas in every national park.

It is difficult for many of us to understand why the Japanese people, well known for their regard for nature, have allowed the destruction of their natural environment to such an extent. This is because most outsiders have not examined the Japanese attitude toward nature and don't understand what appreciation of nature really means to them. The Japanese do not regard nature in the same way as many of us do. I find it a fascinating philosophical concept, and an acquaintance with it explains much that I have seen in the country that I wish had not happened.

Japanese birders don't all have a desire to leave crowds of people behind and go to quiet, undisturbed areas for birding. The purposes and approach to birdwatching of many Japanese are significantly different from those of most Western birders. Many of the places the Japanese go regularly in large groups are unlikely to appeal to a visiting birdwatcher. You may hear about "bird parks" which are not included in the site guides. I found most to be too crowded, too commercial, or otherwise lacking in appeal to visiting birders. There are no species likely to be found in the majority of the bird parks to make it worth overlooking the unpleasant aspects and going anyway. The ones which are excluded have been excluded deliberately.

But don't be discouraged. There are lovely, undisturbed areas and excellent birding spots in Japan. By making your way to them, in addition to birds, gorgeous wildflowers, beautiful scenery, and traditional architecture, you will see aspects of Japanese life and culture completely unknown to most foreign visitors.

WHEN TO COME

There should be good birding in Japan in all seasons, but sometimes the birder must surrender to the great crowds of people. It is necessary to escape from the cities, but, even more important, the birdwatcher must escape from people. During certain times of the year, this is impossible, and birders are better off not to come. The Japanese believe there is a right time for everything, and then they all do it together. This makes the crowds predictable, so the visitor can avoid the problem.

The long school holiday is from the middle of July until the beginning of September. Although birds must be around somewhere, the serious birder should avoid Japan during that period. If families don't take holidays together at that time, they send their children off, usually with school groups. No matter how remote a place you have chosen to visit, you will find it inundated with thousands of children and other assorted groups.

The children in each group wear identical hats. You will be passed on the trail by 200 children in red hats, then, immediately behind them, by perhaps 300 in blue hats. Next will come 250 in yellow. Then the colors will be repeated. There are different shades of blue hats, but seldom any other colors. The time I went to Nikko in August, I found that the children were up at dawn and by 5:30 a.m. were beside a lovely small lake (normally an excellent birding spot) doing calisthenics to an amplified recording of "Stars and Stripes Forever" which carried for miles. I hope they are able to develop an appreciation of nature from these activities, but their invasion of the out-of-doors makes birding impossible.

During the year, there are three periods of about a week each when the Japanese either have long holidays or make their annual pilgrimages to their ancestral homes. The latter, the time of the Obon Festival, occurs in mid-August during the long school holiday, so it doesn't cause additional problems for birdwatchers. The others are the New Year holiday, usually beginning by December 30, and Golden Week, beginning on April 29, the Emperor's Birthday.

During the New Year holiday and Golden Week, almost everybody goes somewhere. Internal transportation is solidly booked, the trains are filled with twice as many people standing as there are sitting, flights into and out of the country are full, and the airports are clogged. If you must come to Japan at either of those times, be sure you are in the country before the holiday starts and that your internal transportation and accommodations are booked far ahead. You must book tickets outside of Japan more than one month in advance. At that time, tickets go on sale in Japan and are immediately taken for any holiday period. You will be happier if you find some place to go which isn't attractive to Japanese tourists and you stay there until everyone else goes back home.

In addition, there are many one-day holidays. When they occur on Saturday or Monday, all public transportation and accommodations are full. These short holidays are easier to deal with, provided you have confirmed reservations. They don't last long enough to cause serious problems with your schedule if you have to stay in one place until they are over.

The other major factor which must be considered in scheduling a trip to Japan is the rainy season. This varies somewhat from place to place. Three of the four main islands, Honshu, Shikoku, and Kyushu, generally experience the rainy season from mid-June to mid-July. Hokkaido is not affected. The smaller islands far to the south are on a different schedule, with the rainy season beginning and ending at least a month earlier.

Unfortunately, the rainy season does interfere with birdwatching for a long period during the breeding season. Of course, it doesn't rain everywhere every day, but the rains can cause landslides and floods and disrupt transportation. Some years they come somewhat earlier or later, so there is no way to predict accurately what the conditions will be at this time of year.

The other weather-related hazard to birdwatching is the typhoon season. It is at its peak in September. The bad weather associated with typhoons usually is of short duration, but it can cause serious problems in the mountains as well as severe flooding and disruption of transportation.

In summary, forget about birdwatching from mid-July to the beginning of September. Beware of monumental logistics problems as well as overcrowding of certain areas from December 30 to January 5 or 6 and from April 29 to May 6. Remember the rainy season, and try to avoid it. The possibility of a typhoon should not keep you out of Japan as long as you are able to make some adjustments in case you get caught in one.

EXPENSE

Don't be frightened away by the reputation Japan has for being expensive. It is possible to spend a lot of money traveling in Japan, but it is not necessary. It depends on your requirements. A Western-style hotel of international standard with an English-speaking staff is expensive, but with the current exchange rates, not out of line with similar hotels in most parts of the world. A twin room in a luxury hotel in Tokyo can be had for about ¥25,000 plus tax and service. (US $100 at an exchange rate of ¥250/$1.) Except for certain famous, elegant *ryokan*, prices go down from there.

On the other extreme, it is possible to stay in a *minshuku* anywhere in Japan for approximately ¥4,500 per night including dinner and breakfast. If you are willing to travel like the Japanese, stay in Japanese-style accommodations, eat Japanese food, and take on the task of doing all this without being able to communicate in a language you know, you can travel in Japan for a reasonable amount of money. In fact, at many of the best birdwatching spots, you will have no other choice.

After hotel costs, you can make the biggest cut in your budget by eating what the Japanese eat. Restaurants catering to foreign tourists are much more expensive than ordinary restaurants. The same meal can cost five times as much in a fine hotel as it does in a Japanese restaurant just down the street. If you stay in a *ryokan* or *minshuku*, dinner and breakfast will be included in the price. Most restaurants have special prices at lunchtime. If you order the day's special, you can eat a good lunch for from ¥600 to ¥1,000. Western food can be difficult or impossible to get in some places, and it will cost more than a typical Japanese lunch.

Transportation costs will account for a major part of your expenditures. Public transportation is efficient and usually the best way to go, but it isn't cheap. Foreigners can buy a pass for the trains on the Japan National Railways (JNR) if they do it before arriving in Japan. This is a great bargain and strongly recommended if you plan to use the trains. Flying also is expensive. Before you come, ask about reduced rates if you include internal flights on your international tickets. Rental cars in almost all cases go for a flat rate except in Hokkaido, where there is a mileage charge. You can get fly-drive specials to Hokkaido which will eliminate that charge. Bring all your rental car discount and identification cards, but don't expect the discounts that you are accustomed to in other parts of the world.

TRANSPORTATION

Japan has efficient, clean public transportation: planes, trains, subways, and buses. Air travel is easy for foreigners, as are subway travel in the major cities and train travel on the three Shinkansen lines (bullet trains) and other major trains. The Japan National Travel Organization (JNTO) publishes the *Condensed Railway Timetable* in English, giving the schedules of the fastest trains on the major lines. When you use the minor lines and slower trains, working out the schedules and changes gets complicated.

Buses are mysterious. No routes, schedules, or instructions are in English. Riding a Japanese bus is fine (but slower than trains) if you know where to catch it, the exact fare, and, most important, where to get off. That is difficult with no knowledge of the area or of the Japanese language.

If your goal is to spend as little money as possible, you can manage almost entirely by public transportation. The final legs by local trains and buses will cost you a great deal of time. They can be excruciatingly slow, the schedules will seldom suit yours, you may have to walk some distance (during which time you are unlikely to see any birds), and it can take what seems forever to make sure you are getting the right train or bus and headed where you really mean to go.

Because buses are difficult and trains can be a problem as well as time-consuming when you are trying to get to some of the out-of-the-way birding spots, the ideal way to travel in Japan is to get close to your destination as quickly as possible by public transportation and then rent a car. I find it is much more convenient, birding is more enjoyable, and it saves time. You can be sure that when I recommend some other way to travel to a site, the problems associated with getting there by car far outweigh the benefits.

Air Travel
The internal airline network is good and fast, but not cheap. There are no bargains. The two main internal airlines are TDA (Toa Domestic Airlines) and ANA (All Nippon Airways). Between them, they cover almost all major cities. JAL (Japan Air Lines) flies from Tokyo to Osaka, Fukuoka, Sapporo, and Okinawa. There are smaller airlines which serve small towns in Hokkaido and some of the islands. If you can set up your itinerary in advance, see if any specials are available or if you can save money by putting your internal flights on your air ticket to Japan.

Driving and Rental Cars
Don't come to Japan without an International Driver's License. You absolutely cannot rent a car without one unless you have a Japanese license (forget that). Even if you are certain you do not want to drive in Japan, unless you are coming with a group tour, get one. If you get to Japan and change your mind, there is nothing you can do about it.

Don't drive in Tokyo. A short-time visitor has little hope of finding the way anywhere, and a car is much slower than the train. In three years in Japan, I drove in Tokyo only once. The 3-km. drive between my house and the freeway entrance almost ruined the whole trip. Once when I was traveling in a car with Japanese companions, it took five hours to get back to Tokyo from a birding spot I had visited the week before. Then, by train and bus, I made the trip in an hour and a half. Driving in Tokyo isn't worth it even when you know the way.

Driving outside of Tokyo is fine, but it is almost always slow. Don't let short distances on the map deceive you. The speed limit on highways is usually no more than 50 km./hour. Most often you are lucky to average 30 km./hour. There are some expressways, but the tolls are expensive. It can take a long time to make a trip entirely by car, but a group of four sharing the cost of a car might save a good deal of money over renting cars plus buying train passes and air tickets.

Driving is on the left in Japan. Most of the roads are narrow and crowded, but the greatest difficulty comes from trying to find the way. Almost all road signs are in Japanese only.

If you are accustomed to driving on the left, have a good sense of direction, and are comfortable with maps, you can manage. It will be much easier with two people, one to drive and the other to read the map and try to find the way. Outside the large cities, it isn't too difficult. Along with your International Driver's License, bring a magnifying glass and a flashlight. Try as I would to avoid night driving, I regularly found myself doing it because I got lost or it took far longer than I expected to reach my destination. Do not plan to drive in the dark. It is too difficult to find the way. No matter how good your eyes are, you will need a magnifying glass to read a Japanese map and to get any idea of the appearance of the *kanji* labels. You can often see Japanese on the subway reading books with a magnifying glass, so you need not feel embarrassed.

There are several major rental car companies, and cars are available in most cities and at most airports. Nippon Rent-a-Car is the Hertz affiliate; Nissan is affiliated with Avis. Other large rental companies are Toyota and Eki Rent-a-Car. (*Eki* is the Japanese word for train station.) Usually that office is next to the station, but the others are nearby, too.

The rates are essentially identical no matter which company you use. Most cars in Japan are rented on an unlimited mileage basis except in Hokkaido. Make every effort to get unlimited mileage there, because that is where you will need it the most. The airlines have fly-drive packages which give unlimited mileage in Hokkaido.

I have used Hertz most often. They currently have the only bargain in rental cars. If you can manage with a tiny car, rent a Honda City or the next grade, Honda Civic (or the equivalent in another brand), for about half the price of the A-grade car (the cheapest of the regular cars). They are fine if your party fits in and you are going only a short distance. I find the smallest car suitable only for two people, though I've survived as one of five in a Honda City on some occasions.

Hertz (Nippon) will give a 10% discount on an A-grade or better car if you have a Hertz No. 1 Club card. This is also useful in getting a 10% discount at all Tokyu Inns and some other hotels. Avis will give a discount to card holders, but not on the first rental. Because of this restriction and the absence of the bargain on the two smallest cars, I started with Hertz and stayed with them most of the time. They are most often near the train stations and have a sign that is easy to recognize.

I have yet to discover people at rental car offices outside of Tokyo who speak English. If possible, make your reservations in Tokyo. Get all the details of rates settled at that time. Then you can present your reservation number and your International Driver's License and get the car with little need to communicate.

You can telephone Tokyo to get reservations if you are unable to plan everything in advance. Or get a brochure of the cars and rates in English and one in Japanese. They almost match. You can point to what you want. With Hertz, the English brochure lists the two small cars as SS and SA. The next size (for which you can use the No. 1 Club card for a 10% discount) is an A. In the Japanese brochure, they are SSS, SSA, and SA respectively. This led to confusion and a couple of arguments before I determined the cause of the problem.

You will have a good chance of getting a car without reservations (in the proper season), but it will take a lot of time. It is probably worthwhile to visit the service department at the Tokyo head office of the agency you choose to deal with and get acquainted with someone there whom you can telephone for help with reservations.

There will be variations in the rental rates at different locations. Some places charge extra in warm weather for air conditioning. All the cars are air-conditioned, so you can't choose one without it. Sometimes you will have to pay extra whether you want or need it. You may encounter other extra charges such as a fee for being driven a short distance from the airport to the rental car office. I encountered this only at Nagasaki. But in every location you face the possibility of a new surprise. After a number of these, I complained to the headquarters and learned that the local agencies sometimes have a good deal of autonomy.

All of this is difficult to deal with when communication is such a problem, but being aware of what might happen helps. In Japan, it is safe to assume that no one is trying to cheat you. So although the charges may vary, they will follow local policy. All the agencies in one location will probably have identical charges.

While I found this inconsistency confusing and annoying, there were many times when I received special treatment because I was a foreigner. An extreme example occurred when I returned my car to the Hertz agency in Okinawa. The agent was concerned that we might have a problem when he learned we intended to purchase a plane ticket at the airport. So he drove us to a travel agency, went in with us to make sure we got the proper ticket, and then drove us to the airport. There was no charge for this, and in Japan there is no tipping. Japanese people tend to take special care of foreigners who don't understand.

One of the procedures for renting cars differs from what is common in most other countries. You must tell exactly when you will return the car and pay the full amount in advance. If you are delayed, you must call and let them know ahead of time that you will not be back with the car when you said you would. An approximate time will not do. Most agencies take American Express cards, but not all. Check this for each location while you are at the Tokyo office. Even with a credit card, before you ever start out, they will fill in the full amount for the time you say you will have the car.

Train Travel
In planning your trip, give serious consideration to train travel. The best bargain in transportation is a pass on the JNR (Japan National Railways). Passes can be obtained for different time periods (7, 14, or 21 days) and can be for regular coaches or Green Cars (first class). The Green Car is more expensive but much more comfortable and less crowded. People are not allowed to stand in the aisles in the Green Cars. During holiday periods, trains often carry several times as many people as there are seats. Even if you have a seat, you won't be comfortable in a car that is stuffed to capacity. The 14-day Green Car pass costs about the same as a round-trip Green Car ticket between Tokyo and Kyoto. Any additional train travel is free.

There are several types of trains with which you must be familiar if you plan to use them. The Shinkansen is commonly known outside Japan as the bullet train. Japan now has three Shinkansen lines: the Tokaido-Sanyo Shinkansen from Tokyo to Hakata (in Kyushu), the Tohoku Shinkansen from Tokyo to Morioka (northeast Honshu), and the Joetsu Shinkansen from Tokyo to Niigata (northwest Honshu). The last two lines come into Tokyo at

Ueno Station and the first at Tokyo Station. These are the fastest and best trains and an excellent way to travel. On each of these lines there are two types of trains, one faster than the other because it stops at fewer stations. These trains have different names on each line. This will be clear when you examine the timetable. Be sure to take the faster train if it stops at the station you want.

Limited Express trains are next in order of speed, with Express trains third. There are extra charges for all these trains, but the JNR pass allows you free travel on all of them. You may need two tickets for these trains: one for the basic fare and one for the express charge. (You must surrender your ticket when you leave the train station. If the ticket taker takes only one of your tickets and leaves you with one, keep it. You will have to pass another ticket taker before you get out of the station, and he will want what you have left.) If you do not have a pass and are cost conscious, check the difference between the Limited Express and the Express. You might save only 10 or 15 minutes for your particular trip, but the price difference could be significant.

Eating on the street is considered rude in Japan, but everyone eats on trains. Most people eat box lunches at their seats. After one meal in the dining car on the Shinkansen, I have always chosen that system. You can select a box lunch in the station, where you can see samples of what is available. People regularly pass through the train selling food and drink. This is a bit more difficult. You must waylay them as they go past, and the box you buy could contain almost anything. The contents are not evident from the wrapper if you can't read. Ask for an *obento*. Then you will have a meal rather than a box of sweets or dried fish.

It may suit your schedule to travel overnight. You will have to pay extra for a sleeping car even if you have a JNR pass. There are at least two styles of sleeping cars: one with bunks two or three deep down both sides of a central aisle, the other with compartments (with four or six bunks) opening off the aisle running down the side of the car. They are curtained, so private. A sheet and a blanket should be provided. You can undress and spend a comfortable night. There is no place to put your luggage except in the bunk with you. The bunks aren't enormous to start with, so be careful what you bring on such a journey.

The sleeping cars are made up for sleeping when you board them. There is no place to sit except in your bunk. Don't loll in bed in the morning after you hear an announcement on the loudspeaker and your neighbors start moving about. Around 7:00 a.m., they start folding up the bunks and preparing the train for daytime use whether you are ready to get up or not.

Pay attention to the time the train will arrive at your destination, and be ready to get off. Usually the trains stop for less than a minute. There is no time for you to realize suddenly after the train arrives in the station that it is your stop, gather up all your belongings, and get off the train. Japanese people have an uncommon ability to get on and off trains and airplanes quickly. You will have to be on your toes to keep up with them.

Only twice in three years of constant travel in Japan did I see a porter in a train station. If there is one, he will most likely be beside the Green Car on the Shinkansen in stations where many foreigners regularly go, such as Tokyo and Kyoto. You must be able to carry everything yourself. In the train stations you must often walk long distances and go up and down several flights of stairs. Folding carts or wheels on your suitcase are no help on stairs. Furthermore, there is no place to store your luggage except in the rack over your seat. Keep it to a minimum.

The main hazard to train travel is the smoke. If you are a non-smoker and sensitive to cigarette smoke, you may be miserable on a long train ride. Most Japanese men smoke all the time. There is one car or part of a car set aside on each Shinkansen train for no smoking, but seats in this area are unreserved. Recently a few other long-distance trains began providing a totally inadequate no-smoking area. There is a movement to get the size of these areas expanded and available on all trains, but the movement is weak since the vast majority of the people smoke. Don't expect significant changes in the near future. If this is important to you, it might help the cause if you express your desire for a non-smoking area when you purchase your tickets.

Smoking is not allowed on subways and on certain commuter trains inside the Tokyo area, but smoking is allowed on all long-distance trains. Airplanes in Japan do have no-smoking areas. If the plane is not filled to capacity, the no-smoking area will be the least crowded.

ACCOMMODATIONS

You will seldom find places to stay in Japan where birds are all around you. Many people have an image of staying in lovely Japanese country inns all alone in the forest. This would be ideal, if only it were possible. The places which do exist at or near the good birding sites are always mentioned in the site guides.

There is a big variation in the type of accommodations you can choose from in Japan, but almost all will be in a city or a built-up area. The kinds most common are unique to Japan and require some detailed explanation. Your choice of accommodations will depend, first of all, on your pocketbook. You can go from a luxury hotel or *ryokan* at the top of the scale to a *minshuku* at the bottom. But if your goal is to stay as close to the birds as possible, you will often find yourself in a *minshuku* because that is all that is nearby.

If cost is not a serious consideration, try different types of accommodations, depending on the location and the circumstances. You can enjoy the full range as you travel through Japan. I have found it interesting to stay in many types of places just to see what they are like. You see different things and different kinds of people and will have totally different experiences, depending upon the accommodations you choose. The places I am familiar with are described in the site guides. My first criterion is to sleep where the birds are. If that is possible, it will be made clear in the site guides. I have also described places which I consider to be special. Some are cheap while others are quite expensive. The information is there. You can decide if you are interested.

Western-style accommodations are available in all large cities. Tokyo is the place to stay in a luxury Western-style hotel if that is on your list. I have discovered a few high-quality Western-style hotels outside of Tokyo which I recommend over the Japanese places, but most of the time I find they have less charm. Some of the more expensive Western hotels outside of Tokyo and other major cities are, to me, quite unattractive. They often cater to large tour groups and will attract them with *pachinko* rooms and souvenir shops.

Most of the luxury hotels, in Tokyo anyway, are like similar quality hotels the world over. You can have anything you want and get it in English. The next level down will be less luxurious with smaller rooms and may well have no English-speaking staff, but everything will look familiar except perhaps the food. The prices of these hotels will depend on the quality and the location. You can expect the rooms to come with bath. Except in the luxury hotels, the bathrooms are prefabricated plastic modules. After you have seen one, you have seen them all. Everything is on a smaller scale than Westerners are accustomed to, especially the bathtub, but everything will be there, including a shower.

Then there are business hotels. These cater to Japanese businessmen and are the least expensive way to get Western-style accommodations. There are no frills, but on the whole the rooms are satisfactory. Here, too, there is variation, with some hotels being much nicer than others. There will be no room service and often no eating facilities, but these hotels are always centrally located with restaurants and shops nearby. Most of the rooms are designed for one person. There will be a single bed, usually a small desk and chair, a reading light, a small bath, and a TV, which most often is coin operated. You will seldom find a closet in any but the most expensive hotels. Japanese travel with a minimum of luggage and have no need for a closet. You will find a couple of pegs hanging on the wall and a clothes hanger or two. There are some double rooms, but in the lower-grade hotels, they can be cramped. Rooms in the cheapest hotels may not always have private baths.

If you want a business hotel, you can usually find one easily when you reach your destination. Then you can see what you are getting before you decide. In this category the price is generally a good indication of the quality. I've stayed in business hotels for as little as ¥3,000, but I prefer something better. Usually a single room will range in price from ¥4,000 to ¥7,000. At this price level, you can expect to be satisfied.

Depending on the location and my mood, I often enjoy staying at a good business hotel. They offer better value for the money and are just as comfortable as most of the higher quality hotels outside of Tokyo. The rooms are usually similar. You give up a large lobby and some services which will not be of particular use to you anyway. Food outside the hotel will be better and cheaper. If you must spend the night in a city, there are times when it is more convenient and less time-consuming to stay at a centrally located hotel. If you are weary of eating whatever is offered and wish to choose your own dinner out, a night in a hotel can be a pleasant break from too much local color.

I have discovered Tokyu Inns, a chain of hotels owned by a giant corporation which also owns the Tokyu Hotels, with which they should not be confused. They are business hotels without room service and without a service charge. In some of the smaller cities, the Tokyu Inn is the nicest hotel in town. All of them in which I have stayed have been a good value. The Tokyu Inn chain is new, so, at least for now, they are exceptionally clean. To the best of my knowledge they all have restaurants. Except for the lack of room service and the lower price, they seem no different from a regular hotel. They are almost always located within a block or two of the train station. A further advantage is their 10% discount to holders of a Hertz No. 1 Club card. Prices vary according to the town. A twin room is usually about ¥10,000 and a single ¥5,500 or ¥6,000.

High-class Japanese-style accommodations can be much more expensive than a luxury Western-style hotel in Tokyo. Staying in a top-quality *ryokan* is a special experience, surely one of the highlights of a trip to Japan. Treat yourself if you have the money, but don't use them exclusively. That would give you as warped a view of Japan as would spending every night in the Hotel Okura in Tokyo. At the best ones you will pay ¥25,000 per person and up. This includes two meals.

When you select one of these places, be sure that it really is what you have in mind. Sometimes these expensive *ryokan* are in *onsen* (hot spring resorts) which for the most part have become extremely commercial and crowded. The *ryokan* may be beautiful inside, but the atmosphere of the *onsen* may not be appealing to people who enjoy beautiful and quiet surroundings. And some of them have cluttered the traditional Japanese decor with some Western additions which ruin the atmosphere.

There are plenty of less expensive *ryokan*. They vary greatly in price and quality. You will have no way of knowing by looking at the outside what they will be like inside. Price alone is not always a good indication. If the *ryokan* is in a popular tourist resort or *onsen*, or if it is the high season, you can pay a lot of money for rather ordinary accommodations.

Occasionally you may encounter a *pension*. These most often are in ski resorts. They will have Western-style beds, but almost everything else will be done in the Japanese manner. They will have Japanese baths and serve Japanese food and seldom have private toilet facilities.

Minshuku are the least expensive accommodations in Japan. A *minshuku* is a bit difficult to define. There isn't a good English word which can be used. In the beginning a *minshuku* was a home where the family took in overnight guests. This is often still the case. In these establishments, the guests share the family table. Now there are those which still are the family home, but the building has been expanded to hold a larger number of people and the family does not eat with the guests. Other *minshuku* have grown to look much like hotels. I have stayed in some *minshuku* which were much nicer than some other places which were called *ryokan*. The only sure difference I have been able to discover has to do with the *futon* (bed). In a *minshuku* you must get your own bed out of the closet, put it together, and next morning take it apart, fold it up, and put it back where you got it. There is no maid service.

In many of the birding spots there will be a *minshuku* or *ryokan* which is affiliated with the Wild Bird Society of Japan (WBSJ) where members can get a 10% discount. These are almost always the lowest-priced accommodations in the area. Often they are places where you will want to stay even if money is no object because they will be in a good birding spot or at least will be where you can meet other birders and get good information.

Some of these places are charming, while others are advantageous only because of the location or because of the fun of being with other birdwatchers. That, by the way, can be a distinct advantage. It will be your best opportunity for getting to know some of the Japanese birders. You can learn a great deal from them. They may be shy at first, but you will have a good chance of finding someone who speaks some English. You will not go wrong staying in one of these places.

Japanese people, including birders, almost always travel with several friends, sometimes a lot of friends. In a *minshuku*, a group will stay together, all the men in one room and all the women in another. If the group is too large, they will get additional rooms, but all are filled to capacity. Sometimes as many as six or even more share one room if there is enough space. The smallest room in a *minshuku* will hold three or four (with no room to spare). When every bit of floor space is covered with *futon*, the room is considered to be full. When my husband and I have traveled alone and stayed in *minshuku*, we have always been given a room of our own, but a group of foreigners might be given rooms on the same basis as the Japanese. If your group is large, you cannot count on being allowed to stay two persons to each room. If there is plenty of room, this will be ok, but many places will not guarantee this in advance. The same is true at Japanese-style hotels and *ryokan*.

If you are the kind of birder who has traveled to the ends of the earth looking for birds, you will certainly have stayed in many places which will make even the worst places in Japan seem luxurious. Sometimes they don't look like much and have no charm, but they are clean and adequate. If you should have the misfortune to discover a place which is truly dirty, as opposed to a bit dingy and tatty looking, leave. You are wrong to assume that is normal and you must put up with it.

In *minshuku* and many *ryokan* the rooms do not have private baths or toilets. Occasionally the rooms will have a washbasin and sometimes a toilet, but most often not. You will share the toilet. There will usually be an area with one long sink with several sets of faucets where everyone goes for face washing, tooth brushing, and shaving.

Your room will have little furniture. The floor will be *tatami* (don't even wear your slippers on *tatami*). There will be a small, low table in the middle of the room beside which you will sit on the floor on cushions. In a *ryokan* your meals will probably be served on this table, but sometimes you must go to the dining room. Later the table will be removed or turned on end to make space for putting down the *futon*.

There could be a small alcove at the window with another table and two chairs. Except for that, you will operate from the floor. Sometimes there is another alcove only a foot or so deep, called a *tokonoma*, which will contain, ideally, a scroll, a flower arrangement, and some other beautiful object. Except in elegant *ryokan*, don't expect much of real beauty. Sometimes traditional Japanese objects have been abandoned and replaced with something garish. But everything should be clean.

Futon (Japanese beds) are comfortable by anyone's standards, so don't worry about sleeping on the floor. First a pad (usually foam) is laid on the *tatami*, then comes another thick soft pad with a sheet over it. You lie on this and cover yourself with a thick, puffy top-covering inside a slip-on case which can be removed for washing. In an elegant place, this top cover will be filled with down. Otherwise it is of some less expensive material. If it is cold, you may have more than one of these and perhaps a blanket to put directly over you for added warmth. No matter what the conditions are in the room, you should be warm in the *futon*.

Tall foreigners are often too long for the *futon*. Sometimes the maid will put two together so you will fit. It is a good idea to bring along heavy socks or down-filled footcovering if you are coming in winter. This will keep you from freezing if your feet get uncovered during the night.

The only problem you are likely to encounter with the bed is the pillow. It is often stuffed with rice hulls and is hard and uncomfortable. A rolled-up sweater or down jacket will be a good substitute.

Almost every place will provide a freshly washed and starched *yukata*. This is a cotton kimono-like wrapping which you can sleep in or use as a bathrobe. You will see Japanese wandering about a hotel in them and sometimes even down the street in a resort town. This is not always appropriate, so foreigners should avoid doing it. It is always permissible, however, to wear your *yukata* between your room and the toilet or *ofuro*. If you are at a *ryokan* where you will eat in your room, have your bath before dinner and change into your *yukata*. It is customary to wear the *yukata* for dinner and all the time you are in your room.

Do bring a small towel and a washcloth with you. Most places will give you a towel about half again the size of a washcloth, but only a quarter the thickness. The Japanese manage with this for both washing and drying. You will probably prefer your own. There will always be a rack in your room where you can hang these to dry.

You are sure to encounter a co-ed toilet while you are in Japan. They usually are a shock to foreigners the first time. The urinals are by the door, so everyone must pass them going to the stalls. You will be the only one disturbed by this. The Japanese consider it normal procedure. You can wait around until the coast is clear or pretend you are Japanese. I have most often found these in restaurants or *minshuku*. Most toilets have pictures on the doors clearly indicating for which sex they are intended. You will feel more secure if you learn the *kanji* for "men" and "women". If there is no mark, the toilet is for both. While on the subject, most Japanese toilets flush two ways. The handle is marked "big" and "little" in Japanese. A turn in one direction produces a small amount of water, in the other direction considerably more. If you don't get what you want, try the other way. The typical Japanese toilet is at floor level, for squatting, not sitting.

Public toilets in Japan almost never provide towels for drying your hands and seldom provide toilet paper. You must remember to carry at all times a handkerchief or cloth for hand drying and a small package of tissues.

If you want to stay in *minshuku* or inexpensive Japanese-style accommodations, you must be firm if an agency makes your reservations. Japanese are reluctant to send foreigners to such places and sometimes insist they don't exist. My husband was told by his company's travel department that there were no Japanese-style accommodations in all of Hokkaido. On another occasion when he asked for the names and phone numbers of places to stay at Lake Shikaribetsu, the written response came back that most tourists preferred to visit Lake Akan which is more famous. Names and phone numbers were supplied for that lake which is well over 100 km. away, with many tourists indeed, but no Blakiston's Fish-Owls. The Japanese always think that, as a foreigner, you couldn't possibly understand what you are asking for and that they know what is best for you. Sadly, most have an inaccurate view of what foreigners require and would like. This causes many visitors to miss some of the most charming and interesting aspects of the country.

The JNTO has a booklet of approved Japanese-style accommodations. These are on the expensive side. They usually have someone on the staff who can speak English, and they are especially eager to have foreign guests. The places which are not on any special list for foreigners tend to be more authentic, though this is not true in all cases.

I have been made to feel welcome in every *minshuku* and *ryokan* where I have stayed. They often expressed concern when I first appeared that I might require a bed or Western food and would be unable to eat with chopsticks. Most are unaccustomed to foreigners and, having fallen for the propaganda, think we always require something special.

They will offer you whatever they have that they think you might like. Take what is offered, and don't ask for anything. This includes scrambled eggs, toast, coffee--everything except hot water. You can bring instant coffee and make your own. If you think you can't manage with chopsticks, bring cutlery too.

Japanese don't operate like most of the rest of us. If you ask for something that isn't available or is difficult to provide, they won't just say so. They will make every effort and sometimes go to great expense to get what you have asked for. You will never be aware of it, but they will remember that foreigners cause a lot of trouble. The next ones won't be so welcome. In fact, I have learned that some hotels have a policy of not accepting foreign guests. The ones I know about are in areas where foreigners often go. They must have had bad experiences.

In a *ryokan* or *minshuku* behave as though you were a guest in someone's home. Always remove your shoes at the front door. You will be given a pair of slippers to wear while walking around indoors. These must be removed before entering your room. Never step on *tatami* with anything more than socks on your feet. When you enter the toilet, you will find different slippers. Step out of your other ones outside the door and into the toilet slippers, which stay on the toilet floor. It is easy to forget and make a mistake with shoes and slippers and *tatami*, but do your best to pay attention. Where you step with which shoes is of prime importance to all Japanese.

In a *minshuku* you will eat with the other guests or with the family. This will be one of the most interesting and enjoyable experiences you will have in Japan. You will be told when to take your bath and when to eat. In a *ryokan* where you will have your meal in your room, you may have a choice of the time, but it will have to conform to the local schedule. Remember, 7:00 p.m. is late for dinner. The food may be cooked ahead, so the earlier you eat, the better it will taste.

Japanese Bath

The *ofuro*, or Japanese bath, is one of the most delightful aspects of life in Japan. Foreigners always seem to be terrified of the *ofuro* until they experience their first one. After that they will seldom choose anything else.

You will find *ofuro* ranging from the one- or two-person-at-a-time size in a small *minshuku* to swimming pool size in a large *ryokan* or Japanese-style hotel. The men's *ofuro* is invariably three times the size of the women's. Upon your arrival they will show you the location of the *ofuro* and toilet and will probably give you detailed instructions regarding the *ofuro*. In a small place, you are assigned your turn in the bath. In a large place, you go when you are ready and share the bath with anyone else who happens to be there. I have never encountered a mixed *ofuro*. They probably still exist, but they are rare enough that you are unlikely to get in one by mistake.

The *ofuro*, like the wearing or not wearing of shoes, is sacred. Go into the anteroom, remove all your clothes, and put them in a basket which is provided. Take in only your washcloth. You will get drier if you leave your towel in the basket and dry yourself in the anteroom.

I have never seen an *ofuro* without soap, but it doesn't hurt to take your own just in case. The tub may have a cover on it. If so, be sure to put it back when you are finished. You will find tiny stools and small pans in the *ofuro*. In a high-class place there will be small wooden buckets instead of plastic dishpans. Sit on the stool, dip water out of the tub, and pour it over your body, carefully, to get accustomed to the heat. It is ok to pour it all over the floor: it all drains away.

Then, fill your pan with water from the tub or the faucets around the edge of the room, and wash yourself with soap, staying well away from the tub to be sure you don't accidentally get any soap in it. After you have washed and thoroughly rinsed off all the soap, get in the tub (remember, the water may be scalding hot) and relax for a while before leaving the *ofuro*. Never, under any circumstances, get soap in the water or pull the plug.

Your fellow bathers may exhibit a great deal of curiosity and interest in you. After the first time or two, you won't pay them any mind.

My *ofuro* experience has been limited, with two exceptions, to the *minshuku*, *ryokan*, or hotel where I was staying. Once in winter I visited an *onsen* with outdoor baths. It was interesting to be outdoors in the bath with deep snow all around the pool. On another occasion when I was traveling with Japanese and staying in a hotel which had nothing but showers, we walked several blocks to the public *ofuro* so we could have a proper bath. This was in a small town on the far side of Japan where plastic hadn't yet taken over. We had wooden tubs for dipping and wicker baskets for our clothes. It was most enjoyable and interesting to see the way a large percentage of the people in Japan still have their daily baths. Many apartments don't have room for a bath, so the people must use the public bath. It is a social event, enjoyed by all.

Camping
Camping is not a good option in Japan. Places where it is possible are rare. It is not worth the trouble to bring your equipment when you may never have a chance to use it.

FOOD

Japanese food, like so much about the country, is distinctive and, to a great extent, unlike that of its neighbors. You will encounter many food items you have never seen before. Often after you have finished a meal, you will still be unable to identify what you have eaten. Coupled with the language problem, this makes finding the sort of restaurant you have in mind and ordering food a real challenge.

If you enjoy trying new food, you will have a fine time in Japan. If you are a finicky eater, this will be the area where your adjustment will be the most difficult. In Tokyo you can get anything you want to eat if you are willing to pay the price. Out where the birds are, you have little choice.

Birders will appreciate that anywhere you go in Japan, you can drink the water and eat the food without fear of its being unclean or bad. But outside of the large cities, you will usually have to eat Japanese food and eat it with chopsticks. (You may take your own knife and fork.) It is a healthy diet, and millions of people get along quite nicely on it. Be open minded and you will be fine.

The one hazard of Japanese food is the high salt content. If a low-salt diet is a necessity for you, get medical advice before you go. There is little way that you can avoid the salt. Japanese pickles and *miso* soup, which are served with every meal, and the soy sauce, which is poured on almost everything and is a basic ingredient in most other sauces, are especially salty. Skip the soup and the pickles, avoid putting soy sauce on anything where the choice is left to you, and beware of the dipping sauces. You will miss out on some good tastes, but that is about all you can do.

Many Japanese dishes will appeal to all. Taste everything. Sometimes the things which look the most unappetizing (to Western eyes) are delicious. I find that the foods which I think aren't especially good are rather bland and tasteless. With few exceptions, nothing tastes really bad. Fish and rice are a basic part of almost every meal. If you cannot eat fish, Japan may not be the place for you. Japanese eat far more rice at each meal than any Westerner can handle. All the rice you can eat (as well as all the Japanese tea you can drink) is provided free of charge. If you find a meal doesn't suit you, you can avoid hunger by filling up on rice.

Coffee is expensive, strong, and served in small cups. It is not available in all restaurants. Only in rare circumstances will you get refills. If you like a lot of coffee, bring some instant coffee and make your own. You should always have a thermos of hot water in your room for making tea (or your own coffee). If not, it is permissible to ask for it.

Many restaurants have displays of plastic food in the window. This is a great help. You can get someone to go outside with you so you can point to what you want to eat. That works fine until you want to eat where there is no plastic food. If you can be satisfied with a meal without being too particular what it is, you can ask for a set meal, or you can ask to eat the same thing that someone near you is eating.

The task of getting something to eat in a restaurant will be much simpler now with the recent publication of *The Guide to Japanese Food and Restaurants* by Russell Marcus and Jack Plimpton, published by Shufunotomo Co., Ltd., Tokyo. This will explain everything you need to know about types of restaurants and food, and most important, it tells you how to order. Important phrases are written in Japanese, so you can point and manage nicely. This same publisher has an older book which you will also find useful,

Eating Cheap in Japan by Kimiko Nagasawa and Camy Condon. Take both of them with you everywhere, and all will be well. If you can obtain and study them before your arrival, that will help. You will need some time to go through the first book before you set out on your own.

Donald Richie's *A Taste of Japan*, published by Kodansha International, explains a great deal about Japanese food. If you enjoy good food and want to know more about what you will be eating or what you should be sure to try, read this book before you go.

A seldom-mentioned fact, but one which you will need to know to avoid confusion, is that, in a Japanese restaurant, the waiter doesn't bring you the bill when you finish your meal. Instead, get up and go to the cash register or some likely-looking spot near the door and your bill will be ready for you.

When you are staying in a *minshuku* or *ryokan*, you are saved the effort of finding food because your breakfast and dinner will be included. You don't get a choice. You eat what they give you. Both meals will most likely include soup, rice, and fish, with the evening meal having a variety of other things, the number and the quality of which are determined by the quality and price of the establishment.

In most *ryokan* and many *minshuku* you can pay extra and get beer or *sake* with your dinner. If your *minshuku* doesn't have it, it is permissible to stop at a nearby store on your way back for dinner and buy some cold beer. Buy enough so that you can share with the others if you do this. It will be difficult to figure this out before your first dinner in a *minshuku*. You may prefer to take your chances and see what happens the first night. Then you will know the proper procedure if you stay longer.

Foreigners have the worst time with Japanese breakfasts. Sometimes you may be offered the choice of a Western breakfast. Decide this according to the intensity of your dislike for Japanese breakfasts. The Western breakfast will be a poor substitute for what you are accustomed to. Japanese breakfasts will vary greatly from one establishment to the next. It is better, even if given a choice, to try the Japanese breakfast first and abandon it for the rest of your stay if you can't bear it.

A staple of Japanese breakfast in most places is a whole egg in a bowl. This egg is not boiled: it is raw. It is to be broken into the bowl and beaten up with some soy sauce. Then it is either drunk as is or poured over a bowl of rice. I have never felt up to this dish. My other great dislike at breakfast is *natto*, fermented soybeans. These are a special favorite of most Japanese and almost universally hated by foreigners. I ate mine three times to be polite and gave it up. I have my worst times at *minshuku* which serve breakfasts limited to soup, *natto*, rice, and raw egg. Fortunately this is not common. Another regular item at breakfast is a small package of rectangular strips of seaweed (*nori*). With skill you can dip a piece of *nori* in soy sauce and with one hand use your chopsticks to make a roll of rice with the *nori* wrapped around it.

If it is that important to you, you could carry your own cereal or other emergency rations, but you will also have to take your own milk. Japanese tea is the normal breakfast drink. Everything will be easier if you can survive on what is offered.

Most times when birdwatching, it will be better to take a packed lunch. I've had foreign visitors say to me, "Oh, don't bother, I don't want anything special. Just a sandwich will do." That translates to, "I really don't want Japanese food, so surely I can have a sandwich, can't I?" Actually, that is often impossible. Japanese are great users of lunchboxes *(obento)*. They are for sale in every train station as well as in many other places. They don't contain sandwiches. The contents can vary greatly, but there usually is a large variety of items: fish, chicken, vegetables, and rice. They come in small disposable boxes, and chopsticks are always included. You can tuck a lunchbox in your pack and throw everything in the trash when you are finished.

When you are staying in a *minshuku* or *ryokan*, ask the night before and they will supply you with a packed lunch at breakfast time. The favorite item, which you are likely to get from your *minshuku*, is *nigiri*. This is what Japanese usually take on a picnic instead of sandwiches. *Nigiri* is a ball of rice with something stuffed in the middle and wrapped with *nori* (seaweed). Often a pickled plum is in the center of the ball of rice. Usually, you will get three or four, each with a different center. Salmon is a popular filling. Occasionally flecks of something will be mixed with the rice. The worst you will get when you order a lunch from your *minshuku* is several balls of *nigiri*, all with a pickled plum center. It isn't bad, but it can get boring.

In certain areas there are plenty of restaurants, so you could give up birding and go inside to eat. In Japan, everything is prepared from scratch when you order it. The food tastes much better this way, but you will often kill an hour indoors over lunch.

Sometimes you can stop in a grocery store and buy snacks, but you must remember that you won't find the kinds of things you can buy when you are at home. You can spend a lot of time in a store searching for something you can recognize and that you think you might like to eat. We often make serious errors when we buy the unfamiliar. What looks like sausage may be fish or, just as easily, something sweet. You can also spend a lot of time searching for a store.

In many areas vending machines with a variety of cold (and sometimes hot) drinks are common along the roads. This is a wonderful convenience. Cans of hot coffee and cold coffee are regularly sold in these machines. You need to be able to read the difference. Usually they have milk and sugar, but sometimes one variety will be without. Consult the list of Essential *Kanji* in the appendix.

Although the food in any Japanese restaurant, no matter how inelegant, is always prepared to order, don't be surprised if the food you are served at a *ryokan* has been prepared several hours in advance and everything is at room temperature. Those of us who like cold things cold and hot things hot are often sadly disappointed. The temperature of the food is not important to Japanese. It is disheartening to see in the halls of some expensive *ryokan* carts of food containing baskets of cold, soggy *tempura* which undoubtedly was delicious when it first came out of the pan. Don't complain or send something back to be reheated. That is simply not done. Remember, you are a guest. Soup is always served hot, and rice is kept warm. Nothing else is sacred.

You may be fortunate to stay in a *ryokan* which takes pride in its food. In those places you will be served exquisitely prepared food, beautifully presented and at the precise temperature it should be. A truly elegant Japanese meal is a work of art and a taste treat, but it is expensive. Ordinary Japanese food is good, fresh, well prepared, and good for you. Don't make judgments about it without tasting it first.

LANGUAGE

People who are accustomed to traveling on their own throughout the world generally manage to get along quite well even when they know nothing of the local language. In most countries it isn't difficult to find someone who speaks English or some other language you are at least acquainted with. If all else fails, sign language usually works. This is not the case in Japan. The difficulties brought about because of the inability to talk with anyone and to read any of the signs are upsetting to many seasoned travelers.

You must understand the extent and seriousness of the problem in order to determine the best way for you to travel in Japan. Many people are unable or unwilling to cope with the language difficulties. Numerous people have told me that, had they not been with a group or with a Japanese friend, despite their previous experiences getting along by themselves, they could not have managed in Japan. People can and do manage in Japan without the language, but you need to make sure that you are suited to the task and that you are willing to face calmly getting lost and being confused and feeling totally helpless a good deal of the time. Of course, you will lose a lot of time in the process. If you are up to the challenge and are not the type to disintegrate the first time you get lost, you will have great pride in your accomplishment when it is over, and you are guaranteed to have fascinating experiences and learn a great deal because you travel on your own. If you are the nervous type or you think this will ruin your holiday, forget it.

I have traveled independently throughout the world for a great many years and have never had communication problems anywhere which would begin to compare with the problems I had in Japan even after I learned some of the language. At the end of three years, with the ability to ask directions and understand the reply, I still got lost or at least confused occasionally and sometimes felt tempted to give it all up and go straight back home to Tokyo. But the experiences I had traveling this way were well worth the trouble--most of the time.

The intent of this book is to give you information and assistance which will save you many of the agonies I experienced. If you are careful in following the directions, you should not get lost, although everybody does it sometime. Knowing what to expect in Japanese restaurants and hotels will eliminate much of the need to understand what is being said to you, but you will still have many tasks to perform where some type of communication is required. In each site guide there is a list of useful *kanji*, and a section of essential *kanji* is in the appendix. You can point to these to show people what you are looking for. They will also enable you to recognize road signs and find where you are on maps.

Most young Japanese have studied some English in school. There are many Japanese who speak excellent English, but you have little chance of finding one of these when you are in need. Most people are simply unable to understand spoken English. Remember, never begin your conversation by asking if the person speaks English. The answer will invariably be no. Even if a Japanese does speak English, he won't admit it. He will think his English is not adequate or that he would be bragging to answer in the affirmative or who knows for what other reasons. If you need help, skip that formality and just ask your question. If the person understands, he will help. If not, he will often try to find someone who does. If you are desperate, write it down, but in simple terms and in clear print. Many times the person you are dealing with will understand what you have written, even though he could not understand what you said. Understanding his answer to your question is another problem. Japanese people are reserved to the point that they do not readily engage in sign language or charades to communicate.

People will help you if they can. Especially if they see you carrying a map and looking confused, they will often step up and offer assistance. But this most often happens in Tokyo where you need help the least.

The signs are written in Japanese. It can be easy to follow signs written in a language you don't know if Roman letters are used; following signs written in Japanese characters is much harder. You have to find your way and recognize when you have arrived by some other means. You must keep your wits about you at all times.

The Japanese use three different writing systems simultaneously. Two of them are phonetic: *hiragana*, used for Japanese words, and *katakana*, used for foreign words. There are 96 symbols, and they can be learned fairly quickly. This is hardly worth the effort for a short-time visitor. You won't know the meaning of words you can sound out in *hiragana* unless you know the Japanese word. It is easier to consult your aids than to try to figure out the foreign words in *katakana*. These will be words imported into the language and written as they sound when pronounced as though they were Japanese. Some examples are *aisu kurimu* for ice cream, *miruku* for milk, and *hanbaga* for hamburger. Then you get to the *kanji* characters, which are derived from the Chinese. There are thousands of them, and they must be learned one at a time. You will often find all three of these writing systems in one sentence. Don't plan to learn to read Japanese without making it a lifetime career.

An additional problem in Japanese is that there are multiple possibilities for pronunciation of the *kanji* characters. If they are proper names--the names of towns or places, for example-- a Japanese will not be sure he is calling it by its correct name unless he is familiar with the place. It is better always to point to the character for the place you want to go than to attempt to sound it out. In order for me to write the names of many of the hotels and the small towns mentioned in this book, a Japanese person had to telephone the hotel or someone in the town to find out how it was pronounced. You will find a few instances in the site guides where two names are given for one place. On these, the Japanese were unable to reach a consensus on the proper pronunciation of the characters.

The Japanese language can be written in Roman letters (*romaji*), though there are several systems for doing this. This is solely for the use of a foreigner trying to learn the language. It is a rare Japanese, indeed, who can make any sense out of a Japanese word written in Roman letters. Even if they read English well, their own language written that way is strange to them. So don't expect to get anywhere by showing someone something written in *romaji*. When you get instructions or directions from someone at your hotel, for instance, they will write the place names in Roman letters for your benefit and in Japanese for the person to whom you must show it. You will usually be much better off showing the written Japanese than trying to pronounce it.

The Tourist's Handbook, which you can get from the JNTO, contains many useful phrases as well as questions and possible answers written in English and Japanese for you to show people to get help. *Travelers' Japanese*, published by the *Japan Times*, has much additional help, but sometimes the Japanese is written only in *romaji*. Get it anyway. The two food guides discussed under Food will also give you many things written in Japanese to which you can point to order what you want to eat. *Reading Your Way Around Japan* by Boye De Mente will help you read signs. You must start off on any expedition with all the aids you can find.

Also remember that you cannot read the telephone book. You might see an English telephone book in your hotel in Tokyo, but you won't find one anywhere else. Be sure to carry with you all the telephone numbers you will need.

The JNTO has a service to help tourists in trouble. You can now make a collect call to the Tourist Information Center from anywhere in Japan to get answers to your questions or assistance in translation if you are trying to communicate with someone. The instructions for the use of this service are in the JNTO publications. You will need to have your emergencies during working hours. The TIC is open from 9-5 on weekdays (except during lunch from 12-1) and from 9-12 on Saturdays.

FINDING YOUR WAY

Traveling in Japan without knowledge of the language is not for the fainthearted or those with poor sense of direction. Roman letters on maps and signs would solve many problems, but they are rare. Occasionally, in certain parts of the country, you will find a sign that you can read. But, except in Okinawa, you cannot get anywhere using these signs exclusively.

The Japan National Travel Organization is attempting to get more signs put up using the Roman alphabet, but it will be long in coming, if ever. Many Japanese resent the intrusion of signs in Roman letters and are actively resisting all efforts to add them. The greatest intellectual challenge facing you will not be in identifying new birds, but in finding your way to them. This book is designed to help you do just that.

The first rule is to be constantly aware of your surroundings: as you travel, note all potential landmarks, making sure at all times that you can make your way back to your starting point. You will often have to go back to point zero and begin again. If you can't find that, you are in real trouble. You cannot use a street sign to help you find your location on a map.

The ability to read Japanese would not help a great deal either. Most streets have no names. The way of designating locations is much different in Japan from what it is in the Western world. If you look at a city map, you will see lines and the spaces between the lines. We name the lines (streets); the Japanese name the spaces between the lines (blocks).

To illustrate, in Tokyo I lived on Meiji-dori (Meiji Street), a major thoroughfare and one of the few in the city with a known name, and a well-known one at that. But my address was not some number on Meiji-dori. It was instead 3-8, Jingumae 1-*chome*, Shibuya-ku, Tokyo. Tokyo is first subdivided into several large sections. Mine was Shibuya-ku. Each of these large divisions is further divided into many small "towns". My town was Jingumae. It is fairly easy to find Shibuya-ku, but locating the town requires more skill. Then each town is divided into a number of *chome*, usually somewhere between 10 and 20. These all have numbers rather than names. All these geographical entities are irregular in shape, and 2-*chome* is certainly not required to be located adjacent to 1-*chome*.

Back to my house: perhaps you have found Shibuya-ku and even Jingumae, but finding 1-*chome* on your own would take uncanny luck. Without a course in finding your way, you wouldn't know how to tell when you had arrived. Every so often you will pass a signboard with a map of the immediate neighborhood on it. But it is all in Japanese, so for your purposes undecipherable. Once you have found 1-*chome*, you must then find block 8, again not necessarily adjacent to either block 7 or block 9, and there you begin to look for house 3. The 3 tells you that it was the third house built on that block but gives you no hint where you will find it. Most of us had maps made showing the exact location of our houses. In a Japanese city you never start out to go to a new place without detailed instructions.

Getting to a good birding spot is not as difficult as finding an address in a large city. But you need to know that, although it varies considerably from area to area, the highways in Japan are poorly marked, if at all. Some highways which are numbered on a map will never have a number on the road and vice versa. The signs will almost always be in *kanji*. Often major highway intersections will not be marked at all, neither with a number nor even with a sign in Japanese. You must be prepared to stop and check the signs against your map. This usually is difficult to do in traffic, but essential. You must also be aware of the configuration of the roads and expected turns so you won't pass up one which is unmarked.

Once I was with Japanese friends driving through Nagoya. The drive seemed endless, and we were constantly making the wrong turn. They had a map, and everyone was participating in the attempt at navigation. Since I was seeing no street signs and no highway numbers, I asked what they were looking for. Their map showed the names of buildings, they said, so everyone was busy trying to read any names he could find. In all the clutter of signs in a large city, picking out the small ones while driving down the road is no easy task. I began to feel better about my own navigational abilities when I realized that, when traveling alone, I did not get lost any more, and perhaps less, than my Japanese friends who could read when I couldn't.

Take heart. It would be unfair not to point out the difficulties, but you can find your way. On the other hand, people who have trouble staying on course when they can read and speak the language will be far better off birding in Japan with a group. Those who become terribly frustrated and nervous when they run into problems and delays while traveling are also advised to join an organized tour. If your time is limited and you want to cover a large area of the country, you can't do it as quickly and efficiently on your own. But for those who prefer to travel independently and who feel up to the challenge, the problems are not insurmountable.

The main thrust of this book, besides telling where the birds are, is to give explicit directions on how to get to them, with the full understanding that you cannot read the signs or ask for help. In many cases, the directions and the accompanying maps in this book will be adequate (along with the Useful *Kanji*) for getting to a birding spot. In other cases you will feel more secure if you have a map of a larger area or a map of a larger scale than can be included here. If you are driving any distance, a highway map is essential.

In addition, national maps are sometimes useful. National map is my translation of a series of maps covering the entire country done by a government agency. Many are available on a scale of 1:25,000, and all of Japan is mapped on a scale of 1:50,000. There are two problems with these maps: they are in Japanese, and some of them are so old they lack many new roads. If you are going where the birding is good over a fairly large area, an up-to-date national map will show all the small roads you can explore and will be quite helpful. Once you get located on one of these maps, you should have no trouble keeping up with where you are. But getting them mixed up is a problem. You will have to match the *kanji* title with the name in this book. When you purchase a map, write something on it immediately to identify the area it covers.

You may want to check the date on any map that you buy, but reading a date in Japan requires some instruction. Years in Japan are numbered according to where they fall in the reign of an emperor. The reign of the current emperor is known as the Showa Era, and 1986 is the 61st year of his reign, or Showa 61. A search will reveal the date of publication on every map. You will recognize the month and date, and you can determine the year by adding the other number to 1925 (1926 was the year 1 in the Showa Era). Some of the national maps may be updated by the time you go to Japan and need them. If I have indicated that the current map is old, it might be worth checking to see if there is a new one.

The JNTO publishes some maps in English which they will give to you. Write them before you go and get the Tourist Map of Japan, the Tourist Map of Tokyo, and others noted throughout this book which are of interest to you. The Tourist Map of Japan is excellent for acquainting you with the geography of the country, but it is of little value for actual travel. You will find that if you are doing much traveling, you will need to use several maps in conjunction. This is another reason why you need a driver and a navigator to get around. It is too much for one person to handle alone.

While I was living in Japan, the only good highway maps available with any English on them were published by the Buyodo Map Company on a scale of 1:250,000. These maps were not available for every part of Japan. (There are several tourist maps in English which cover the country, but I found them either inadequate or inaccurate, and the towns were named only in Roman letters. You need to have names in both Japanese and in Roman letters so you can work out the highway signs which you encounter.)   The Buyodo maps are indicated for each birding site where they are useful. These maps fold in rather an interesting manner, but they easily fall open all over the car, further complicating your travel. Carry some large clips with you. When you get the map folded to the place you want, clip it so it will stay there until you want to turn to the next area.

A new series of maps, called Champion Maps, has recently been published by the Buyodo Company. I believe they are the best currently available. They come in four volumes and cover all of Japan. These booklets are slightly larger than 7 x 10 inches, and the maps are on a scale of 1:250,000. They show the latest roads and have more place names in Roman letters than the other Buyodo maps. You will still need a larger map all in one piece to help you find the page you are looking for in each booklet. If you order these four booklets from a bookstore and the maps from the JNTO before you leave home and study them along with the maps in this book, you will save a great deal of time after you arrive in Japan. If it makes sense to you at home, you will not have an excessive amount of trouble in Japan. If, after studying the Champion maps and this book, you are hopelessly confused, you are a prime candidate for an organized birding tour of Japan. If you pass that test, you can purchase any additional maps you need when you arrive in Tokyo.

The Champion booklets also contain maps of the major cities. All are labeled only in *kanji*, so you will have to match the names to those on the main maps. Some of the booklets have sketches of exits from freeways, as well as sketches showing how particular highways are routed through some small towns. Guessing at these Japanese symbols will be a test of your ability, but these sketches are helpful if you can figure them out.

This book attempts to keep you out of as many difficult situations as possible. Driving in the country is far easier than going through a large city. My recommendation is to get as close as you can to your birding spot by public transportation before setting out in a car. Then instructions are given on how to get from the airport or train station to the highway you need. If you are especially brave, after you practice a bit and you see you are doing fairly well, you can make longer trips by car if you prefer. But never forget that long-distance travel by car is extremely slow in Japan.

Essential items which you must bring with you are a small flashlight and a magnifying glass. You cannot see the *kanji* on the maps well enough to match it with road signs without a magnifying glass. And you are sure to find yourself trying to read in the dark despite all your good intentions not to be driving at night. A compass would be useful as well.

The clue to success with all this is to work out your route and be sure you understand where you are trying to go and how you plan to get there before you start off. Mark the route on your map and become as familiar as possible with the *kanji* you will need to recognize. Your preparation will be rewarded. Getting started is the worst part. It is difficult when you leave a subway or train station or a car rental office to figure out which way to go. Try to verify that you are starting off correctly. In as simple terms as possible, ask only enough to get yourself pointed in the right direction to the road you want or even out the correct exit of a train station. If you ask too much, unless you have had the luck to approach a Japanese who is fluent in English and good with directions, you will get in deeper than you mean to.

You will always do better to work out everything possible for yourself. You are asking for trouble every time you stop and ask for directions. You will inevitably get lost and have to ask, but you must be careful whom you ask. There is no way to know in advance if you have made a good choice, but it helps to know what you are up against. Asking directions will always take far more time than you think is necessary, and even when you find someone with whom you can communicate, you will seldom get a satisfactory answer.

I started off traveling about Japan thinking that, if I showed someone a map in Japanese with my destination marked on it, he could tell me which way to go, or at least show me on the map where we were. Most of the time this doesn't work. I haven't been able to determine exactly why this is so, but I have some theories. Almost every time you hand a person a map, he will turn it around and around and often end with it upside down. Maps published in Japan don't always have north at the top. This may contribute to the problem, but also I believe that the general public is not skilled in map reading. Usually the people who look confused with your map will be. They will consider and consult and may even make some suggestions, but don't depend on their accuracy.

I decided that perhaps I was asking people who did not drive and therefore had little experience with maps. After I became more experienced, I limited my questioning to gasoline station attendants or policemen. (Taxi drivers should be good sources, but I wasn't successful with the few I questioned.) This brought better results, but still it is risky. Japanese people will seldom tell you they don't know and suggest you ask someone else. Nor will they tell you anything precise even if they know it. With vagueness being a primary goal in the language and nobody wanting to take responsibility, you will seldom get anyone to say positively how you can find your road. After consulting with all their associates, they will give you at least two choices. Be prepared to spend a minimum of 15 minutes when you ask for help.

Policemen are the best sources, but they can be hard to find if you are on a highway, and they, too, come up with strange answers sometimes. Once I was searching for an office building in Tokyo and passed a large police station, not a small *koban*. I went in and was sent to an old gentleman standing behind a counter which held a huge book of maps containing drawings of every block and every building in the area. He appeared to have spent all his career standing right there directing the lost. I told him what I was looking for; he turned to the right map and referred to it as he drew a map for me. I had to begin by crossing a bridge which we could see out of the window. I verified that was the bridge and which way I should go, but when I got outside and over the bridge, nothing looked quite like the map he had drawn. Eventually I found the place and ascertained that he had drawn an exact mirror image of what the map should have been.

As you explore, you will gradually figure out good ways of getting yourself out of trouble. Even in the small towns, there is a chance of finding someone in an airline office who can understand a little English. But an airline office may not be readily available. Another excellent source of help, even if not always in English, is the post office. The people employed there should be familiar with the neighborhood and helpful if they understand what you want. When I have been far away from cities, I have found the local post office to be a good place to ask about restaurants and almost anything else I needed and couldn't find on my own.

I have found Japanese people willing and eager to help when I needed it. They will usually accompany you to where you are trying to go, if it isn't too far away, because they are certain you can't be trusted to get there on your own. I have encountered nothing but kindness in these situations. Once you make a request, you must stay there until the process is finished. You can't just say "oh, never mind" and run off when you see that real help is not going to be forthcoming. When you have lost 30 minutes while all this has been taking place, you will tend to get frustrated and upset. It is easy to forget in such circumstances that they also lost 30 minutes. So don't take off with the idea of making inquiries all along the way. Do it only when you are desperate.

WHAT TO BRING

Bring as little with you as possible. This is most important if you want an enjoyable and stress-free trip in Japan. Everything is on a smaller scale than most Westerners are used to, and you need to fit in. You, yourself, are likely to be far out of scale. The struggle to fit your oversized body and all your possessions into small spaces can be frustrating. With as many other problems as you will have while traveling, you don't need to be burdened with excess baggage. You will have to carry everything yourself (often for long distances), and there is little place to put it in your room, on a train, or in a car.

I know it is difficult to limit your baggage since you need boots, rain gear, a telescope, bird books, maps, etc., but you will regret every extra item you take. One solution is to plan your itinerary so you are in and out of Tokyo a few times. You can store some luggage at your hotel and go for several days at a time with, at most, a small bag and an airline flight bag. With all the extras birders require, at least keep your clothes to an absolute minimum.

I have watched the Japanese carefully and have tried to learn to pack as they do. I have made progress, but I am still unable to limit myself to one piece no larger than a flight bag. My award for best packing goes to a Japanese woman with whom I traveled for a week. She had everything, including binoculars, in a large purse. And it was large only by Japanese standards; an American would consider its size quite normal. She did not have a telescope, but she seemed to have everything she needed, as well as a few necessary things that some of the rest of us lacked.

Essential items are a magnifying glass and a small flashlight for reading maps, an International Driver's License, a towel, a washcloth, something for hand drying in public washrooms, and a small package of tissues. You will not be given a napkin in most restaurants, and you are likely to need one badly. Many public toilets do not provide toilet paper. Be prepared. Clips for holding folding maps together are a great convenience if you are driving. Carry your passport with you at all times.

Credit cards will be useful in Tokyo and in some major hotels elsewhere. They are becoming more widely used, but don't count on being able to use them. American Express and Visa and, sometimes, Mastercard are accepted. Your car rental cards may be helpful in getting discounts on cars and rooms in some hotels, but gasoline credit cards are useless. Most Japanese pay for everything with cash and are accustomed to carrying large sums of money.

It is easy to cash traveler's checks in Tokyo, though sometimes it seems to take much more time than is necessary. The last time I was assisting a friend with this process, we discovered that the exchange rate in the hotels matched that in the banks. Major hotels in Tokyo usually handle this transaction much more swiftly than banks. It gets more difficult and time-consuming when you leave Tokyo or a large city accustomed to many foreign visitors. You will usually have to find a bank and wait for some time. Your hotel or *ryokan* will seldom be able to do this for you. It is best to take plenty of cash when you start off on an expedition.

If you come in warm weather, and especially if you are going to any of the southern islands, carry mosquito coils. They can be bought cheaply in any pharmacy and are called *katori-senko*.

In winter, take advantage of what many birders consider one of Japan's greatest products: hand warmers. These, too, can be bought in any pharmacy. They are small packages of chemicals sealed in plastic. Remove the plastic wrapper and shake the package vigorously for a few seconds. It will then produce heat for about 24 hours. Put them in your pockets. In bitter cold, the Japanese slip one into an old nylon stocking and tie it around their waist with the warmer at the small of the back. Ask for a *poketto kairo* (pocket warmer). A popular brand is Hokaron. Another is Naisu Hotto (nice hot).

Kodak and other brands of film can be bought cheaply at one of the two discount camera shops across from Shinjuku Station in Tokyo. They are Sakura and Yodobashi. Go out the east exit of the station and look to your right. Ask anybody if you don't find them. This takes time, so you may prefer bringing film from home. These prices are much better than elsewhere in Japan.

First-time visitors to Japan are always impressed with how well dressed everyone is all the time. Japanese birders regularly go out in designer sports clothes. I have never seen any evidence that Japanese possess any old worn-out clothes. If they did, they certainly wouldn't wear them birdwatching. This is simply a warning that you will be even more conspicuous if you are accustomed to birding in anything but your newest and finest. Although they are impeccably dressed, they do wear the same costume throughout a trip. They never seem to fall in the mud or rip their clothes climbing over or through fences.

There is no need to change clothes for the evening if you are staying in a *minshuku*. In a *ryokan* where you have dinner in your room, you can wear the *yukata* which is provided. Only when you are staying in the finer hotels where you will be eating in a nice restaurant either inside or outside the hotel will you want different clothes for evening. Most of the time men will not feel out of place without a coat and tie. In a fine resort hotel, women will want a skirt, or at least more fashionable slacks than those they wear birding. Men will be comfortable in a nice sport shirt or sweater. Save the coat and tie for Tokyo. Even there, you can manage without it under most circumstances and save room in your luggage. Japanese men wear suits and ties during the day, but not necessarily in the evenings. Nevertheless, they are always elegantly dressed.

If you come in winter, remember that it is cold, and most traditional Japanese buildings do not have central heating. In a *minshuku* or *ryokan* there will be a heater somewhere, though not necessarily in your room. You will be warm inside your *futon*, but be sure to have plenty of warm clothes. The entire country is cold in winter except for the southern islands, so warm clothes are essential for birding as well as for evenings in your *minshuku*. Hokkaido, northern Honshu, and most areas along the Japan Sea coast have bitterly cold winters with much snow.

SAFETY & THE POLICE

It is doubtful that there is any country you could visit where you would be in less danger than in Japan. There certainly is crime in the country, but it so seldom affects a foreigner that we soon begin to feel it doesn't exist. There is almost no chance that you will be the victim of robbery or violence of any kind. But don't let this cause you to become careless and take foolish risks.

You will seldom be alone in Japan even when birdwatching. In the few places where this is possible, it is probably wiser, at least for a woman, not to go without a companion. I have done it, but I still believe it is best to be cautious at all times, even when there is no need for fear.

If you do encounter something unpleasant, it is most likely to be just that: unpleasant rather than dangerous. Most often, the unpleasantness will be in the form of a group of drunks. What you will suffer is harassment rather than harm. Public drunkenness is socially acceptable in Japan, and a drunk is usually excused from any responsibility for his actions.

I suspect that a man alone will attract little attention of an objectionable sort. A woman alone in Japan is in a little different situation. I have traveled all over Japan by myself with no problems, but I always take care to be where I am supposed to be by nightfall. If I am having dinner outside my hotel, I make sure the place is an appropriate one for me to go to alone, and I am careful to give no indication of any interest in the other patrons. Most of the time the other patrons will be groups of men. Women stay home in the evenings. You rarely see a family going out for dinner together. Again, it is not a question of being in danger, but of being subjected to unwanted and often rude attentions. According to many things I have heard and read, in Japan the sympathy of the police is seldom with a woman if there is an incident.

I never rode a train or a subway by myself late at night. The behavior of many of the men on the last train home is notorious. It is a scene to be avoided.

Japan has a system of neighborhood police boxes, called *koban*, which many believe to be a significant contributing factor to the general safety of the country. It is the business of the police at the local *koban* to know everyone in the neighborhood and be aware of everything that goes on. Policemen spend much of their time giving directions (Japanese people can't find their way either) and otherwise tending to small problems. Their conspicuous presence apparently serves as a major deterrent to crime.

This is where you should go if you need help. The problem is that you will need a bit of practice to recognize the *koban*. The *kanji* is given in the appendix under Essential *Kanji*, but few have signs which are obvious. Usually the *koban* will occupy a tiny building on a corner. These can be minute, but a uniformed policeman is usually in sight. In Tokyo there is a fair chance that a *koban* will have at least one policeman who can speak a few words of English, enough to help you in an emergency anyway. Don't count on this outside of Tokyo. If you go to the police for help and are polite and respectful, you can be sure to be treated courteously and given the help that you need, provided you can make yourself understood.

It is imperative that you carry your passport with you at all times. There is a good chance that the police will stop you and ask for it. They have every right to do this. In fact, they are instructed, so I understand, to stop every foreigner they see. If you don't have it, there is bound to be trouble. You will be subject to a fine which is seldom waived, and you will lose a considerable amount of time before you are finally released.

The first time I was stopped was in Tsushima. I had walked no more than 20 feet from the end of the gangplank after disembarking from the ferry, when two men in plain clothes stopped me, said they were policemen, and asked for my passport. I didn't believe them at first, and then wanted to know what I had done to cause them to detain me. Righteous indignation is not the way to handle these situations. The Japanese friends with me told me to be absolutely quiet and let them handle it. I presented my resident's permit. They didn't just look to see that I had it, they read every word and questioned my friends about me at length. The questioning covered a wide range of personal and what I considered unrelated information, especially details about my husband and his work in Japan. (Most Japanese men, at least, think a woman has no identity of her own. What matters most about her is who her husband is.) When they had satisfied themselves that my husband was employed by a well-known and respectable company, I was released. This took some time.

I could count on being stopped when I was birdwatching outside Tokyo. Birding gets you to places where foreigners seldom go, so you are sure to be noticed by the local police. But, once in Tokyo, a friend and I were walking on the sidewalk just outside the entrance to Oi Bird Park when a police car came to a screeching halt beside us. Two policemen jumped out and raced toward us. I looked around to see whom they were after and was surprised to discover that they wanted us. These two were less than polite. After they were satisfied and started to leave, I asked why they had stopped us. The answer was that it was their duty. If you accept it as just that, are polite even if they aren't, and answer all their questions even if you think it is none of their business, all will be well, provided you do have your passport with you. Remember, it is their country and the law of the land. The police attention, which you may resent, could be the reason why Japan is such a safe country.

Police, from time to time, set up road blocks to check all drivers' licenses. If you are stopped, you will also have to produce your passport and explain where you are going and what you are doing. Show your binoculars and your bird book, and they will probably understand. I am not aware of any sensitive areas you are likely to get into where the use of binoculars will cause trouble. The sensitive areas I know of are so well guarded you won't get in by mistake.

You should be especially cautious while driving and obey all traffic regulations. It is easy to make mistakes because of the confusion of trying to find your way and to decipher all the warning signs. The speed limits are usually extraordinarily low. If you aren't sure, guess on the conservative side.

If you should be stopped for a traffic violation, you will be far better off if you handle the situation the Japanese way. That is to be excessively humble and apologize profusely to the policeman for your error. If you have committed a minor offense and are properly remorseful and apologetic, you may be let go because you are a foreigner and the policeman doesn't want to get deeply involved trying to communicate with you.

I did not behave properly the one time I was stopped for a traffic violation. I was, and still am, convinced that I did not speed through a radar trap. I had traveled only about 50 meters from a dead stop at a light. During that short journey I was passed by three cars, all of which honked because I was going so slowly. I had just recovered from a wrong turn and was attempting to avoid making another by creeping down the highway so I could read the signs. I expected the policeman who flagged me down to want to check my identification since he could see that I was a foreigner. Other than that, the only thing I could think of was that I would be reprimanded for obstructing traffic.

When I found out what the charge was, especially considering that the three cars which sped past me were not stopped, I insisted that there was a mistake. If you can restrain yourself, do not ever suggest to a policeman in Japan that he might have made a mistake. We spent 45 minutes by the side of the highway while I was made to answer endless questions about why I was so far away from home alone, where I was going, what I was going to do there, when I was going to return to Tokyo, etc. Then I was told to sign a ticket which was an admission of guilt. When I refused and asked what recourse I had, I was taken to the main police headquarters where the questioning continued for another three hours.

All I was trying to do was find out if I could tell my story to a traffic judge or the equivalent who would decide, after hearing the evidence, if I was guilty. The ensuing events are material for quite another story. Another part of it which could be useful for you to know is that a police interpreter was eventually called in who wanted me to make a statement in English which he would write down in Japanese. The situation deteriorated even more when I refused to sign anything I couldn't read. It was a memorable experience, but in retrospect I see that it was extremely foolish for me to argue. I don't recommend it at all.

When I got back to Tokyo and recounted my experience to Japanese friends, they were overcome with disbelief that I would even consider arguing with the police. The answer is there is no recourse, or at least none worth pursuing. They all said that I would have been much better off to apologize immediately even though I was positive I had not exceeded the speed limit.

My advice to you is to obey the rules scrupulously so you will not be stopped. If you are stopped, besides being apologetic, don't give any indication that you can speak or understand Japanese, even if you can. Don't sign anything you cannot read. Signing the traffic ticket, according to my sources, is an admission of guilt. If the situation is serious, call your embassy or consulate for help. You will need an interpreter who will be on your side.

In addition to being safe from bodily harm and not having to worry about being robbed, there is no need to fear being cheated. If an extensive search were made, a few people would surely be found who might try to take advantage of you. I never encountered one in three years of travel. You will never see Japanese people count their change. They always assume the salesperson is honest and accurate. Sometimes they do make mistakes, but you can be sure it is unintentional. I once had a salesgirl follow me three blocks to return ¥10 (about two and a half cents) which she realized I was due.

A friend pointed out the importance of visitors being aware that cheating is not a problem. Once when he was on a train, the conductor made him buy an extra ticket. He didn't know that, besides a ticket for the regular fare, he needed a ticket to cover the extra charge for a fast train. His tendency was to argue. In many countries where he travels regularly, he would be safe to assume the conductor was trying to pocket some extra money.

It is best to know the situation in Japan. If someone demands extra payment, it is legitimate. You can relax, and the Japanese will be relieved of having to deal with an angry and suspicious foreigner. This will help the encounters between our cultures to be smoother.

GOOD MANNERS & MEETING JAPANESE

The Japanese probably are no more and no less polite than any other people, despite their reputation for extreme politeness. Japanese politeness manifests itself in ways which are different from those of most other cultures and in ways which are obvious and impressive to foreigners. We are interested to see all the bowing and the rest of the ritual which takes place when people meet. A translation of all the set phrases which are repeated like a lengthy litany would amaze you. But it has as much sincerity as "How are you?" does in English; it is just much longer.

To watch a group of Japanese try to go through a door can be great entertainment. Everyone gets deeply involved in multiple repetitions of "Please, you go first." Much time is wasted before they finally go through in an order which they all knew well before the discussion started. Position and age will decide the order, from the highest ranked to the lowest. Japanese always know exactly where they stand in relation to every member of any group in which they find themselves. This determines their speech and behavior.

This extreme politeness occurs only among people who are acquainted. The rudeness of an anonymous Japanese subway passenger can equal that of the most infamous city dwellers anywhere in the world. A Japanese has no obligations of any kind to someone he has not met. Although you will see many evidences of politeness, you will discover that there are a couple of things the Japanese commonly do which are considered unacceptable to the point of being unmentionable in Western societies.

Now that I've warned you so you won't be surprised when you do see rude behavior, I must emphasize that you will see relatively little of it. You will, instead, be treated with such courtesy that you will probably have re-entry problems when you return to your own country.

Where else in the world is there an announcement on the public address system in the train or subway station (where the trains run every four minutes) which says "Good morning, welcome to X Station. We are sorry to have kept you waiting, but your train is now coming. Because it is dangerous, please step behind the white line while the train is coming in..."? Young women stand outside elevators to bow to you as you get on and off. This is in addition to the elevator operator who does the same thing. Someone usually stands by the door in the grocery store to bow and thank you for your patronage as you leave. A favorite activity for foreign visitors in Tokyo is to be the first in the door when a department store opens. If you are in the first wave of customers on the escalators and go all the way to the top, a welcoming committee at the front door plus every salesperson on each floor will bow in unison as you make your appearance.

When you are the customer or the visitor, people cannot do enough for you. There will be an abundance of sales people or waiters to serve you cheerfully. In Japan there is no tipping, so you have the feeling that everyone is treating you well because they want to. It all makes for a most pleasant stay. No matter who you are and what standards of behavior you are accustomed to, you will have a task before you to keep up with the Japanese.

Outwardly life in a Japanese city looks much the same as that in any modern city, but many Westerners fail to realize and probably none of us fully appreciates the extent and seriousness of the social and cultural differences. Most of the time we simply don't

understand each other and often aren't even aware of it. Things
are seldom as they seem.

Your behavior and manners can be impeccable by the standards of
your own culture and still be offensive to the Japanese. You can't
always expect them to understand that you mean well; your
customs are simply different. Japan is an insular and homogeneous
society. Most Japanese have had little or no experience with
foreigners and know as little about other cultures as most of us
know about theirs. Like many of the rest of us, many Japanese
believe theirs is the best and only way. They can be unforgiving
to those who do not conform.

To the Japanese, you will look strange and your behavior will
seem even more strange. While we all need to learn to respect
customs of people different from ourselves, we should not be the
ones to try to force this on the Japanese. We who are visitors in
Japan should make every effort to conform to their principles of
good behavior and perhaps show them a few others in addition.

A Westerner has little chance of ever learning to behave in true
Japanese fashion. But risking oversimplification, here are a few
pointers which, if you follow them, will let the Japanese know
that you are at least making an effort.

1. When you meet a person do not shake hands unless
   that person, in recognition of your custom, offers
   his hand first. Japanese do not shake hands. You
   will win points by not rushing forward with your
   hand extended; you will make an even bigger hit if
   you will bow. Don't worry about bowing low or
   properly; they will notice and appreciate your
   effort.

2. Preliminaries are important. If you want to ask a
   question or begin a conversation, don't just blurt it
   out. Always begin with "Excuse me" and continue
   with as many phrases as you can manage, such as "I
   am sorry to bother you. I know I am being rude by
   interrupting you, but would you be so kind as to
   allow me to ask you a question..." This ritual goes
   on for some length in Japanese. You will appear
   rude if you neglect at least an attempt at it.

If you are meeting someone you have met before, remember to begin with some comment about the last time you met and thank him for what he did for you at that time. Surely you can figure out something. At least thank him for being kind to you the last time you met. Then inquire about his family and discuss the weather. The Japanese do not ask about each other's health, but weather and the season (cherry blossoms, autumn leaves, full moon, etc.) are commonly discussed at length.

3. Never call a Japanese by his first name or insist that he use yours. After the age of five, even children call each other by their last names. A Japanese told me of his extreme discomfort when he spent a week in an office in England working on a project. The person in charge announced to him that he would be called by his first name because that was the custom there. He said he continued to be startled every time someone addressed him. His father was the only person who had ever called him by his first name. His mother did not, his brothers and sisters did not, and his wife did not.

The most common form of address and the one which is always acceptable is the last name followed by *san*. This is suitable for men, women, and children. There are other designations, such as *sensei* for teachers and doctors and *chan* for young children and dogs, but you would never be expected to know that. It is possible that you will encounter a Japanese who will tell you to call him by his first name, either because he has lived outside of Japan and has been called by his first name often or because he is aware of your habits and is trying to make you comfortable. Don't.

4. Speak quietly at all times. I know, the Japanese don't always, but they expect you to. Japanese groups can be rowdy. Sometimes I believe there is nothing a Japanese loves more than an excuse to use a microphone or a bullhorn, but in general, they are quiet. Foreigners get a great deal of criticism for

speaking louder than the Japanese think is appropriate for them. A group of foreigners in a public place laughing noisily or otherwise attracting attention to themselves will never be forgiven. A Japanese associate has described to me in great detail his dislike of foreigners who come into his office shaking hands, speaking loudly, and speaking directly (more about the latter later). When you initiate a conversation, be sure to speak only slightly above a whisper as you remember to say all your "excuse me's". This will get you started off much better and will increase your chances of getting the results you seek.

5. This next one is surely the most difficult for a Westerner to understand and certainly to follow. You must be indirect in all things. This aspect of the Japanese character is fascinating, but much too complicated to take up here. While we are taught to get to the point, especially in a business situation, in order not to waste another person's time, getting directly to the point is the height of rudeness to a Japanese.

After you finish all the preliminaries, do your best to avoid making any definite or strong statements. Try to sneak up on your subject, endeavoring to accomplish what you need to with gentle hints. If this is all going well, the person to whom you are talking will catch on and help you. Try to let him suggest what you are trying to say. It is best to avoid expressing definite opinions. I am not talking about saying what you think when your honesty might give offense; I am talking about simply saying what you think. Japanese are reluctant to commit themselves. The goal in Japanese is to speak in as vague terms as possible. They learn to do this and to understand each other in the process. You will never catch on to this one, but you must be aware that your positive statements and your directness will grate on the nerves of the Japanese. At least try to soften it.

A Japanese who speaks English well may have had enough experience with foreign ways to forgive you. But you will get much better results if you try to conform.

6. Don't ask for anything. If you want to make a request, hint. Then if what you want is possible, it will be done. Otherwise it will never be mentioned outright, and nobody will be uncomfortable about it. We are accustomed to stating what we want and asking if it is possible or convenient. The Japanese will never do this. They do not want to be told no, and they will not say no. This goes for business as well as social situations. They will always figure out a way to determine that the answer is not no (by using an intermediary if necessary) before they will ask the question.

If you do make a request, a Japanese will never say no, that it is impossible, that it is inconvenient, or that he doesn't want to. He will, instead, do everything in his power to give you what you have asked for. This may take him a great deal of time or even a great deal of money or require some other sacrifice, but he will do it if he can. Since foreigners don't understand this, or at least don't understand the extent of it, they often put Japanese people in difficult situations. This is one reason why some Japanese don't want to talk to foreigners. This is an area where our basic approaches clash severely, often resulting in serious problems.

To put this on a level where a visitor will most often be involved, when staying in a *ryokan* or *minshuku*, don't ask for something which isn't offered. If they are prepared to give you scrambled eggs or coffee or even bread instead of rice, they will offer it. If you are sitting at the table and see that there is salt on the table, certainly you may ask someone to pass it to you. But be sure you do not ask for something that is not readily available. Be careful of making assumptions. What you consider to be a staple item found in every household may not exist in a Japanese house.

The Japanese have many signals which they send out so others can recognize if the conversation is heading toward difficulty of some kind or other. These will be much too subtle for you to recognize, but there is a warning sign you can notice. If a Japanese person sucks in his breath, back off of whatever you are saying, asking, or doing. He may be smiling and saying "yes, yes," but the sucking in of breath is an absolute indication that a problem exists. In conjunction with this, you need to know that when a Japanese person says "yes" (*hai*), he means "yes, I hear you," and it does not indicate agreement.

Be careful of wishing aloud. You may consider yourself to be making an idle comment, but the listener may feel an obligation to try to make your wish come true. All of us who have had the opportunity have probably made the terrible error of admiring something which belonged to a Japanese and had him give it to us. Once you have done this, it usually is impossible to refuse to take it. Instead, give him a gift in return.

7. Never wear shoes in a Japanese home or in many Japanese buildings. Every time you enter a Japanese building, stop and look around you to determine what is required regarding shoes. In a hotel or public building where you should remove your shoes, you will see shoes lined up in the entry or a cabinet for shoes nearby. There should also be slippers handy for you to put on when you remove your shoes. You will seldom enter such a building without someone being at the door whom you can ask to make sure. When you enter a home, *ryokan*, or *minshuku*, don't ask, just take off your shoes. The importance of this custom cannot be overemphasized. Foreigners who wear shoes when they shouldn't, greatly offend the Japanese.

8. There is no tipping in Japan. Enjoy it while you can. We can only hope that this custom will spread to more countries and thus make life more pleasant for us all. Handing money to someone other than a salesperson is considered rude. When money is given for some reason, it must be properly wrapped in a   special kind of envelope expressly for that purpose. There is one right way to give a gift of money. Surely you will not find yourself in a situation where it is required.

I've noticed Japanese friends are even uncomfortable if they have made a purchase for me at my request and I hand them the money to pay for it. Your change will always be given to you on a tray. If your bill is presented on a tray, be sure to put the money on the tray rather than hand it to the person. Occasionally your receipt and your change will be given to you in an envelope.

9. To end this brief lesson in proper behavior, you will come out ahead in almost all situations if you do nothing to call attention to yourself. With your foreign features and coloring, you will always be obvious in Japan. You can't get lost in the crowd. This is enough attention. Try to be as inconspicuous as possible, but also do your best to keep from advertising your talents or your reputation. The goal for a Japanese is to do nothing to stand out. If you arrive and announce that you are an expert of some sort, you will not be received with favor. If the Japanese already know of your reputation, they will call attention to it at some length. Then your job is to deny the importance of what you have accomplished and certainly that you are well known.

The gracious acceptance of a compliment is unacceptable in Japan. A simple example is if someone says you are wearing a lovely dress, you must say something to the effect that it is very old and certainly never was nice, even if you spent a fortune for it that very day. And if you are giving a gift, you must present it with many apologies, saying that it is nothing special, but despite its unworthiness, you hope it will be accepted.

Bear all these things in mind, and try to be sensitive to what is going on around you. Then be on your best behavior by the standards of your own culture. That is all that you can do, and, of course, all that should be expected of you. If the Japanese recognize that you have some familiarity with their ways and are attempting to adjust your behavior to conform somewhat to their standards, you will be welcome wherever you go. But another aspect of the Japanese sense of propriety is that they will never let a foreigner know that he is not liked or has given offense. While having totally negative feelings toward you, they may treat you in such a way as to make you think you have been adopted into the family. Sincerity and intellectual honesty are not traits which are regarded highly in Japan. You will think everything is wonderful, but be aware that reality and appearances in Japan are often widely divergent.

MAKING ARRANGEMENTS & GETTING HELP

Please do not ask for help from the WBSJ. This organization is not equipped to deal with inquiries and requests for assistance from visiting birders. They do not have the English-speaking staff to handle inquiries. Even if communication were not so difficult, no one has the time to devote to this activity. There is no guide service available. An announcement of your impending visit with a request for suggestions on where you should go and what birds you can expect to see is well beyond their capacity.

They specifically discourage telephone calls. The communication problem is even more severe over the phone. One of the few members of the staff who is able to handle such a situation will have to be called from his work to deal with your inquiry.

You may want to visit the offices of the WBSJ when you are in Tokyo. The bookshop is stocked with assorted items which may be of interest to you. While there, certainly introduce yourself. If you have some specific question for which you are unable to find an answer, ask, of course, but do not go in with general questions or requests for someone to show you around. Be considerate of their time.

The staff of the WBSJ assisted me in my work on this book in the hope that if this information were available to the birders of the world, they would no longer receive so many inquiries.

Advance Planning
If you travel independently, it is important to plan everything you can before you leave home, or you will spend a great deal of time in Tokyo doing just that. Order the books and maps you need from Tokyo and get maps and information from the Japan National Travel Organization in your home country or write to Tokyo. The publications which will be helpful if you have them before your arrival are mentioned in other sections. Familiarity with the food guides and the books with language aids will not help you plan your trip, but will make everything easier for you on your arrival.

You need to plan your itinerary and decide how you will travel. Of course, you can make adjustments, but it is best to have a good idea of where you will go. If you will be using trains enough to warrant a JNR pass, you must buy it before you arrive in Japan. This can be done through either Japan Air Lines or a travel agent.

If you want to have all arrangements made ahead, get in touch with the foreign independent tourist department of a major travel agency in Japan or go through your own travel agency. This will be expensive. If you deal directly with a Japanese travel agency, their charges will add at least 10 - 15% to the total cost of your trip. If you go through a local travel agency, it will be even more. Everyone makes something out of this.

If you prefer to travel with this kind of security, choose a well-run birding tour. It will surely cost you less money, and your trip should be trouble free. If you have everything done in advance by a travel agency, you will lose all flexibility and you will still have the worry of finding your way around on your own.

If you are making your own arrangements, you can write in English for reservations at major hotels in Tokyo and to several other hotels. These are noted in the site guides. You could also try writing to the two *minshuku* in Nemuro. If reservations are required for other places, you must get someone to make them for you in Japanese. Letters in English will be ignored. In most instances, you will not need a reservation far ahead of time. Tokyo, however, can get crowded, and the luxury hotels are often fully booked well in advance. It is best to make reservations at all the places you can deal with in English, and take care of the rest when you arrive in Japan.

Planning and Assistance in Tokyo
When you arrive in Tokyo, first visit the TIC (Tourist Information Center) which belongs to the JNTO. Here you can get answers to all your questions, though the TIC will make no arrangements for you. Collect any additional literature they have available on the places you will visit and check schedules and accommodations. They will cheerfully assist you at some length if necessary.

Then get someone to help you make the additional reservations which are necessary. If you go through a travel agency for reservations, you must be firm when you request accommodations at some of the places recommended in this book. They are likely to tell you that the places you have chosen are not suitable for you and suggest substitutes.

Find out ahead of time what the travel agency will charge for helping you. Some will add a flat percentage of the cost of all your accommodations and tickets. Others will charge you for telephone calls and a bit more for the time they spend on your behalf. You may have to shop around. In Tokyo, you will have no trouble finding a number of travel agencies which can assist you in English. If you wish to stay as flexible as possible, you may be lucky enough to find someone at an agency whom you could call from time to time as you travel throughout the country, getting them to make your next reservations for you.

The luxury hotels in Tokyo have service desks where their guests can get assistance with a great many things. If you are staying at one of these hotels and you don't require an excessive amount of help, see if they are willing to make your calls for you. If you know exactly where you want to stay, when, and the telephone number, it might cost you no more than the price of the telephone calls.

You will need to make arrangements for rental cars while you are in Tokyo. This is discussed in detail under Transportation. Do not fail to establish a contact with the headquarters of a rental car company before you leave town.

If you need additional maps, some of the national maps for example, go to the Maruzen Bookstore in Nihonbashi or the Taiseido Book Center in Shibuya. The national maps are available in many stores in Tokyo (don't count on finding them somewhere else), but these two are easy to find and they usually have most of the maps in stock.

Maruzen is across the street from the Nihonbashi Takashimaya Department Store. It is centrally located and is at a subway stop. Anyone can direct you. The maps are on the second floor; the foreign language books are on the third. If you haven't found help somewhere else, you can locate someone in the inquiries section on the third floor who will speak English and will see that you get assistance in finding the maps and anything else you need.

Taiseido Book Center is near Shibuya Station (both subway and JNR). It is across the street from the Seibu Department Store annex, and is a bit difficult to spot. Search for a small "Book Center" sign or look in all the shops until you find a book store.

The map department is on the fifth floor. When you run out of escalators, use the stairs. On the fifth floor you will find the alcove containing the map department on your right and to the back. I have almost always found all the maps I needed in stock here. Since the maps are in a separate area with a large counter where they can be spread out and examined away from the crowds and general commotion, getting what you need is easier here than in many shops. You may not find a salesperson who speaks English, but you need only to point in this book to the maps you want. All the people who have served me at Taiseido have been particularly knowledgeable about the maps and willing to help.

In case you encounter a salesperson who is not very familiar with the maps, it will help if you know generally where in Japan the area in question is located and can point it out on a map of Japan. By the time you go shopping for maps, you should know enough Japanese geography to do this.

When you have done all this, go by the WBSJ office and see what is for sale. I suggest that you pay ¥4,000 and become a member. This will probably come back to you in discounts at WBSJ associated accommodations. Anyway, you will be supporting the preservation of birds and habitat in Japan. It is sorely needed. If you still have some questions, see if you can get an answer there. Then you are ready to be on your way.

Outside Tokyo
Try to think of everything before you leave Tokyo, for once you have gone, you are, for the most part, on your own. There are additional sources of aid, but it is best to plan to use them only for emergencies. You will have more need of them than you want anyway.

If you have a problem during office hours, you can telephone collect to the TIC in Tokyo for help. They probably won't be able to tell you which way you should turn at the intersection, but they can serve as interpreters to help you talk to someone who can give you local information or assistance.

A local information office will be inside or near many train stations. You are unlikely to find any tourist information in English or a person who can speak English. But since their job is to give information, they will know the answers and make every effort to understand and help you. If you have the time to make a stop and struggle with the communication, you can sometimes find a local map which, though entirely in Japanese, will be of some assistance.

There are police boxes everywhere. This is discussed in Safety and the Police. Don't count on finding a policeman who speaks English, but this is an excellent place to go in an emergency or if you are lost. A distinct advantage here is that the police are on duty around the clock.

If you are fortunate enough to be near an airline office when you have a problem, you will have a good chance of finding someone inside with whom you can communicate. They aren't there to give general assistance, but they can usually help if you are lost or if you want to know where to find a nearby hotel or restaurant.

A post office is another good place to ask directions or for local information. Depending, of course, on where you are, you will have a fair chance of finding someone in a post office who can understand your plight. They will be friendly. Often all the customers will get involved in trying to understand you, and someone will turn up who can help. Learn the post office symbol (see the appendix) so you can easily find the local post office.

I never had any problems with a car I rented in Japan, so I can give no advice on what that is likely to involve. Car trouble could be a disaster if you cannot communicate. Every time you rent a car you will get a telephone number to call if there is a problem, but I think you will have almost no chance of getting someone on the other end who can understand a word you say. This is an important subject for you to cover when you visit the rental car agency before you leave Tokyo.

SAPPORO AREA

Sapporo, the principal city of Hokkaido, is a popular destination for tourists. Most visitors to Hokkaido will find themselves in Sapporo anyway because it is the main point of entry by air. It is also a good place for birdwatching.

The main airport is at Chitose, about an hour south of Sapporo. Utonai Sanctuary is 15 minutes by car from the airport in the other direction. Any visit to Sapporo should be combined with a visit to Utonai. Nopporo Forest Park is the most important birding spot in the Sapporo area, followed by Nishioka Suigenchi. These three places will give you a chance at seeing most of the species which occur in this part of Hokkaido. If you are spending a lot of time in Sapporo and come in the right season, a trip to the mouth of the Ishikari River would be worth a day.

It is possible to visit Utonai while staying in Sapporo, but it is more convenient to stay near the sanctuary. For all the other places in the Sapporo area, it is best to stay in the city center. This is convenient if you are using public transportation. If you are driving, it is easier to find your way and quicker to reach your destination if you start from a central location.

Transportation:
It is easy to get to Sapporo (Chitose Airport) by plane. There are frequent flights to and from Tokyo (Haneda Airport). JAL has 12 flights each way daily, ANA has 11, and TDA has three. This trip takes 1½ hours. In addition, JAL has one flight to Narita, three to Osaka, and one to Fukuoka (2 hours, 20 minutes). ANA has three to Osaka, three to Nagoya, four to Sendai, two to Niigata, and one to Komatsu. TDA has five flights to Kushiro (40 minutes) as well as flights to Memanbetsu, Hakodate, Aomori, Misawa, Akita, Hanamaki, and Yamagata. The small Sapporo Airport, on the north side of the city, is served by NKA with flights to Nemuro Nakashibetsu, Monbetsu, Wakkanai, and Hakodate.

You can get to all the Sapporo birdwatching places by public transportation. If you have rented a car for Hokkaido under a fly-drive arrangement, use it in Sapporo. It is easy to find your way around, and a car will save you time.

Food:
Be sure to try the local seafood while you are in Hokkaido. Crab and salmon are specialties. Ishikari *nabe*, salmon and seasonal vegetables cooked in broth in a big pot on your table, is one of the famous dishes of the area. There are plenty of good restaurants. I can recommend Ezogoten in Tanukikoji, a shopping arcade in the center of town. The food is delicious and not too expensive. Everything about the place is in traditional Hokkaido style. It is interesting and full of local color. The telephone number is 011-241-8451. Ask directions at your hotel.

Accommodations:
Sapporo has all kinds of accommodations, including a number of first-class hotels. The tourist information lists numerous places. The Tokyu Inn in central Sapporo (¥11,000 for a twin room before discount) is a comfortable hotel which is less expensive than some of the others. The telephone number is 011-531-0109.

Maps and Information:
The most helpful thing I've found for finding the way around Sapporo is "Your Guide to Sapporo", an excellent map of Sapporo with subway, bus, and other information in English. I got mine from the Sapporo Tourist Association in the City Hall, telephone 011-211-3341. It is published by Iay Press, Hinode Building, Minami 1, Nishi 4, Chuo-ku, Sapporo 060, Japan, telephone 011-281-5188. It is worth going to some trouble, if necessary, to obtain one.

>   Champion Maps, Vol. 1, Hokkaido
>   JNTO Information Sheet MG-011
>   Welcome to Sapporo, (Tourism Dept., City of Sapporo)

NOPPORO FOREST PARK

Season: May - July, all year
Specialties: Hazel Grouse, Black Woodpecker

Most of Hokkaido's forest birds occur in Nopporo Forest Park (Nopporo Shinrin Koen). More than 100 species are recorded here each year.

Transportation:
There are several ways to get here by public transportation. By bus, it takes at least 45 minutes, plus another 25 minutes on foot. By train, it takes about an hour, plus the same walk. It takes 30 minutes to drive from the center of Sapporo.

Nopporo Forest Park

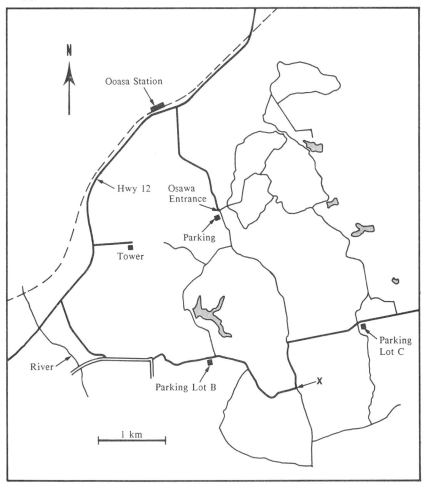

Directions:
At the Sapporo Station Bus Terminal take the Kokutetsu Bus (JNR) bound for Ebetsu. Get off at Joshi-Tandai bus stop. Walk from there to the Osawa entrance to the park. Alternately, take the Tozai Line Subway to Shin-Sapporo Station and catch the bus

for Ebetsu there. At Sapporo Station you can get a train on the JNR Hakodate Line and get off at Ooasa. This takes an hour. The train station is near the bus stop, so the walking time is the same.

By car, take Hwy. 12 from Sapporo. You will cross the Toyohira River at the Azuma Bridge. From this bridge, it is 16.3 km. to the Osawa entrance to Nopporo Forest Park. The sign on Hwy. 12 indicating a right turn over the Azuma Bridge does not show a highway number, but it shows (in Roman letters) Asahikawa and Iwamizawa to the right and Numata and Tobetsu straight ahead. Turn right and stay on Hwy. 12.

Shortly before you reach the turnoff to Nopporo Forest Park, you will see a tall, dark monolith (the Hokkaido Centennial Tower) on the right, back some distance from the highway. Then you will see, in this order, a Kazama Ski sign on the right, a pedestrian bridge over the highway, and a 15 km. sign on the left. Watch for the 16 km. sign, near which is a sign over the highway indicating a right turn. Turn right at that sign. It is 14.2 km. from the Azuma Bridge.

After you turn, you will pass a chapel on your left. Its tall steeple with the cross on top is easy to spot. Beyond that is an agricultural college with barns and silos. When you have the opportunity, curve to the left in order to keep the forest edge on your left and a housing area on your right. After 1.8 km., you will reach the Osawa entrance and a parking area. This entrance is the easiest one to find by car and the one closest to the area you should explore first if your time is limited.

If you wish to go to parking lot B or C, go back down the highway toward Sapporo past the dark monolith and look for a tall, white smokestack and the Hotel Sapporo Emperor III on your left. The hotel is on the highway; the smokestack is set back some distance. Turn left at the hotel corner and follow that road until it comes out on a wide major road. Go to the left. Where the major road makes a sharp right turn, go straight ahead on a small road which leads uphill past a large building with the sign "The Truth Shall Liberate You." Continue on that road to parking lot B.

The road winds around a bit, and there are some intersections between parking lots B and C. By this time you will have encountered several signboards showing a map of Nopporo Forest

Park, usually indicating where you are. Don't be confused when you get to point X on the map. The map on that signboard is drawn exactly upside down from all the others.

To get a better idea of where you are, look on the "Your Guide to Sapporo" map. You can find an edge of the forest at F-10.

Site and Birds:
This enórmous forest is beautiful in any season. It is covered with deep snow in winter, but a trip on cross-country skis would be a delight. This is a popular place on weekends with various groups including huge groups of school children. This shouldn't be a serious problem if you get here early, but a weekday is always best.

There is a considerable variety of habitat in this forest with ponds, marsh, streams, hills, and many kinds of trees. If you can't check everything, the recommended route is to start at the Osawa entrance and cover those paths, then head toward parking lot C and explore as much of that area as you can. In 3½ hours, I was unable to cover all the paths near the Osawa entrance.

This is one of the best places in Japan to look for the Black Woodpecker, but even here, it is not easy to find. Probably the area near the Osawa entrance is the place to look first. Other residents of interest include Sparrow Hawk, Common Buzzard, Hazel Grouse, Gray-headed Woodpecker, White-backed Woodpecker, Goldcrest, Long-tailed Tit, Marsh Tit, Varied Tit, Brown Creeper, and Jay.

The greatest number of species is here in spring and early summer. Look for Hobby, Latham's Snipe, Japanese Green Pigeon, Common Cuckoo, Ural Owl, Jungle Nightjar, White-throated Needle-tailed Swift, Ruddy Kingfisher, Skylark, Brown Shrike, Siberian Blue Robin, Stonechat, White's Ground Thrush, Gray Thrush, Brown Thrush, Short-tailed Bush Warbler, Bush Warbler, Crowned Willow Warbler, Narcissus Flycatcher, Blue-and-White Flycatcher, Siberian Meadow Bunting, Japanese Grosbeak, Russet Sparrow, and Red-cheeked Myna.

In spring and fall, some ducks, including Mandarin, gather on the ponds. In winter, besides the resident birds, look for Bohemian and Japanese Waxwings, Winter Wren, Dusky Thrush, Brambling,

Siskin, Common Redpoll, and Bullfinch.

Time:
This park is so large, it is not possible at birding pace to cover every path in one day. Even if you are on a rushed schedule, allow at least half a day. It is not necessary to wait for opening hours; you can walk in as early as you wish.

Food:
You can get a snack at the playground area near parking lot C. There are restaurants along Hwy. 12, but it is best to bring food and drink with you.

Useful Kanji:
Nopporo Forest Park (Nopporo Shinrin Koen)　野幌森林公園
Osawa Entrance　大沢口
Ebetsu　　　　　江別
Joshi-Tandai　　女子短大
Ooasa Station　 大麻駅

NISHIOKA SUIGENCHI

Season: spring and summer
Specialties: Hazel Grouse, Common Kingfisher

This park surrounds a lake which supplies water to Sapporo. It is a lovely area with a variety of habitat. It is certainly worth a visit if you have time in Sapporo.

Transportation:
By public transportation you can come by bus or a combination of subway and bus. The exact time is unclear. By car, it takes 30 minutes from the center of Sapporo in rush hour, probably half that at other times.

Directions:
Take the Namboku Line Subway to Sumikawa Station. Change there for the Nishioka Kanjo Line bus #80. Get off at the Nishioka Suigenchi bus stop. You will be at the entrance.

You can catch the Chuo Bus to Nishioka on the south side of the Tokyu Department Store in Sapporo. From the Nishioka bus stop you must walk ten minutes to get to Nishioka Suigenchi.

By car, start from the center of Sapporo on Hwy. 36, headed
south toward Chitose Airport. Hwy. 36 crosses the Toyohira River
at the Toyohira Bridge. From the bridge, go about 0.5 km. and
turn right onto a broad cross street and go until you reach the
first major intersection. This will be about 1 km. from the bridge.
Turn left at that intersection and go 5.9 km. On your right is what
appears to be an army training center. You will see a highway sign
indicating Hwy. 230 to the right. Turn *left*. Go 1.6 km. until you
reach a T-junction, where you will see a golf sign. Turn right and
go 0.9 km. There is another golf sign. Turn left and go 0.5 km.
and Nishioka Suigenchi will be on your right. Go a few meters
farther to get to the parking lot.

You will find Nishioka Suigenchi on the "Your Guide to Sapporo"
map at I-5 and 6. Nishioka Headwaters is written in large blue
letters. The road you want for the longest part of this drive runs
alongside the subway track near Sumikawa Station. The map will
add to your confidence.

Site and Birds:
There are maps on signboards strategically placed around this area.
Check one when you enter. If you are pressed for time, walk
around the lake, but try also to allow time for walking along the
boardwalk. From the entrance, go down a steep, forested hill to
the lake. The boardwalk winds about through a marshy area with
a stream running through it beyond the right end of the lake (as
you face it where you enter). From the edge of the park near the
entrance you can look over the fence into grassy fields and open
areas where you are likely to see different birds.

This is a popular place on weekends, so go early or on a weekday.
On a cold autumn Saturday afternoon when I went, there were
many visitors, including children fishing in the lake. On the first
Sunday of the month, you might encounter a group from the
Sapporo Chapter of the WBSJ.

In spring and autumn there is a small flock of ducks on the lake.
In winter look for Goldcrest, Brown Creeper, Siskin, Bullfinch,
and Jay. Summer visitors include Common Sandpiper, Common

Cuckoo, Oriental Cuckoo, White-throated Needle-tailed Swift, Gray Wagtail, White Wagtail, Siberian Blue Robin, Gray Thrush, Bush Warbler, Blue-and-White Flycatcher, and Black-faced Bunting. Sparrow Hawk and Common Buzzard are resident. You should be able to find a Common Kingfisher. Ruddy Kingfisher is supposed to summer here, but it will be difficult to find. Hazel Grouse is resident. If you get here early when there are no visitors, you may see it. Look for red fox and two kinds of squirrels.

Time:
A half day is enough. If rushed for time, two hours will do.

Food:
Bring it with you.

Useful Kanji:
Nishioka Suigenchi	西岡水源池
Nishioka Kanjo Line	西岡環状線
Sumikawa Station	澄川駅

MOIWAYAMA (MT. MOIWA)

This mountain, near the city center, is 530 meters high. (See F- and G-10 on the "Your Guide to Sapporo" map.) A toll road leads to the summit and is used by sightseeing buses and many tourists going up to get a good view of Sapporo. There is no point in trying to see birds on this road or at the top in either the parking lot or the souvenir shops. If you are willing to walk down (or up) the mountain, the birding should be good. This trip is for someone who is in Sapporo anyway. Don't stay over just to do this.

Transportation:
Go up the mountain on the Moiwayama Ropeway, walk down the mountain by one of four trails, and take a bus back to Sapporo. None of the trails reaches the bottom near the foot of the ropeway, so it will be of little help if you drive yourself. You can go in both directions by bus or by taxi.

Directions:
Ask for specific directions at your hotel. You can go by bus or streetcar. The bus (Ropeway Line #12) from Maruyama Koen

subway station (Tozai Line) takes 15 minutes to reach the ropeway. The ride to the top takes seven minutes. The problem comes in finding the bus at the end of the trail you have chosen to take to the bottom. One trail recommended for birdwatching is the one which goes down to the Jikeikai Byoinmae bus stop. Get the best information you can before you start up. If you don't get to the bottom exactly where you intended, it is probably easiest to take a taxi back.

Site and Birds:
I have not walked down this mountain, but I have driven to the top. The view is nice, but there is nothing else to recommend it. It can be extremely cold, so dress appropriately.

Resident birds include Gray-headed Woodpecker, Great Spotted Woodpecker, and several tits. Black Woodpecker has been reported, but it is not a confirmed resident. Spend your time searching for it somewhere else.

In summer, look for Rufous Turtle Dove, Oriental Cuckoo, White-throated Needle-tailed Swift, White-rumped Swift, Winter Wren, Siberian Blue Robin, White's Ground Thrush, Short-tailed Bush Warbler, Crowned Willow Warbler, Narcissus Flycatcher, Blue-and-White Flycatcher, Black-faced Bunting, and Japanese Grosbeak. Sometimes Peregrine Falcon occurs.

In fall and winter, there could be both Bohemian and Japanese Waxwings, Dusky Thrush, Brambling, Siskin, Common Redpoll, Rosy Finch, and Hawfinch. In mid-winter, the snow is deep.

Time:
Allow at least four hours to walk down from the top.

Food:
Bring it with you.

MARUYAMA KOEN

This wooded park, which contains the zoo and the ski-jump hills used for the Winter Olympics in 1972, is at the foot of Mt. Maru, 225 meters, and close to the center of Sapporo. It is not important for birdwatching, but it is a place you can go when you aren't able to visit one of the better locations. Visitors to Sapporo in

winter can easily see some of the resident birds which gather at
feeding stations in this park.

Transportation:
Take the Tozai Line subway to Maruyama Koen Station. Then
walk five minutes to the park. You can drive from the center of
Sapporo in less than ten minutes. If you are near the subway line,
it may be more convenient to take the train and be free of the
need to find a parking place.

Site and Birds:
Despite the large crowds here in good weather visiting the zoo, a
shrine, or several playgrounds and baseball fields, there are birds
in the forest. You can stroll around in open areas on the edge of
the forest or take trails up the mountain.

Resident birds include Sparrow Hawk, Gray-headed Woodpecker,
Great Spotted Woodpecker, White-backed Woodpecker, Japanese
Pygmy Woodpecker, five species of tits, Nuthatch, and Jay.

In summer you might see Gray Thrush, Brown Thrush, Siberian
Blue Robin, Bush Warbler, Crowned Willow Warbler, Narcissus
Flycatcher, Blue-and-White Flycatcher, Brown Flycatcher, and
Black-faced Bunting.

In winter, Bohemian and Japanese Waxwings, Dusky Thrush,
Brambling, Siskin, Common Redpoll, and Bullfinch occur.
Sometimes it is possible to see Rosy Finch and Red Crossbill.

Time:
You can walk around the park in an hour. If you want to climb
up, you can spend more time.

SAPPORO BOTANIC GARDEN

The Botanic Garden is in the center of Sapporo about 0.5 km.
from the station. It contains some virgin forest and plants from all
over Hokkaido. It is not an important birding spot, but it is
convenient if you have a little time with nothing else to do. It is
open from April to November from 9:00 a.m. to 4:00 p.m. It is on
all the maps and is easy to find.

A Blakiston's Fish-Owl was seen here in about 1920. Now you

will have to be content with more common birds. In spring and early summer you might see some woodpeckers, Brown Thrush, Crowned Willow Warbler, Narcissus Flycatcher, tits, Oriental Greenfinch, Japanese Grosbeak, and Red-cheeked Myna. In the fall the birds are limited to such familiar species as Rufous Turtle Dove, Great Spotted Woodpecker, Japanese Pygmy Woodpecker, White Wagtail, Goldcrest, Marsh Tit, Great Tit, Nuthatch, and Gray Starling.

MOUTH OF ISHIKARI RIVER

If you are in the area during shorebird migration, go to Ishikari, north of Sapporo. (See Champion Maps, page 16.) A narrow spit of land which extends for several kilometers between the ocean and the Ishikari River and a marshy area just after Hwy. 231 crosses the Ishikari River are excellent places for birds. This is on the way if you are driving to Teuri Island or Sarobetsu Plain. If you are passing by anyway, it is worth a stop in any season.

Before you get to the Ishikari River on Hwy. 231, you will come to a huge sign with a fish on it, where a road branches off to the left. Go left to get onto this spit of land. Drive toward the lighthouse. Park where the road is blocked and walk the rest of the way. To the right is a mudflat. There are supposed to be more shorebirds here in the fall migration than in the spring. The point is grassland, which is excellent for buntings.

To get here by bus from Sapporo, take the bus for Ishikari at the Sapporo Terminal of the Chuo Bus. Get off at the final stop. It takes one hour, plus another 20 minutes on foot to reach the lighthouse.

UTONAI SANCTUARY AND VICINITY

Season: all year
Specialties: geese, swans, ducks

Utonai is the first WBSJ sanctuary in Japan, created in 1981. It consists of a shallow lake, reed marsh, grassland, and woods. This site is important for wintering as well as for breeding birds in Hokkaido. Since it is only a few minutes from the main airport which serves Sapporo, it is convenient for almost every visitor to Hokkaido and is worth a visit in any season.

Utonai Area

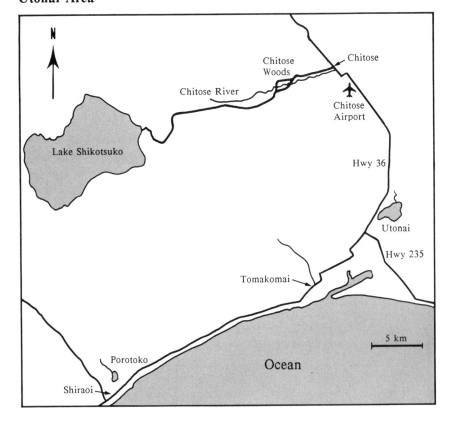

Transportation:
It takes about 15 minutes by car from Chitose Airport to Utonai. A rental car would allow you to visit other areas nearby, but you

can easily get here by taxi. There is also a bus from the airport, but a taxi is much less complicated.

Directions:
Go south from Chitose Airport on Hwy. 36 for about 15 km. Utonai is on the left of Hwy. 36 before it intersects Hwy. 235. To get to the sanctuary, turn left on a dirt road next to a yellow building with a blue roof. There is an orange sign near this road with "24" on it. On the opposite side of the highway there is a long concrete-block fence with pink on the top and bottom and white stripes in the middle. After you turn on this road, you will be able to see a small Utonai sign at the corner with a picture of a Gray Heron on it.

If you miss the turn (which is easy to do), you will soon see the entrance to the Utonai Lake Hotel on the left. There is a large blue sign with a swan on it. You can also see the nearby amusement park. If you get that far, turn around and try again.

After you go down the sanctuary road for a kilometer or so, you will come to a parking area on the left. Leave your car there and walk through the woods to the nature center.

Site and Birds:
The nature center is open 9:00 a.m. to 5:00 p.m. throughout the year except on Tuesdays and Wednesdays and from December 26 through January 1. The view of the lake is excellent from this building. There are trails in the woods you walked through from the parking lot and one which goes along the lakeshore to a hide. The ranger and his assistants will gladly help you. They will tell you what birds are around and will also give you directions for getting to other good birding spots nearby.

Gray Heron is present throughout the year. There are wintering ducks, but more species during migration. In both spring and fall, but especially in March and April, there are many White-fronted and Bean Geese as well as ducks on Utonai Lake. White-tailed Eagle and Steller's Sea-Eagle occur in small numbers in winter. Woodpeckers are resident, along with tits. In summer you should see Latham's Snipe, Wryneck, Siberian Rubythroat, Stonechat, Black-browed Reed Warbler, Gray-headed Bunting, Yellow-breasted Bunting, Reed Bunting, Long-tailed Rose Finch, and Red-cheeked Myna. Look for the three grasshopper warblers.

Listen for Gray's Grasshopper Warbler along the path between the parking lot and the nature center. The bird list for Utonai is quite long. In some seasons there won't be many species, but it is always worth a visit.

If you have a car, time, and a detailed map of the area, make your way around the lake outside of the sanctuary to look for more good habitat. You should find many birds in the immediate neighborhood. If you will go back to the highway, turn right (toward the airport), and then take the next left, you can find a nice patch of woods by following that road a little way. Short-tailed Bush Warbler occurs there. Ask the ranger for directions.

Porotoko (Lake Poroto) is about 45 minutes farther down Hwy. 36 and not difficult to find. It is behind the Ainu Village at Shiraoi. This is a little more than 30 km. from Utonai. Turn off the highway to the right near a Saito store. The Ainu Village is well advertised and obvious. You can't miss the huge totem pole in front and all the souvenir shops.

At the front of the Ainu Village, go left and then right along the west side of the lake. Check the lake for birds (Red-necked Grebe in summer), but your destination is beyond the lake. After about 2 km., there is a place to park by a bridge. Cross to your right and walk along the trail. Ruddy Kingfisher is here in summer. It is never easy to see, but listen for the call. Among birds in this forest, you might find Brown Hawk-Owl and Ural Owl. But don't go on weekends or holidays.

Chitose Woods, north of Chitose Airport, is one of the best places in the area. Go north on Hwy. 36 past the airport. Stay on Hwy. 36 as it turns left and then right. Then take the first left turn after Hwy. 36 crosses the Chitose River. This road goes to Shikotsuko. Just before that road crosses the Chitose River (perhaps in another 4 km.), take the road to the right. This road goes by a salmon hatchery and through a forest. The birding is excellent along this road. The ranger at Utonai can give you the latest information about this area too. Ural Owl is resident here.

Time:
You could see a lot in two hours at Utonai. With more time you would want to explore farther afield. A full day should give you enough time for everything. You might want to spend the night,

especially in spring and summer, in order to enjoy the dawn birding.

Chitose Woods

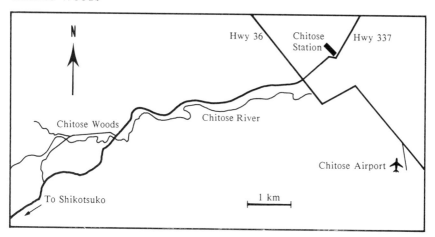

Food:
There is no food available at Utonai Sanctuary. The Utonai Lake Restaurant is near the Utonai Lake Hotel. There are some places to eat on Hwy. 36.

Accommodations:
The Utonai Lake Hotel (0144-58-2111) gives a discount to WBSJ members. The price is about ¥6,000 per person with two meals. Most rooms are Japanese style. It is on Hwy. 36 about 1 km. from the turnoff to the sanctuary. Birdwatching is great from the *ofuro*. It is on the top floor with a huge window overlooking the lake.

Maps and Information:
   Champion Maps, Vol. 1, Hokkaido
   Hokkaido Map and Colour Guide 1:400,000
   National Map: 1:50,000 Chitose 千歳

Useful Kanji:
Utonai Sanctuary	ウトナイ湖サンクチュアリ
Shiraoi Ainu Village	白老アイ又村
Porotoko	ポロト湖
Chitose	千歳
Shikotsuko	支笏湖

TEURI ISLAND

Season: June - July
Specialties: Rhinoceros Auklet, Thin-billed Murre, Spectacled
Guillemot

Teuri Island is important to birdwatchers primarily for its breeding colonies of seabirds. It is popular with tourists so has ample accommodations as well as a sightseeing boat which circles the island, enabling birdwatchers to get a better look at the birds.

Transportation:
The boat for Teuri leaves from Haboro and takes 1 hour, 35 minutes. Getting to Haboro is the main problem. It is possible to go by train, but it is slow with an inconvenient schedule. The best way is by car. From Sapporo, allow at least four hours to drive to Haboro, plus time to check shorebirds at the Ishikari River during migration. If you are going up to Sarobetsu Plain, near Wakkanai, this is on the way.

Directions:
It would be most convenient to leave Sapporo on Hwy. 231, stop by the Ishikari River, continue along the coast meeting Hwy. 232 at Rumoi, and go on to Haboro. I added rental car agents to my list of instruction-givers not to trust without double checking when mine assured me that the dots on my map were meaningless, the road was complete all the way, and I could easily drive from Chitose Airport to Haboro in two hours. It was almost dark when I found myself at the absolute end of the road with no alternative but to retrace my route a long distance and then go 60 km. across the mountains on a back road before reaching a highway which would eventually get me to Haboro. The farmer I found at the end of the road predicted it would take me four hours to reach Haboro; it only took three and a half.

The road ended at a tunnel under construction. In October of 1983, there was not much distance left to cover. By the time you want to drive that way, the road may be finished. Do your best to make sure before you start out, or allow yourself a lot of extra time.

If you are going straight to Teuri Island, you must turn off the highway in the middle of Haboro to get to the ferry. There are several clues for finding your turn. Probably the easiest one is the highway sign which shows 62 km. straight, 0.6 km. to the right (to the station), and 0.9 km. to the left. You want to turn left. Just before you reach that intersection, you will see a Caltex sign on the right, then another gasoline station on the right corner of your intersection. The building on the left at the corner has a microwave tower on the top. Across the intersection on the right is a Honda sign. Turn left, go three blocks until you reach the waterfront, turn right, and in about three more blocks you will be at the ferry terminal. You probably can leave your car in a parking area on the pier while you go to Teuri Island.

The ferry stops at Yagishiri Island on the way to Teuri, so be sure to get off at the right place. In June, July, and August there are four trips each day. In May and September there are two trips, and only one during the other months. Try to confirm the schedule with a tourist information office. The phone number for information (in Japanese) is 01648-3-5422.

Site and Birds:
I failed in my October attempt to get to Teuri Island. The seabirds are not there then, but interesting migrants come through for about two weeks beginning around the 20th of October. Large flocks of Bohemian Waxwings, buntings, Lapland Longspurs, and Common Redpolls are possible, as well as some Steller's Sea-Eagles and Rough-legged Buzzards. Since I was in Hokkaido and wanted to visit the island, I decided to make the attempt. The sea was extremely rough, there was a strong wind, and it was sleeting and sometimes snowing. Only ten minutes before departure time, the ferry company decided to make the trip anyway. A severe storm was coming, and it was certain that the ferry couldn't make the trip the following day. I gave up. I don't recommend that a birder visiting Hokkaido under normal circumstances attempt a visit to Teuri in this season. The weather is always uncertain, and you risk seeing no migrants and being stranded besides. If your time is limited, you can spend it better elsewhere.

During June and July, however, the weather is fine. From the looks of the brochures, the island is lovely, with birds flying all about. Temminck's Cormorant, Slaty-backed Gull, Black-tailed Gull, Thin-billed Murre, Spectacled Guillemot, and Rhinoceros Auklet breed here. Thin-billed Murre used to be common, but now there are only a few. Besides the seabirds, you might see such land birds as White Wagtail, Siberian Rubythroat, Gray's Grasshopper Warbler, Middendorff's Grasshopper Warbler, Black-browed Reed Warbler, Great Reed Warbler, Yellow-breasted Bunting, and Red-cheeked Myna.

Walk around the island, being careful to look out for snakes. The far end of the island is a good place to go with your telescope and look at the birds around the offshore rocks and flying out over the sea. The sightseeing boat, which circles the island in 1½ hours, leaves from a different dock from where you arrived. You will get a good look at many of the birds from this boat. About 7:00 p.m., if you are down on the far end of the island, you will see great numbers of Rhinoceros Auklets returning to their nests.

Time:
You will want at least half a day to walk around the island and additional time for the trip on the sightseeing boat. If you are on the first boat in the morning, it is possible to go and come back in the same day and still see what you need to. That way, though, you will miss seeing the returning Rhinoceros Auklets in the evening. If you do it in one day, you will be spending two nights in Haboro. Possibly a more efficient schedule would be to leave Sapporo (or the Sarobetsu area) in the morning, take the ferry at midday or in the afternoon, and leave Teuri around midday the next day. That will allow time to get to your next destination from Haboro before nightfall.

Food:
There are plenty of day-trippers to Teuri, so there must be places to eat. If you are staying overnight, you will be having breakfast and dinner, at least, at your *minshuku* or *ryokan*.

Accommodations:
There are *ryokan*, *minshuku*, and youth hostels on Teuri. Especially after the middle of July when students are on holiday, reservations are advised.

If you stay in Haboro, I can recommend the Kumagai Ryokan. After we arrived in Haboro around 7:30, well after dark and after the customary dinner hour, we drove around the town several times looking over all the lodgings we could find. On the basis of appearance in the dark, we selected this one. The owners were especially kind to us, prepared our meal while we had our baths, and served us in our room. The food was good, and our *tatami* room was clean and attractively decorated. There was a heater in our room which we could adjust to suit ourselves.

The next morning we had breakfast in the dining room downstairs. The owners took a great interest in our proposed trip to Teuri. Without being asked, they made several phone calls to the weather bureau and the ferry terminal, keeping us posted on developments and making suggestions. We paid ¥4,600 each for the room and two meals, but that was the off-season rate. The tourist brochure lists their prices as ¥5,000 to ¥6,000 per person. They spoke no English, but seemed to understand a few words when our Japanese was exhausted.

The Kumagai Ryokan is easy to find. At the intersection where you turn left off Hwy. 232 for the ferry, turn right instead toward the station. The *ryokan* is on the second corner on your right, before you cross the intersection. The telephone number is 01646-2-2248 or 2-2896. They can accommodate 50 people, so it would do nicely for a tour group.

Useful Kanji:

Haboro	羽幌
Teuri Island	天売島
Kumagai Ryokan	熊谷旅館

SAROBETSU PLAIN

Season: June - July, migration
Specialties: Smew, Black Woodpecker, Yellow Wagtail, Yellow-
breasted Bunting

Sarobetsu Plain, part of the Rishiri-Rebun-Sarobetsu National Park, is a vast expanse of marshland with some scattered woods. It was set aside to preserve its spectacular wildflowers, which are at their peak in July. It is a unique area in Japan and interesting to birdwatchers as well as to botanists. But except for the breeding Smew and the Yellow Wagtail, all the birds here can also be found in eastern Hokkaido. Since it is so out of the way, it is difficult for birders with limited time to justify the trip.

Transportation:
This area, like Teuri Island, can be reached by train, but it takes a long time to get here from Sapporo. You can fly from Sapporo to Wakkanai and drive or take the train from there. If you make the effort to get here, you probably should include Teuri Island on your route. This, then, gets you almost halfway between Wakkanai and Sapporo. You could fly one way and go by rented car the other, but you will have to decide whether that is worth the extra expense.

The Sarobetsu Plain stretches for almost 30 km. from north to south. The southern limit is about 85 km. and 1½ hours from Haboro. You could get to the plain by bus from Toyotomi, but you would have to walk a long way. A car is required to get the full value from birding this area. From Toyotomi, it takes about 45 minutes to reach Wakkanai.

Directions:
From Haboro, continue north on Hwy. 232. After you pass Teshio, the area looks good for birds. Hwy. 232 curves inland and then meets Hwy. 40 about 83 km. from Haboro. Cross the bridge over the river and continue north on Hwy. 40. Coming from this direction, you should first try to get to Panketo (Lake Panke), which is normally accessible by car. At the 200 km. post, there is a highway sign indicating 51 km. straight ahead and 10 km. to the left. Turn left. Stay on this road when it makes a sharp right turn. A little farther ahead is an intersection with a sign to a train station to the right. Turn left and you should get to the lake.

Sarobetsu Plain

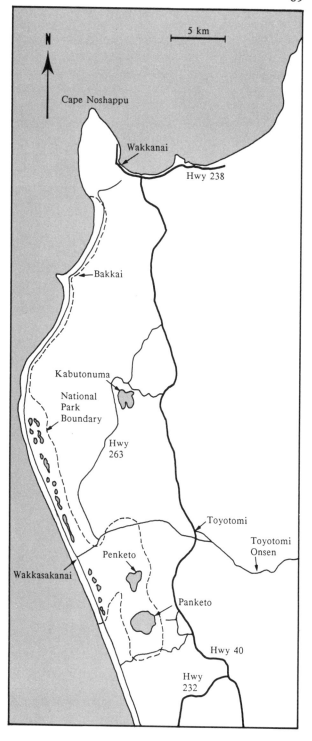

There was extensive road construction throughout the area when I came, and the road to the lake was totally blocked. The principal road crossing the Sarobetsu Plain goes to the west from Toyotomi.

Site and Birds:
The birds are not concentrated in any particular areas, so you are on your own to explore and see what you can find. The national maps are useful because they will give you a good idea of the topography. I encountered so much road construction when I was there that I am sure these maps are out of date as far as roads are concerned. But they should still give you some clues to where you might like to go.

If you are traveling along the main road from Toyotomi to Wakkasakanai, when you get in the middle of the plain, you will notice a building on your left with a boardwalk nearby leading out into the marsh. Have a look around here and continue toward the coast. When you leave the marsh, you will come to some mixed woods. There are several trails leading into the woods from this road, but they aren't obvious. There is no place to park at the entrance to any of the trails I found, so park your car where you can find a place and walk. Check the different habitats you find along this road, and then start exploring.

I drove south from Wakkasakanai in a fruitless attempt to get to Panketo. The road which goes from the coast back to the highway south of Panketo had some interesting habitat and birds. Next I drove on Hwy. 263 going north from the Toyotomi-Wakkasakanai road, eventually meeting Hwy. 40 again. This, too, was a promising area.

Explore all the small roads you can. Many do not have a hard surface and can be rough and muddy. You may want to set out on foot to reach some of the lakes, in which case high boots would be essential. Since the area is so large, I recommend driving around it first before starting off on a long hike. Don't overlook the wet areas just inland from the beach, the woods, the cultivated lands, and the small hills surrounding the plain. Much of the plain remains in its natural state because there are few clear trails and, as a result, few people.

Among the breeding birds are Smew, Osprey, Black Woodpecker, Great Spotted Woodpecker, Japanese Robin, Siberian Bluechat,

Stonechat, Blue-and-White Flycatcher, tits, and Yellow-breasted Bunting. This is on a migration route, so many birds come through in spring and autumn. At that time it is a gathering place for geese, swans, and ducks.

I can't imagine a foreign visitor making it all the way up here in the winter, but just in case, the birding sounds good then too. Of course, there is much snow. You need skis to get into the area. Once there, though, you might see Gyrfalcon or Snowy Owl.

Time:
Allow at least one full day. If you come in June or July, with all the birds and the wildflowers, there is enough to keep you occupied for two days.

Food:
Bring it with you. I saw no restaurants outside of Toyotomi.

Accommodations:
Toyotomi Onsen is 7 km. east of Toyotomi on Hwy. 724. It is nothing special, unattractive as a matter of fact, but it is out in the country. I did not continue down the highway, but it is possible that beyond the *onsen* there could be some birding possibilities for an early morning outing before breakfast.

By far the best-looking place to stay in this *onsen* is the New Hotel Sarobetsu (0162-82-1211). It is large and, as its name implies, new. The rates are from ¥8,000 to ¥12,000.

There may be a place to stay in Toyotomi itself, but I never was able to find one. Hinjuku Ashitanoshiro (or Ashitanojo) is associated with the WBSJ. The telephone number is 01628-5-2155, and the cost is ¥3,300. It is in Hotoku, Toyotomi, which is probably nearby.

If you are coming back to the Sarobetsu Plain for birding the next day, don't go to Wakkanai for the night. You will waste a lot of time in the congested traffic in town.

Maps and Information:
  Champion Maps, Vol. 1, Hokkaido
  Japan Guide Map Co. Ltd., Handy Map of Hokkaido
  Hokkaido Map and Colour Guide 1:400,000

National Maps: 1:50,000   Wakkasakanai 稚咲内

                           Bakkai   抜海

Useful Kanji:

Sarobetsu Plain   サロベツ原野
Toyotomi   豊富
Toyotomi Onsen   豊富温泉
New Hotel Sarobetsu   ニューホテルサロベツ

Note:

If you go to Wakkanai to spend a night or to catch a plane, it is
worth driving out to the point of Cape Noshappu. At Wakkanai
harbor, get off the main road and drive next to the water all the
way out. The houses, fishermen, and boats are picturesque. In
October there were many interesting gulls. The Wakkanai map on
the back of the Handy Map of Hokkaido will help.

KUSHIRO AREA

Season: all year
Specialties: Japanese Crane

Kushiro is the starting point for birding in eastern Hokkaido. Whether you fly or come or go by ferry for birding in this part of Hokkaido, you will pass through Kushiro and probably spend at least one night here. The Japanese Crane winters near the city, and you may also find some breeding in the area.

Transportation:
There are several ferry runs each week between Tokyo and Kushiro. See the Tokyo - Hokkaido Ferry chapter. There are direct flights to Kushiro from Tokyo on ANA and TDA (1 hour, 40 minutes) and on TDA from Sapporo (45 minutes).

It is possible to get around eastern Hokkaido by public transportation, but avoid it if you have any other choice. It is extremely slow and complicated. You can see far more in a fraction of the time if you have a car. Hokkaido is probably the easiest place to drive in all Japan. In winter there is the problem with snow, but the roads are wider and far less congested than elsewhere. This is a big area to explore, and a car makes that possible.

Directions:
If you arrive in Kushiro by ferry, try to persuade the rental car company to pick you up at the dock. If that fails, come with the exact location of the rental car office written in Japanese. You can then take a taxi to meet your car.

Nippon, Nissan, and Toyota Rent-a-Car have offices at Kushiro Airport. It takes slightly more than 30 minutes to drive to Kushiro from the airport, which is on the west side of town. Directions for getting into town will come first. But if you are already comfortable driving in Japan, you may want to investigate some birding spots before you find the city.

From the terminal building, go to the left past the building with the rent car offices. A road branches off to the left, but stay on the road to the right which goes downhill. About halfway down, there is a Hwy. 426 sign. At 2.2 km. you will reach a signal light where you should turn right. Later on you will see a sign showing that you are on Hwy. 240. A little farther a sign in *kanji* shows Kushiro 20 km. ahead.

Kushiro Area

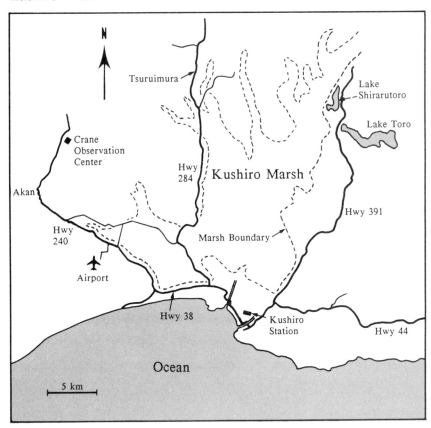

After a while you will see statues of two cows on the left and a sign on the right (which you can read) pointing out the Kushiro Technical College. Before the big intersection (approximately 11 km. from the airport) where you should turn left, you will see a Hwy. 38 sign. When you turn left, you will be on Hwy. 38. The road immediately crosses a river, and a sign shows Kushiro 13 km. ahead.

You need to be familiar with the *kanji* for train station. At something close to 18 km. from the airport, a sign will indicate

Kushiro Station (in *kanji*) 5 km. ahead (over a bridge) and some other station 2 km. to the right. At this point you want to turn right, even if you mean to go to Kushiro Station. Hwy. 38 turns to the right here and goes down the west side of a waterway. This is a good place to look for gulls and perhaps other birds. There are a couple of places where you can pull off the road and look. At the next bridge, Hwy. 38 turns left over the bridge. If you are going on through Kushiro, stay on Hwy. 38 until it gets to Hwy. 44. If you are going to stop in Kushiro, go to the left at the fork in the road which you will encounter 2 km. from that last bridge. In 0.5 km., you will be in front of Kushiro Station. To stay on Hwy. 38, take the road to the right at that fork.

Site and Birds:
There are several places near Kushiro where the cranes are fed in winter, two or three where you can see large numbers of them. The place I saw was near Tsuruimura. The cranes come to eat the food which is put out in a large field. Viewers must stay behind a fence at the edge of this field. This particular place looks completely natural: fields almost always have fences around them. Unlike so many similar situations in Japan, this one didn't look like a zoo. With the absence of souvenir shops and snack bars, I felt as though I had happened on some cranes in a field beside the road.

When I went, there were 65 cranes in the field, quite close to the fence, dancing and looking simply spectacular. It is worth a whole trip to Japan to see these birds. If you see a group of these cranes at close range dancing in the snow, you will never forget it.

To get to this place near Tsuruimura, you need to find the highway which is between Hwy. 240 and Hwy. 391. The number is marked on only one of the many maps I have. That one shows it as Hwy. 284. On the Champion map and the large Hokkaido Colour Guide map, this road is green, while the other two are red. The feeding place is on Hwy. 284, probably slightly more than 20 km. north of Hwy. 38. You should look for cranes all along this green road. You may see pairs or family groups here and there in the fields, or you may find some other feeding stations.

Another place where large numbers of cranes come is on Hwy. 240 between 10 and 15 km. north of Kushiro Airport. I have not seen this place, but I have seen the crane park a short distance

north of the airport. Don't go there. Tour buses take tourists to see
the cranes. I suspect they go to this feeding station and crane
observation center north of Akan. It is highly developed with all
the usual things that you find where tourist buses stop. If you go
there and are disappointed, try the road to Tsuruimura.

If you come when it isn't winter and want to see cranes near here,
you need to drive through the marshy area between Hwy. 284 and
Hwy. 391. Few maps show the road. On Hwy. 391 about 23 km.
north of the intersection with Hwy. 44 going to Nemuro, Lake
Toro is to the right (east) and Toro Station is to the left. About 2
km. farther north, a road goes to the left (west) over the railroad
track. It soon turns to the northwest. For the next 5 to 10 km.
look carefully in the marsh for cranes. They will no longer be in
large groups. You will need a telescope because you will be
looking down on the marsh from a distance.

Farther down the road, you will have some options, so a good map
will help. This area is excellent for birds in all seasons. The road
may not always be passable in winter, so be careful. I went in late
March when there was still plenty of snow, but the roads had
been cleared. One pair of cranes was already in this marsh. Hazel
Grouse was easy to see along the road, as were Rosy Finch and
many other interesting species.

Lake Toro and Lake Shirarutoro (just north and west of Lake
Toro) are probably worth investigating in any season if you have
time. Falcated Teal breed here. Sometimes it is possible to get a
good look at them from Hwy. 391. Drive slowly along the eastern
shore of Lake Shirarutoro and check all ducks. If you have plenty
of time, explore the southern shore of Lake Toro. Birding is good
in the area.

Don't take time away from eastern Hokkaido to spend it here. If
you are waiting for your ferry or airplane, birding around
Kushiro is a good way to spend the time. The whole area between
Lake Toro and Hwy. 240 down to Hwy. 38 is worth driving
through if you have a good map or a good sense of direction. A
thorough investigation of this area will take some time.

In spring, the fields on the east side of Hwy. 240 opposite the
airport are excellent. It is a good area for birds of prey, including

Hobby. In early June while they are still on migration, Latham's Snipe are abundant here.

If there is time, check the rivermouth near the ferry terminal. This is near where you drove along the river on your way into town.

Time:

Allow plenty of time in winter to find the cranes, photograph them, and enjoy watching them. Most of them winter in the area, so you will surely find them. In other seasons if you are going on to Nemuro, you will probably see them somewhere else. I do not budget time for staying in Kushiro for birding. I have had a lot of birding time here when I have arrived in the afternoon and preferred to wait until the next day before starting to Nemuro. Especially in winter, I want to get back to Kushiro the night before my departure by plane or ferry. A snowstorm could make that drive impossible at the last minute. So there is always birding time in the morning before leaving.

Kushiro Airport, being near that marsh, is susceptible to being fogged in. Be careful of tight connections.

Food:

There are plenty of restaurants in Kushiro. If you don't plan to be in town at mealtime, take a lunch.

If you like *sushi*, you are in for a treat. If you have never tried it, start here. Hokkaido *sushi* and *sashimi* are said to be best of all because the fish come from colder water and can be eaten immediately rather than having first to go through the Tokyo fish market. There are some excellent *sushi* restaurants in Hokkaido, and Sakae in Kushiro is one of them. It is a tiny, family restaurant with a few stools at the counter and a couple of small tables. Large groups can use one of the private rooms upstairs. There is nothing at all fancy about this place, but the food is wonderful. On a recent trip, my *sushi* vocabulary had increased along with my knowledge of and appetite for the things they usually serve. I had everything delicious I could order with no regard to what I was spending or whether I needed that much food. Besides all the *sushi*, my meal included a lovely assortment of *sashimi* as a starter. Even so, the bill was under ¥5,000.

Sakae's telephone number is 0154-22-2631. It is closed on Tuesdays. Ask directions at your hotel. If that is a problem, start with your back to Kushiro Station and walk down the big street which runs into it at the side nearest the bus station (the name of the street is Kita Oodori). Walk down the left-hand side of this street. Cross four narrow streets, then a larger one which runs at an angle, then two more narrow ones. Then cross a big street and turn to your left. Go along this big street, crossing two more narrow streets (one block is double size). When you get to the third street, cross it and turn right. Cross two more streets, and Sakae is in the middle of the next block on the left. It has a large sign with the name in *kanji*. It takes no more than ten minutes to walk from the station. All these blocks are short.

Accommodations:
The Tokyu Inn (0154-22-0109) is across the street from Kushiro Station, easy to find, reasonably priced, and perfectly comfortable. A single room is about ¥5,000. A Hertz No. 1 Club card will get you a 10% discount. If the local restaurants don't interest you, it has a restaurant where you can get food which is somewhat Western.

Maps and Information:
Champion Maps, Vol. 1, Hokkaido
Hokkaido Map and Colour Guide 1:400,000

National Map: 1:200,000 Kushiro 釧路

Britton and Hayashida. *The Japanese Crane, Bird of Happiness.* Tokyo: Kodansha International, 1981.

Useful Kanji:

Kushiro	釧路
Kushiro Station	釧路駅
Tsuruimura	鶴居村
Akan	阿寒
Lake Toro	塘路湖
Lake Shirarutoro	シラルトロ湖
Tokyu Inn	東急イン
Sakae	栄寿司

NEMURO - EASTERN HOKKAIDO

Season: all year
*Specialties: Steller's Eider, Hazel Grouse, Spectacled Guillemot,
Tufted Puffin, Blakiston's Fish-Owl, Black
Woodpecker, Lesser Spotted Woodpecker, Siberian
Rubythroat, Gray's Grasshopper Warbler,
Middendorff's Grasshopper Warbler, Lanceolated
Grasshopper Warbler, Marsh Tit, Yellow-breasted
Bunting*

Eastern Hokkaido is the finest area for birdwatching in Japan.
Under no circumstances should it be missed by any serious birder.
Nemuro is the name of a peninsula, a city, and an area of
Hokkaido. This chapter's boundaries do not match any of those.
They were determined solely for convenience. This chapter covers
the best birding spots between Kushiro and Cape Nosappu at the
tip of the Nemuro Peninsula and north to the Notsuke Peninsula.

Transportation:
From Kushiro, you will need a car if you are to cover this area
efficiently and enjoy it to the fullest. Public transportation is slow
and complicated, and will not allow you to visit every place of
interest.

Directions:
From Kushiro, take Hwy. 44 to the east. It turns off Hwy. 391
east and north of the city. At that turn, the sign shows Nemuro in
Roman letters. You will turn right; a bridge is to your left. All
further directions are given in the next section.

Site and Birds:
This area is marvelous at any season. There are special birds in
winter which make it well worth putting up with the cold. Eastern
Hokkaido has far less snow than does the western part, but be
prepared for temperatures at least as low as -10°C. The sky is
often blue, and everything is lovely. But when you get in the wind
out on a cape overlooking sea ice, you will think it is impossible
to be any colder.

You must also allow extra time for driving in snow and ice. If you
are careful and don't have such a tight schedule that you are
forced to drive in a snowstorm, there is no particular worry. On

my first winter trip, we were in a small van driving after dark to reach our next stop. The drive shaft froze. When we stopped for a traffic light and tried to shift gears, nothing would move. Fortunately, the man who lived in the one house near this traffic light in the middle of nowhere helped us determine the cause of our problem, provided the equipment, and assisted in chipping away the block of ice which had formed on the underside of our vehicle. At that time, I knew almost no Japanese and wondered throughout the crisis what I would have done had I been alone in that situation. Try to do all your traveling in the daylight when you have a far better chance of getting help if you need it. It is lonely in these places in the dark and cold.

Nemuro

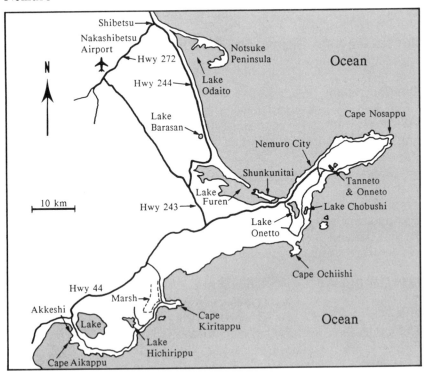

In winter, you could see loons (including Yellow-billed, though it isn't easy), grebes (including Red-necked), Brant, Whooper Swan, and such ducks as scoters, Harlequin Duck, Oldsquaw, Common Goldeneye, Smew, and mergansers. Steller's Eider occurs from

January to late February. Probably the most exciting species for most birders are White-tailed Eagle and Steller's Sea-Eagle. In winter, you can see both of these birds in this area, but you should go to Rausu and see the large concentration of them. Rausu is part of Nemuro too, but it is covered in the next chapter.

Hazel Grouse is resident, but may be easier to see in winter when it is often out in the open eating berries or seeds. Herring, Slaty-backed, Glaucous-winged, Glaucous, and Mew Gulls and Black-legged Kittiwake are all easy to see. Thin-billed and Thick-billed Murres, Pigeon and Spectacled Guillemots, and Marbled and Ancient Murrelets can be seen from the capes along with Crested, Least, and Rhinoceros Auklets. Tufted Puffin is resident in small numbers. Horned Puffin also occurs, but it is rare. Bohemian and Japanese Waxwings come in winter. Lapland Longspur, Snow Bunting, Brambling, Common Redpoll, Rosy Finch, and Red Crossbill are also possible. Red Crossbill sometimes occurs in summer too, but that cannot be expected. Most birders want to find Pallas's Rosy Finch. Some winters it isn't reported anywhere in Japan. When it occurs, it often occurs in Nemuro. Inquire when you get here. The resident woods birds, such as woodpeckers and tits, may be easier to see in this season. All things considered, the best time for winter birding is probably from mid-January through February. Any time in January is fine; a bit later gives a chance for any stragglers to have found their way here.

Many geese and ducks pass on migration, as do shorebirds. There are not so many shorebirds in the spring. The fall migration is best for them, but the period during which they come through is limited to about ten days from late August to early September.

If you plan your trip to see the summer visitors, you will miss the spring migration. The three grasshopper warblers (Gray's, Middendorff's, and Lanceolated), important to most foreign visitors, are late arrivals. They all may not arrive until after the tenth of June. The ideal time to see the summer visitors is late June, from about the 20th to the 30th. They stay longer, of course, but they stop singing after a while. And in July the crowds come. Nemuro doesn't have a lot of tourists, but the birdwatchers descend on the place during the summer holidays. Summer is also the time to enjoy the wildflowers in Nemuro.

In summer you may see Red-faced Cormorant (possibly in winter too), Garganey, Japanese Crane, Water Rail, Redshank, Woodcock, Latham's Snipe, Japanese Green Pigeon, Common Cuckoo, Oriental Cuckoo, White-throated Needle-tailed Swift, White-rumped Swift, Wryneck, Red-rumped Swallow, House Martin, Indian Tree Pipit, Siberian Rubythroat, Siberian Blue Robin, Siberian Bluechat, Stonechat, White's Ground Thrush, Gray Thrush, Brown Thrush, Bush Warbler, Black-browed Reed Warbler, Pale-legged Willow Warbler, Crowned Willow Warbler, Narcissus Flycatcher, Sooty Flycatcher, Brown Flycatcher, Gray-headed Bunting, Yellow-breasted Bunting, Black-faced Bunting, Reed Bunting, Long-tailed Rose Finch, Russet Sparrow, and Red-cheeked Myna.

To complete the picture, resident birds of interest include Temminck's Cormorant, Hazel Grouse, Blakiston's Fish-Owl, Gray-headed Woodpecker, Black Woodpecker, Great Spotted Woodpecker, White-backed Woodpecker, Lesser Spotted Woodpecker, Japanese Pygmy Woodpecker, Long-tailed Tit, Marsh Tit, Willow Tit, Coal Tit, Bullfinch, Hawfinch, and Jay. Of these, Hazel Grouse, Blakiston's Fish-Owl, Gray-headed Woodpecker, and Marsh Tit in Japan are limited to Hokkaido. The Hokkaido subspecies of Long-tailed Tit and Jay are distinctly different from those in the rest of Japan.

Blakiston's Fish-Owl is difficult to see. (According to a recent census, there are only 29 pairs of these owls known to be in Japan.) Some say it is easier to see in the fall when it fishes for salmon in the rivers. It stays in deep forests near water. Listen for them at night. You are not likely to find one in the forest. Your best chance is to pick a good spot in the open on a road (a highway will do) near water with a dense forest nearby. Wait there at dusk, and hope one flies out. It does happen.

There are a number of these owls in Nemuro, but I know of only one place to tell you to look which can be published. You will find the information under Lake Onetto. The local experts have assured me that birders visiting this place will not endanger the owl. This spot has been widely publicized in Japan and is well known to all Japanese birders.

The local people are extremely protective of these birds, as they should be. Also, they don't respond favorably to foreign visitors asking for information about where to find them or asking to be shown one. Japanese never like to be asked direct questions, especially on sensitive subjects. Your best chance is to express your interest in these birds as indirectly as you can and leave it to fate. There are some notorious tales of what happened to certain people who have shown too much interest in these birds. You will most likely find this bird on your own if you are to see it. And the less to-do you make about it, the better. (See Lake Shikaribetsu.)

AKKESHI

Akkeshi is the first stop on the way to Nemuro from Kushiro. About 42 km. from where you turned onto Hwy. 44 east of Kushiro, you should turn off the highway to the right to go into Akkeshi. You will see the bay and a bridge to your right before you get to the turn. You want to cross that bridge. As soon as you cross the bridge, take the first left turn. This will take you behind some fishermen's houses. At the end of that short road you can park and look over the lake. In winter there is a good chance of seeing Brant, Whooper Swan, assorted ducks, White-tailed Eagle, and Steller's Sea-Eagle.

Come back to the road and continue in the same direction. At the first big intersection, the main road, which you want eventually, goes to the left. This road is the one nearest the coast. You will follow it for some distance before rejoining Hwy. 44. To the best of my knowledge, this road has no number.

Before you do this, if you have the time to spare, go out to Cape Aikappu. Instead of turning left on the main road, go straight. This will take you through Akkeshi. You will come to a hill with a road going up it to a park. It goes through some woods where you could find birds in any season. At the end of the road, you can park your car and walk out to the cape, where you can see some rocky islands offshore. Look for cormorants, sea ducks, eagles, gulls, and guillemots.

LAKE HICHIRIPPU

Lake Hichirippu is the next significant place for looking, though you may find something interesting anywhere along this route. At the lake, the road crosses a waterway. In winter there will be birds to your right and left. You might see swans, ducks, eagles, and gulls here. Along the small road which goes through the woods on the east side of the lake is a good place to look for woodpeckers. That road appears to go all the way back to Hwy. 44. I doubt that it is open in winter. Anyway, this is a side trip. There are more important stops to make before you return to the highway.

CAPE KIRITAPPU

Cape Kiritappu is important in any season. Before you get there you should investigate the marsh to the left of the road. This is a breeding area for Japanese Crane. Between Lake Hichirippu and the turn for Cape Kiritappu, you will notice a parking area on the right side of the highway at the top of a hill. Stop here, cross the road, and look down in the marsh for cranes (except in winter). After the road goes back down the hill, you can drive through some of this marshy area near a small village.

There are no outstanding landmarks around here except for Kiritappu itself. You will see it to your right. There is a four-way stop where your main road turns to the left. You should be able to see a causeway straight ahead leading to Kiritappu. Before you leave this area, you will want to explore to find places where you can look out over the ocean in all directions. To get to the tip of the cape, however, take the left fork after you cross the causeway. At a T-junction go right and then twist around eventually to your left to get on the road which goes out to the end. It is fairly obvious. You can't get far lost.

The grassland is good for Latham's Snipe, Siberian Rubythroat, Middendorff's Grasshopper Warbler, Stonechat, and Yellow-breasted Bunting. Lanceolated Grasshopper Warbler is possible. Park in the last parking lot and walk all the way to the tip of the cape. In summer you will see nesting Slaty-backed Gulls at arm's length. Tufted Puffins nest in holes in the big rock at the end. Late in the afternoon they swim around between the cape and the rock. There are not many, so look carefully. Leach's Storm Petrel flies about at night. Temminck's Cormorant, Pelagic Cormorant, and Spectacled Guillemot should be common.

In winter you might see cormorants, Black and White-winged Scoters, Harlequin Duck, Oldsquaw, Common Goldeneye, Slaty-backed Gull, murres, guillemots, murrelets, and auklets. Tufted

Puffin is possible. Horned Puffin is rare, but it does occur.

Back near the entrance to Kiritappu, look in the marshy areas for Black-browed Reed Warbler and Reed Bunting in summer. Shorebirds are possible here in the right season.

LAKE FUREN

Lake Furen is next, keeping the route orderly and easy to follow. Recommended lodgings are near here. If you started from Kushiro at mid-day, you may be ready to stop by the time you check things in the vicinity of Lake Furen.

After crossing back over the causeway to Kiritappu and rejoining the main road, continue on it for approximately 11.5 km. to where it meets Hwy. 44. At that intersection there are two coffee shops and a building on the north side of the highway with a huge "WC" painted on it. Turn right and go to the east on Hwy. 44. A sign shows 51 km. to Nemuro. The kilometer signs all along this highway will help your navigation.

About 35 km. from where you joined Hwy. 44 and near the 106 km. sign, turn off to the left to a parking area overlooking Lake Furen. Walk down the path and look down at the lake and across to the other side. In summer, 20 to 30 Japanese Cranes may be here. They won't be close. Use your telescope.

SHUNKUNITAI

Shunkunitai is a long, narrow island which separates Lake Furen from the ocean. It may become a sanctuary soon. Just beyond the 110 km. sign on the highway, take the small road downhill to your left. This passes a few houses in a tiny village. Near the end of that road, turn left over a bridge to Shunkunitai. If it is winter, you may get no farther with a car. In summer, you can drive on a sandy track almost to the end. This may change if Shunkunitai becomes a sanctuary. It is about 5 km. from the bridge to the end. In winter, this hike can be a struggle if the snow is deep. Usually the snow is not deep here, but I made this expedition once in snow well above my knees. Cross-country skis or snowshoes would be wonderful in such circumstances.

Shunkunitai

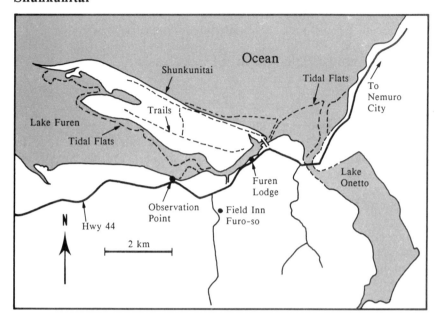

Snow Buntings and Lapland Longspurs like the far end of Shunkunitai in winter. Along the ocean side of the island there are usually some White-tailed Eagles and occasionally some Steller's Sea-Eagles in winter. Black Woodpecker is resident in the woods on the island and is said to be easier to see in winter. I have tried in all seasons and failed to find it, but others succeed.

Shunkunitai is excellent for shorebirds, especially in the fall. During migration, there will also be swans, geese, and ducks.

In summer also, this area is worth a lot of your time. Wear boots. To get the full pleasure from Shunkunitai, you need to get off the sandy track near the eastern edge and get into the woods. To do that, you must cross the marshland in between. This marshland is always good, but especially so in summer. Toward the far end there are some small ponds where Redshanks breed. You might also find a few ducks. Black-browed Reed Warbler, Yellow-breasted Bunting, and Reed Bunting are here. Look for Lanceolated Grasshopper Warbler.

About halfway down the track on Shunkunitai, near a fisherman's house, a path goes across the marsh. The path is difficult to find, and it is difficult to get all the way across without getting wet feet. Make your way over and into the forest where another path goes the length of the forest. There are actually two large patches of forest separated by an open area. You should find many birds in here, including several kinds of woodpeckers. This and Lake Shikaribetsu are supposed to be the most likely spots to find Black Woodpecker. It occurs also in Nopporo (see Sapporo) and on the Shiretoko Peninsula, but it should be easier to find here.

LAKE ONETTO

Lake Onetto and the forest on the west side of it are fine at any season. When you leave Shunkunitai, go slightly to your left to join Hwy. 44 instead of retracing your route through the village. After you have gone about 1 km., you will come to a large lake on your right. Slow down and look carefully for a small road going off to the right before the bridge. Along the first part of this road there are small trees on the right and the marsh and lake on the left. This marsh is a good place to see Water Rail. After a kilometer or so, the road goes slightly uphill and into a thick forest. It eventually gets to a road which, if you turn left, will take you to Cape Ochiishi. But, all along through the forest, there are roads branching off, many of which have chains across them. You can walk down these roads, however. This is an excellent forest, especially good for Hazel Grouse. This road is often blocked by snow in winter, so you must walk.

This is the best place I know of besides Lake Shikaribetsu to see Blakiston's Fish-Owl. People who see it here see it from the beginning of the road near Hwy. 44. From that point there is a clear view across a large open area to the forest edge. You can see the owl if it chooses to come out, and you are far enough away from the forest not to disturb the owl by your presence. If you are staying in the neighborhood, check this area first thing in the morning and the last thing before dark. I once arrived here at 5:30 in the evening to see about 15 excited Japanese birders who had just seen the owl. They were standing only a few meters off the highway and saw it flying along the edge of the forest. I have heard it calling from the forest. The owl is almost impossible to find in the deep forest. You are unlikely to see this bird, but your best approach is to find a good spot to wait and hope it reveals itself.

CAPE OCHIISHI

Cape Ochiishi is on the southern coast of the Nemuro Peninsula. Find the location on the accompanying map and work out on your map the best way to get there. If you take the road along the west side of Lake Onetto, turn left, and then turn right when you get to the main road on the other side of the railroad track, you will find it easily. You will want to look out from both the east and west sides of this peninsula and then make your way to the end by the lighthouse. On the east side there are rocks offshore where Red-faced Cormorants nest. On the west side, you may see a lot of sea ducks in the bay, and it is a good place to look for murrelets. It is a long walk out to the end from where you must leave your car. At least half of this is on a boardwalk, which helps if you are going out there in the snow.

In winter, expect to see Pelagic Cormorant, Black Scoter, White-winged Scoter, Harlequin Duck, Oldsquaw, Common Goldeneye, Slaty-backed Gull, Thin-billed Murre, Thick-billed Murre, Pigeon Guillemot, Spectacled Guillemot, and Ancient Murrelet. Other birds are possible. In summer, the peninsula is a good place for Siberian Rubythroat, grasshopper warblers, and buntings.

LAKE CHOBUSHI

Lake Chobushi became famous recently when three Lesser Frigatebirds (accidental in Japan) chose to spend the summer there. It is a good place to go even without frigatebirds. From Cape Ochiishi, take the road to the northeast which goes close to the coastline. You will stay on this road for a little more than 10 km. A bit more than halfway, soon after you cross a railroad track, there is a sign with Konbu Mori in Roman letters. After you have gone 4.7 km. past that sign, you will get to a sign showing 9 km. straight ahead to somewhere and 2 km. to the right to somewhere else, all in Japanese. Turn to the right at this intersection. When you reach the end of that road, turn right again and you can make your way to the lake.

You can see a lot from where you must stop your car. If you have the energy, take the path uphill to a shrine. There are birds along the way. From the top you can survey more of the lake and decide if you want to hike around it through the forest. Black-tailed Gulls are not easy to find in Nemuro in the summer, but they usually are at this lake.

LAKES TANNETO AND ONNETO

Lakes Tanneto and Onneto and their surroundings are worth a look if you can gain access to them. Get back on the main road from Lake Chobushi and keep going to the northeast. If you have a detailed map, you may figure out how to avoid Nemuro City by taking a shortcut to the road on the south side of the peninsula which leads to Cape Nosappu. If not, you can find it from Nemuro. A narrow lane goes off to the left from this road to a small building and a parking area next to Lake Tanneto. The fields between the road and the lake are good for birds, and something interesting usually is on the lake. Red-necked Grebe breeds here. The last time I came, this lane was blocked. It is worth a try to get in here and also around the edge of Onneto.

CAPE NOSAPPU

Cape Nosappu is excellent in winter, but extremely cold. Don't bother to go in summer unless you want a good look at the neighboring islands which were taken by the Soviet Union after World War II. Many Japanese still passionately desire the return of these islands. There is a monument here, and many visitors come in summer.

There is a building at the cape from which you can look over the ocean. If you can stand the cold, you will see a lot more by walking to the end of the cape near the lighthouse (with your telescope). Look for loons (especially Yellow-billed), grebes, cormorants, and sea ducks. This is where you will see Steller's Eider if it is around. Sometimes in winter, White-tailed Eagle and Steller's Sea-Eagle are here. There is a good chance for murres, guillemots, murrelets, and puffins. Look around on the cape for Common Redpoll and Rosy Finch. Before going out here, you will want to be wrapped in all your warmest clothes with nothing but your eyes exposed.

LAKE ODAITO AND THE NOTSUKE PENINSULA

Lake Odaito and the Notsuke Peninsula are about halfway up the coast between Nemuro and Rausu. If you are going on to Rausu or the Shiretoko Peninsula, stop here on the way. It is close enough, however, for an easy day or half-day trip from Nemuro.

Go back to the east on Hwy. 44 and turn right (north) on Hwy. 243. After 10.5 km., turn to the right on Hwy. 244. This road goes around the north side of Lake Furen. After 13 km. on Hwy. 244, the road reaches the coast. You can detour here and follow the road south along the peninsula between Lake Furen and the ocean.

If you are inclined to explore, about 5.4 km. to the north of where Hwy. 244 meets the ocean and the road to the south along the peninsula (or 19.3 km. from where you turned off Hwy. 243 onto Hwy. 244), a road goes left to Lake Barasan. It is a small lake, not far off the highway, but definitely not obvious. A pair of Japanese Cranes usually breeds here. It is a peaceful place with a variety of habitat, well worth some time.

Keep watch as you drive along the coast in winter, and you will see the place at Odaito where Whooper Swans are fed. You can turn off the highway into a parking area, walk up to the shore, and almost touch the swans. Odaito has the largest number of wintering Whooper Swans in Japan. There will be a few ducks here and some gulls nearby.

At the north end of Lake Odaito, find the road which goes out on the peninsula. You can go for several kilometers on Notsuke Hanto (peninsula). In winter, look for the same birds as at Cape Nosappu. There should be a lot of gulls and sea ducks and perhaps some eagles and other birds of prey. Like Cape Nosappu, it is extremely cold. Gyrfalcon and Snowy Owl have occurred.

During migration, this is an excellent area for geese and ducks and certainly for shorebirds. In summer, the birds to be expected are similar to those at the other capes. You should see Siberian Rubythroat, Middendorff's Grasshopper Warbler, and buntings. Redshanks breed here. Sometimes Japanese Cranes come to feed when the tide is low. A Siberian White Crane occurred in the summer of 1985. This was the second record for Hokkaido.

Time:
Give this as much time as you can. Don't try to visit every place in Japan if you are on a short trip. Pick a few places like this one where there are lots of birds, and give yourself time to find them. Nemuro has almost all the birds which occur in Hokkaido. The

rest of Hokkaido is interesting. Some people would enjoy exploring Hokkaido for several weeks, but if your time is limited, spend most of what you can allow for Hokkaido here.

You will be unhappy if you are unable to stay at least three days. I went once in summer intending to move on quickly to other areas and wound up staying a week. I wasn't sorry, but in winter, that would be too long.

Food:
Take a packed lunch. You will have to go into Nemuro City to find a restaurant, and you definitely do not want to do that. On the way from Kushiro, if the time is right, Akkeshi is a good place to find a restaurant if it isn't convenient to start out with a packed lunch. It is possible, but not preferable, to eat lunch at Cape Nosappu. Here and there you may find a little store in a village where you can buy drinks, but it is better to start off with what you need.

Accommodations:
Nemuro City has some hotels and *ryokan*. There are two *minshuku* near Lake Furen which cater to birdwatchers. Some of the accommodations in Nemuro City may be more luxurious, but they can't be as pleasant for birders as these two places near the birds.

Field Inn Furo-so (249-1 Tobai, Nemuro City, Hokkaido 086, telephone 01532-5-3905) is associated with the WBSJ. It is the home of Masaru Takada, his wife, and two daughters. They can accommodate only a small number of people. You will be lucky if you can stay here. Takada-san has neither the room nor the inclination to take groups. There are a couple of rooms where several people can be stacked on two levels and another small room or so. If you stay here, you will be treated as the guest of this lovely family and will have your meals with them. Takada-san is a naturalist and a writer and is an expert on the birds of Nemuro. I spent some of my happiest hours in Japan in this home.

To get here, turn right off Hwy. 44 near the 108 km. sign. There is also a Hwy. 44 sign at the same place. Takada-san's house is the second building on the left. You can recognize it by the wide porch on the side and all the bird feeders.

Furen Lodge (213-7 Tobai, Nemuro City, Hokkaido 086,

telephone 01532-5-3919) is nearby, overlooking Lake Furen. It is owned by Takeyoshi Matsuo, also a knowledgeable birdwatcher. This place is larger, so you may have better luck getting in. Matsuo-san and his wife are popular with foreigners, and they welcome groups. I stayed there recently when I went to Japan to accompany a group. Furen Lodge has three rooms for guests. One room holds three, one holds six, and the largest has space for eight. Matsuo-san is exceptionally helpful in assisting his guests and sharing information about the local birds.

To get to Furen Lodge, turn off Hwy. 44 beyond the 110 km. sign and go down into the village on the way to the bridge to Shunkunitai. Furen Lodge is on the left. It is a brown, one-story building with a red roof. There aren't many houses, so you will soon find it by trial and error if you have a problem.

At Notsuke Peninsula there is another *minshuku* associated with the WBSJ. It is Minshuku Notsuke, telephone 01538-2-3023.

Maps and Information:
   Champion Maps, Vol. 1, Hokkaido
   Hokkaido Map and Colour Guide 1:400,000

   National Maps: 1:50,000   Notsukesaki   野付崎
                              Shibetsu   標津
                              Nemuronanbu   根室南部
                              (There are two by this name.
                              You want NK-55-26-5.6.10.)
                              Kiritappu   霧多布
                              Attoko   厚床

Useful Kanji:
   Nemuro   根室
   Akkeshi   厚岸
   Cape Aikappu   アイカップ岬
   Lake Hichirippu 火散布沼
   Cape Kiritappu   霧多布岬
   Lake Furen   風蓮湖
   Shunkunitai   春国岱
   Lake Onetto   温根沼
   Cape Ochiishi   落石岬
   Chobushi   長節

Tanneto	丹根沼
Onneto	オンネ沼
Cape Nosappu	納沙布岬
Lake Barasan	茨散沼
Odaito	尾岱沼
Notsuke Hanto	野付半島

114

RAUSU AND THE SHIRETOKO PENINSULA

Season: January - March, mid-May - June
Specialties: White-tailed Eagle, Steller's Sea-Eagle

Rausu, on the east coast of Hokkaido, is famous for its large numbers of wintering Steller's Sea-Eagles. Most years there are a few hundred, but recently more than 2,000 have come. Many White-tailed Eagles are in the same area. For birdwatchers, this is one of Japan's most important sights. Don't miss it.

Transportation:
It is best to come by car from Kushiro, Nemuro, or from Nemuro Nakashibetsu Airport. It is difficult to estimate driving time in winter, but it might be possible to get to Rausu from Kushiro in five hours. It is not a difficult drive from Nemuro in a day with time for birding on the way.

NKA has two flights daily from Sapporo Airport (different from Chitose, the principal airport for Sapporo) to Nemuro Nakashibetsu Airport. There are no rental cars available at the airport, but Toyota has an agency at Nakashibetsu Station. The phone number is 01537-2-3238. The Akan Bus Company has service between the airport and Nakashibetsu Station. You might persuade Toyota to meet you at the airport.

Getting from Kushiro to Rausu by public transportation requires two trains and two buses. Travel time, not counting time for connections, is 4½ hours.

If you wish to start from the other direction in summer, or if you want to visit the Utoro, Shari, Lake Tofutsu area in winter when the road from Utoro to Rausu is closed, you can use Memanbetsu Airport. From there, TDA has four flights daily to Sapporo's Chitose Airport (one hour) as well as two direct flights to Tokyo (three hours).

Directions:
By car, take Hwy. 335 along the coast from Nemuro Shibetsu. Go northeast along the coast from Rausu. In winter the road is clear of snow as far as the Rusa River. The eagles roost in the trees at the cliffs along the coast and at the mouths of the rivers.

Shiretoko Peninsula

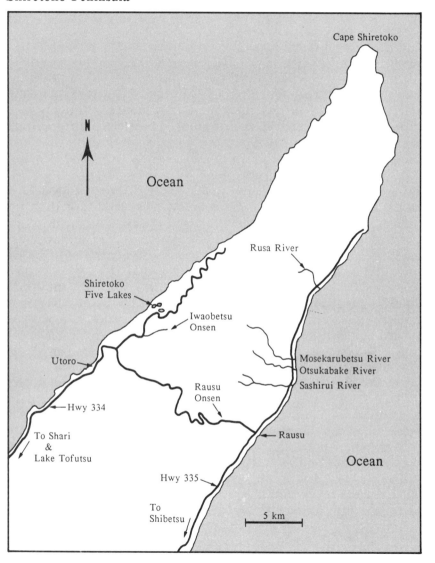

Site and Birds:
The best time to see the eagles is during the first hour after sunrise, probably from 6:00 to 7:00 a.m. when they leave their roosts and fly out over the ocean to get food. For a while there is much flying back and forth over the road, and you can get

excellent views of these birds from close range. Many of them will sit on the floating ice to eat their catch.

The first river beyond the lighthouse by the tunnel is the Sashirui River. Otsukabake River is next, followed by the Mosekarubetsu River. Most of the eagles roost near the mouths of the Sashirui and the Mosekarubetsu rivers, where you will also find many photographers and birdwatchers (especially at the Sashirui River). It is a beautiful scene. Even if you aren't a photographer, bring your camera to record this one. With a telephoto lens, you should be able to get excellent shots of these eagles.

After the early morning activity, the eagles disperse. They return about 2:00 or 3:00 in the afternoon. It gets dark early here in winter.

Look for other birds in the forests and streams near Rausu Onsen and along the rivers near the coast, if the snow conditions permit it. Brown Dippers are common in the winter. Along the coast you should see scoters, Harlequin Duck, Oldsquaw, Common Goldeneye, mergansers, and Herring, Slaty-backed, Glaucous-winged, Glaucous, and Mew Gulls.

You might see a Raven along the cliffs near the tunnel by the lighthouse. This is the only place in Japan where this bird occurs.

The Shiretoko Peninsula is probably the wildest area left in Japan. Most of it can be reached only by a long trek. My Japanese friends talk of bears and other wild creatures and consider most of it a no-man's land. But now the road from Rausu goes about halfway to the end of the peninsula, and there is a road from Utoro on the other side of the peninsula which goes to Shiretoko Five Lakes and beyond. In Japan, roads bring tourists.

The road from Rausu to Utoro is open from June until the beginning of October. The road from Utoro to Shiretoko Five Lakes is open from sometime in April. Birds to look for around these lakes include breeding Mandarin Ducks, White-backed Woodpecker, Indian Tree Pipit, Gray's Grasshopper Warbler, Crowned Willow Warbler, and Nuthatch. You can get to Shiretoko Five Lakes by bus from Utoro, but, with a car, you can go as far as the road does and explore other areas.

I did not manage to get to the Shiretoko Five Lakes until June of 1985. We stayed at Iwaobetsu Onsen and got over to the lakes by 8:00 a.m. I had long heard how remote this all was, so I was shocked to find that 28 tour buses had arrived before we did. I can't imagine where they came from, but most had brought school groups-- hundreds of teenagers all dressed in identical sweat suits. We attempted to make the circuit of the lakes backwards, but people were everywhere. The groups were extremely noisy. The noise level increased considerably when they discovered a group of foreigners. There were no birds to be seen, much less heard, so we quickly left without even looking at all five lakes. Try to visit this place either very early or very late.

The road which branches off the road to Shiretoko Five Lakes and goes farther out the peninsula was too narrow for our bus. This indicates to me that it should be free of crowds. In late spring and summer when this road is clear of snow, it should be well worth exploring. I suggest driving as far as possible out the Shiretoko Peninsula, both along this road past the Shiretoko Five Lakes and along the road on the other side of the peninsula beyond Rausu. You will probably find trails you can explore, but be extremely careful not to get lost, and be prepared for sudden changes in the weather. And do remember there are bears.

It has been reported that Black Woodpeckers are resident at Iwaobetsu Onsen, but we saw no signs of them. It may be that they are up the trail behind the hotel. This trail is rather steep even near the hotel. It goes over the mountains and all the way to Rausu. If you should climb to the top (a major expedition), you should see along the way Japanese Accentor, Japanese Robin, Siberian Bluechat, Pale-legged Willow Warbler, Blue-and-White Flycatcher, Gray Bunting, Pine Grosbeak, and Bullfinch.

The highway between Utoro and Rausu passes through some good habitat. Allow time to stop occasionally to look for birds.

There is a sightseeing boat which goes from Utoro to the end of the peninsula and back. The round trip takes about four hours. The boat makes two trips daily. It is a comfortable boat with an enclosed cabin where you can go for shelter if you get too cold. Not far from Utoro you will see hundreds of Spectacled Guillemots in summer. On our trip a heavy fog came in when we were about halfway to the cape. Before this happened, we were

beginning to see large numbers of Fulmars. I suspect the birding is
better nearer the cape. When you can see, the scenery is lovely.
Look for Short-tailed Shearwater, Temminck's Cormorant, White-
tailed Eagle, Slaty-backed Gull, Black-legged Kittiwake, and
Rhinoceros Auklet.

If you are driving between Utoro and Memanbetsu Airport, it
would be well to allow time to look at Lake Tofutsu, on Hwy. 244
a few kilometers east of Abashiri. The lake is about 6 km. long,
but narrow, with the long side running parallel to the highway.
Apparently, the best birding is on each side of the road, between
the ocean and the lake. This should be a good place in all seasons.

Time:
If you are going to Rausu in the winter, you can arrive in the
early afternoon and see the eagles before dark, observe them again
in the morning for as long as you like, and then be on your way.
Use any extra time to explore some of the forests. Blakiston's
Fish-Owl may be in this area, but nobody is willing to discuss it.
Pursuing it here is a job for an adventurer with plenty of time.

From Rausu, it is impossible to get to the coast near Utoro in
winter without going all the way back to Nemuro Shibetsu and
taking Hwy. 244 to Shari. That is a separate expedition requiring a
great deal more time.

The boat trip in summer takes half a day. The drive from
Memanbetsu Airport to Iwaobetsu Onsen takes half a day. The rest
will depend on how much time you can allow for exploring.
Driving will be slow.

Food:
In an unpopulated area like this, you should take your lunch.

Accommodations:
At Rausu Onsen, there is the Shiretoko Kanko Hotel (01538-7-
2181) which will accommodate 300 people, with prices from
¥8,000 to ¥12,000, and the Rausu Dai-ichi Hotel (01538-7-2259)
which accommodates 60 people, with prices from ¥8,000 to
¥10,000. These rates include two meals. Ryokan Shiga (01538-7-
2101) is in Rausu. It costs from ¥7,000 to ¥8,000. There is a
youth hostel, as well as other cheaper accommodations, in Rausu.

In Iwaobetsu Onsen (near Shiretoko Five Lakes) there is the Hotel Chinohate (01522-4-2331) with rates from ¥8,000 to ¥10,000. In Utoro there is the Shiretoko Park Hotel (01522-4-2321), the Shiretoko Grand Hotel (01522-4-2021), and 16 other inns. The prices in Utoro range from ¥9,000 to ¥25,000.

Maps and Information:
Champion Maps, Vol. 1, Hokkaido
Hokkaido Map and Colour Guide 1:400,000

National Maps: 1:50,000 Rausu   羅臼

Koshimizu 小清水

Useful Kanji:

Rausu	羅臼
Rausu Onsen	羅臼温泉
Sashirui River	サシルイ川
Otsukabake River	オツカバケ川
Mosekarubetsu River	モセカルベツ川
Shiretoko Peninsula	知床半島
Utoro	宇登呂
Shiretoko Five Lakes	知床五湖
Shari	斜里
Lake Tofutsu	涛沸湖
Nemuro Nakashibetsu Airport	中標津空港
Memanbetsu Airport	女満別空港

LAKE SHIKARIBETSU

Season: late May - June
Specialties: Blakiston's Fish-Owl, Black Woodpecker

This lake in central Hokkaido (southern part of Daisetsuzan National Park) is out of the way for a visitor in a hurry, but it is worth serious consideration. The chances of seeing Blakiston's Fish-Owl and Black Woodpecker are slim, but they are as good here as anywhere else in Japan.

Transportation:
There is no quick way to get here. Obihiro Airport is near, but the only flights are from Tokyo (1 hour, 25 minutes). This would be convenient if your only other destination were eastern Hokkaido. If you plan to visit both Sapporo and Nemuro, start on one side and drive all the way across, stopping at Lake Shikaribetsu on the way. It takes the better part of a day to drive from Nemuro to Lake Shikaribetsu or from Lake Shikaribetsu to Utonai.

Directions:
From Obihiro, take Hwy. 273 to the north. It branches off from Hwy. 241 north of Obihiro where Hwy. 241 turns to the east. After about 23 km. on Hwy. 273, near the south end of Lake Nukabira, turn left on Hwy. 726 to Lake Shikaribetsu. It is not far, but it may take about 45 minutes from Nukabira.

Site and Birds:
This lake is surrounded by lovely vegetation. That on the south end of the lake up the mountain is the typical mixed forest for this area. There are rhododendrons, ferns, mosses, and wildflowers. Around the lake is wetland. On the north end, between the lake and Yamada Onsen, is a thick coniferous forest.

You are most likely to find the owl and the woodpecker on the north end of the lake between the campground and Yamada Onsen. You cannot get into the forest except on two narrow roads which go in for only a short distance. It would be next to impossible to see these birds in the thick forest anyway, so you must hope they come out.

The woodpecker nests in the campground. I saw the nest hole, but no woodpecker. There should be several pairs around the lake, so you will have other chances if you don't see these. Lesser Spotted Woodpecker and White's Ground Thrush also are possible around the campground.

Everyone I have ever heard of who has seen the owl here has seen it on the highway between the lake and the *onsen*. I heard the owl calling about 7:00 p.m. I spent two days looking for it and failed to find it. A friend went later, walked down the highway, and the owl flew out and perched within 50 feet of him. There is really nothing you can do but stand on this road at dawn and dusk and hope for the best.

Lake Shikaribetsu Area

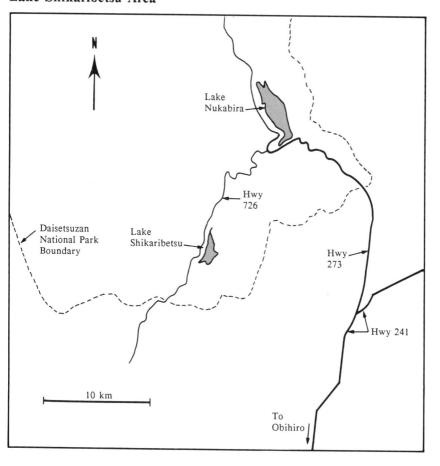

Lake Shikaribetsu

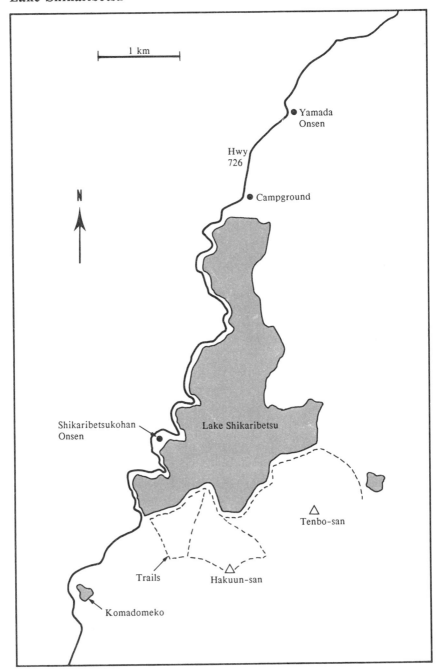

The path around the south end of the lake is easy and pleasant, but going up the mountains can be a problem. I know from experience that it is easy to get lost. There are some signs in *kanji*, but it all gets confusing after a few forks in the trail. The trail up Hakuun-san was muddy and slippery and, occasionally, extremely narrow with long steep drops. While we were on the mountain a cloud descended, and we could see absolutely nothing. Especially if it is wet, don't go up there thinking it is a simple stroll. Most of us have climbed things much more difficult, but in this case there is no warning of the conditions and the need for proper equipment.

There are not so many birds here, but the beautiful vegetation and the outside chance of the owl and the woodpecker make up for that. Woodcock is common in the wetland. Other possible birds include Common Merganser, Hazel Grouse, Common Cuckoo, House Martin, Indian Tree Pipit, Winter Wren, Japanese Robin, Siberian Bluechat, Crowned Willow Warbler, Goldcrest, tits, Brown Creeper, Black-faced Bunting, Jay, and Nutcracker. Also check the area along the road going to the southwest from the south of the lake. Look around Komadomeko and the open highlands area to the south. You might find a Long-tailed Rose Finch.

During the tourist season a sightseeing boat plies the lake, starting from Shikaribetsukohan Onsen. The loudspeaker is annoying, but it has little effect on the birds.

Time:
If you bother to come, spend the night. That gives you a chance to see the owl out on the road. Come one afternoon, look around the area, wait for the owl, and stay alert for the woodpecker. The next morning, finish checking and rechecking, and leave when you are ready. A stay of 24 hours is ample. Waiting for the owl and the woodpecker is not a worthwhile way to spend your time.

Food:
There is a restaurant at the campground. You can probably get food at Shikaribetsukohan Onsen. It is better to take your lunch, but there are alternatives.

Accommodations:
You can stay at Yamada Onsen and patrol the highway between there and the lake on foot. The rates at Yamada Onsen are from

¥4,500 to ¥7,000, and the telephone number is 01566-6-2741. The Central Lodge is at the campground. It has no phone, so you cannot make reservations. It is basic, but adequate, and has a restaurant.

There are two large hotels at Shikaribetsukohan Onsen. They are the Shikaribetsu Royal Hotel Fukuhara (01566-7-2301), ¥10,000-¥20,000, and the Shikaribetsukohan Onsen Hotel (01566-7-2211), ¥8,500-¥15,000.

Maps and Information:
Champion Maps, Vol. 1, Hokkaido
Hokkaido Map and Colour Guide 1:400,000

Useful Kanji:
Nukabira	糠平
Lake Shikaribetsu	然別湖
Yamada Onsen	山田温泉
Shikaribetsukohan Onsen	然別湖畔温泉
Hakuun-san	白雲山
Tenbo-san	天望山
Higashi-Daisetsu-Hakubutsukan	東大雪博物館

Note:
Daisetsuzan is the largest national park in Japan and probably the one containing the most territory still in its natural state. If you have ample time and are willing to do some hiking, it is a beautiful area where you will certainly find some birds and have a fine time if you don't require a lot of birds in a hurry.

There are many tourists, but most come in buses and stay along the main road going through the park. If you come after mid-July, you will encounter many hikers in the mountains. Come earlier, and you can see some of the 150 species of birds which have occurred here. You are unlikely to see anything you can't see elsewhere, but it is a lovely place.

Mt. Midori (2019 meters) can be reached by a two-hour hike from Kogen Onsen. This is a good place to see Japanese Accentor, Gray Bunting, Siskin, Red Crossbill (not easy), and Nutcracker. If you intend to explore more, you will require detailed maps and assistance in selecting a hiking route.

If you go through Nukabira, visit the natural history museum. Its name in Japanese is Higashi-Daisetsu-Hakubutsukan.

TOKYO - HOKKAIDO FERRY

Season: *all year*
Specialties: *seabirds*

The long ferry trip between Tokyo and Hokkaido provides the best pelagic birding in Japan. Every birder who visits Japan should seriously consider making this trip at least in one direction.

Transportation:
The trip takes about 33 hours from Tokyo to Kushiro and about 31 hours from Tokyo to Tomakomai. The boats leave Tokyo late at night and arrive in Hokkaido early the second morning, with excellent birding from dawn until arrival. They leave Hokkaido around noon and arrive in Tokyo the evening of the second day.

Directions:
Kinkai Yusen Ferry (03-447-6551) goes from Tokyo to Kushiro. This route is the most popular for birders who are on their way to or from birding in eastern Hokkaido. Nihon Enkai Ferry (03-574-9561) goes from Tokyo to Tomakomai, which is near Utonai Sanctuary and Chitose Airport, about 1 hour, 30 minutes south of Sapporo. Both ferries make two trips every three days. The schedule is available about six months in advance.

I have been only on the ferry to Kushiro. I am guessing that it is a nicer ferry because the price is considerably higher, even though the distance is about the same. At the time of writing, the Kushiro ferry leaves Tokyo at 11:00 p.m. and arrives in Kushiro at 8:30 a.m. the second day. First class, a bedroom for two to four people, costs ¥28,000 per person, one way. Second class, six people sleeping on *tatami*, costs ¥18,500 per person. And the bottom class, described later, is ¥14,000 per person.

The ferry for Tomakomai leaves Tokyo at 11:30 p.m. and arrives at 6:45 on the second morning. First class costs ¥16,000 per person with two to four people per room, ¥14,500 with six people per room. Second class is ¥11,500.

Site and Birds:
I have made this trip a number of times, mostly in winter. The birding is exciting then, but the voyage is much more pleasant in spring and summer.

The ferry is huge, but the sea can be rough. Birding must be done from the deck. Be prepared for extreme cold in winter, even if the weather is fine. Dress for severe arctic conditions with complete rain gear on top. You will still have to take regular trips inside to thaw out. On one of my trips, the sea was so rough we could find no place on deck where we could escape the waves, which would splash all over us and immediately turn to ice. This made birding impossible for part of the trip. It usually isn't that bad.

First-class cabins do have windows. In good weather it is possible to see some birds from them, but, of course, this is not an ideal way to do pelagic birding. If the weather is fine, the front windows of the restaurant provide a good view over a larger area. You are supposed to be in the restaurant only during the times meals are being served. On my last trip with a group of foreigners traveling first class, we managed to use these windows in the restaurant throughout the day. The Japanese would never ask. We didn't ask, we just didn't leave, and nothing was said. As long as foreign birders are rare on the ferry and are cooperative while the tables are being cleaned, it is possible exceptions to the rule will be made. Late in the afternoon they close the curtains over the front windows. This is so the light will not interfere with the vision of the person who is steering the ship, so don't complain.

In addition to the sea off Hokkaido, the best areas for birds on this trip are off the coast of Chiba Prefecture (east of Tokyo) and off Iwate Prefecture at the north of Honshu. You can follow your course on a large map on the ship. If you are traveling from Tokyo to Kushiro, you will be in these areas in the morning after your departure, that afternoon, and early the following morning. In the other direction, you will also pass through these areas in daylight. Besides birds, look for seals, sea lions, and whales.

Like most good pelagic trips, this one is fun no matter how many times you do it, because anything could turn up. Red-throated, Arctic, and Pacific Loons are possible. Laysan Albatross and Black-footed Albatross occur throughout the year, but are in greater numbers in spring and summer. (Short-tailed Albatross is seen so seldom that there is no way to even make a try for it. It has, however, been seen from this ferry. At least be aware that the bird exists. Pay attention; you might be lucky.) Fulmar may be seen in any season, usually near Hokkaido. Stejneger's Petrel is rare, but most likely to occur from June through August. Streaked Shearwater occurs all year. Wedge-tailed Shearwater occurs, but is uncommon. Look for Flesh-footed Shearwater, Sooty Shearwater, and Short-tailed Shearwater in spring and summer.

Storm petrels are most often seen from the ferry when seas are rough. May or June is a good time to see Leach's, Swinhoe's, Band-rumped, and Sooty Storm Petrels. Fork-tailed is rare. Band-rumped breeds on small islands off Iwate Prefecture. Your best chance of seeing it is from the ferry.

Red and Northern Phalaropes occur during migration. Pomarine, Parasitic, and Long-tailed Jaegers could turn up almost anytime. Gulls occur throughout the year, but in winter you will have a chance to see Glaucous-winged and Glaucous, if not from the ferry, at least in Hokkaido. Black-legged Kittiwake is common in winter.

Winter is the best time to see Thin-billed and Thick-billed Murres, Pigeon and Spectacled Guillemots, Marbled and Ancient Murrelets, and Crested and Least Auklets. When the Sea of Okhotsk is iced (January through March), many birds come south into this area. Besides the birds already mentioned, there are cormorants and sea ducks, including Black Scoter, White-winged Scoter, Harlequin Duck, and Oldsquaw.

Food:
A restaurant on board serves meals at set hours. At other times, snacks are for sale at a counter in the lobby. There are drink machines. If you aren't overly fond of unexciting Japanese food, you might want to bring your own snacks to supplement what you can buy on board.

You must select your food before entering the restaurant and buy a ticket for each item desired, including drinks. Then you place the tickets on your table. Someone will collect them and eventually bring what you ordered. There should be photographs or plastic models to help your selection process. Don't count on anyone speaking English.

Accommodations:
The cheapest way to make this trip is to pay ¥14,000 (one way) and sleep on the floor. In this class, a large open area is divided

into smaller spaces by walls about two feet high. The floor is carpeted, so you remove your shoes before entering. Each little area is supplied with about 12 to 15 blankets, one for each person if it is full. I have done this in winter when the ship is not crowded. If your party is big enough to lay claim to one of these sections and keep others from moving in, it isn't such a bad way to travel. You probably need to be in a group of at least six to accomplish this. We have always boarded the ferry about two hours ahead of departure, as soon as it is allowed, in order to get our place. In seasons other than the dead of winter, the ferry has many more passengers. I imagine this is far less pleasant then.

Unless you are part of a large party and this sounds like fun for the group, I recommend going first class where you will have a private cabin and beds as well as a wash basin. The cabins have a table and chairs and a window. They are comfortable and larger than some Japanese hotel rooms. On the first-class deck there are toilets and showers opposite the cabins. The ferry has a large *ofuro*.

SHIMOKITA PENINSULA

Season: spring and summer, December - March
Specialties: Yellow-billed Loon, Schrenck's Little Bittern, Brant,
Spectacled Guillemot, Japanese Marsh Warbler,
Japanese Reed Bunting

Much of the Shimokita Peninsula, at the northeastern tip of Honshu, remains in its natural state with good habitat extending for more than 80 km. You will have a chance to see the Japanese Marsh Warbler only here and at Hachirogata Lagoon. Birding is good in winter, but it can be extraordinarily cold with heavy snow. Travel is slow, and good birds must be hunted for. Especially in summer when conditions are easier, it is a fine place for a birder who has the time and desire to explore.

Transportation:
TDA has four flights daily each way between Tokyo and Misawa (1 hour, 15 minutes) and one flight between Misawa and Sapporo (50 minutes). One-way fare from Tokyo is ¥23,000 and from Sapporo is ¥15,900. You will need a rental car from Misawa Airport. Alternately, you could take the Shinkansen (train) to Morioka and drive from there, but the slow driving will take much of your time.

Directions:
Misawa Airport is within a few kilometers of where you will start birding. Check all around Lake Ogawara, but spend most of your time examining all the good-looking places up the eastern side of the peninsula along Hwy. 338 north of Misawa. Then go all the way to Cape Shiriya at the northeastern tip. If you go in winter, you will also want to visit Ominato, at the northwest corner of Mutsu Bay. If you go in summer and have plenty of time, you might want to explore Usoriyamako (lake) and the mountainous regions of the western bulge of Shimokita Peninsula and maybe go as far as Cape Oma. This is very slow, so don't attempt it if you are in the least bit of a hurry.

Shimokita Peninsula

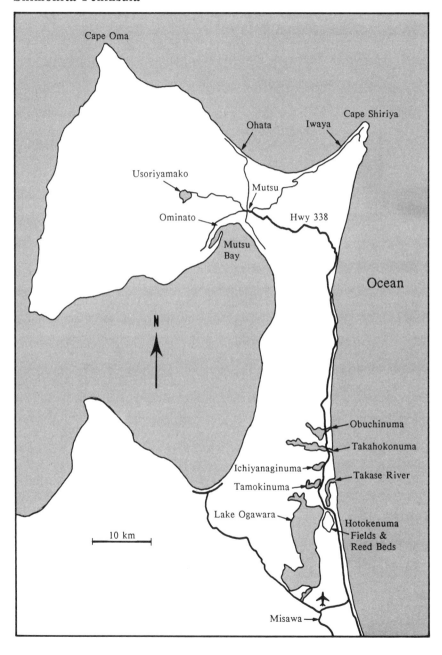

Cape Oma

Ohata

Iwaya

Cape Shiriya

Usoriyamako

Mutsu

Ominato

Hwy 338

Mutsu Bay

Ocean

N

Obuchinuma

Takahokonuma

Ichiyanaginuma

Takase River

Tamokinuma

Lake Ogawara

Hotokenuma Fields & Reed Beds

10 km

Misawa

Site and Birds:
In winter, the primary places of interest are Ominato, Cape Shiriya, and the lakes in the south of the peninsula. It is cold. The day I visited Ominato, it snowed 75 cm. Driving across the peninsula from the east side to Ominato in the snow the day before (and in the dark because it took much longer than we had expected) was terrifying. We were on narrow, twisting mountain roads and couldn't see the road, much less birds, for all the snow.

Lapland Longspur and Snow Bunting winter around Lake Ogawara. If you can bear to get close to the ocean in the cold, look for loons (including a possible Yellow-billed) where Obuchinuma opens into the ocean. This is the northernmost of the lakes. You might see a White-tailed Eagle anywhere, but it is most likely at Cape Shiriya. You should find many species of ducks and birds of prey. Drive to Cape Shiriya and walk around the point. Some people who are immune to the cold walk all the way from Iwaya. You might see Red-necked Grebe, Pelagic and Temminck's Cormorants, scoters, Harlequin Duck, Glaucous-winged and Glaucous Gulls, Lapland Longspur, Snow Bunting, and Common Redpoll.

From Ominato go west along the bay as far as the entrance to the naval base. You cannot enter the spit of land across the water because it belongs to the naval base. You must check the birds over there with a telescope. Along the waterfront you should be able to see Pelagic Cormorant, 100 to 200 wintering Brant (rare in Japan), Whooper Swan, Falcated Teal, Oldsquaw, and gulls.

If the weather and snow conditions permit you to enter the mountain areas, you might see waxwings and crossbills. The north coast between Ohata and the rivermouth about 2 km. to the east is a good place to look for Yellow-billed Loon and sea ducks.

In summer your prime target will be the Japanese Marsh Warbler, with Schrenck's Little Bittern and Japanese Reed Warbler as probable secondary targets. The Japanese Marsh Warbler is extremely local. At the time of this writing, the best places to look were southwest of Lake Ogawara, at Hotokenuma, at the northeast corner of Lake Ogawara, at the southeast of Tamokinuma, to the east of the highway between Ichiyanaginuma and Tamokinuma, and at Cape Oma at the northwestern tip of the peninsula. Although the Japanese Marsh Warbler is said to be next to impossible to find, we found it immediately in mid-June. Start by turning off Hwy. 338 onto the first good road going into the fields at Hotokenuma. Find some reeds, and there is a good chance you will discover one engaging in its characteristic song flight.

Look in the grassland east of the highway between Obuchinuma and Takahokonuma for Japanese Reed Bunting. Schrenck's Little Bittern should be in the area east of the highway between Ichiyanaginuma and Tamokinuma. All three of these species could be in any of the areas mentioned. There are a few Chinese Little Bitterns. They fly more often after they have finished nesting, so are easier to see in August.

Spectacled Guillemot breeds on Cape Shiriya. This is an interesting area, said to be pleasant for walking in the summer.

Hotokenuma is no longer a pond, but has been reclaimed. In summer you might see Japanese Marsh Warbler, Black-browed Reed Warbler, Great Reed Warbler, and Japanese Reed Bunting.

Great Crested Grebe breeds around Ichiyanaginuma and Tamokinuma. Anywhere around these lakes you might find Little Grebe, Gray Heron, Common Pheasant, Latham's Snipe, Stonechat, Great Reed Warbler, Reed Bunting, and Azure-winged Magpie. Great Cormorant breeds at Ichiyanaginuma and at a small lake to the east of Ominato. This species is easier to see at Shinobazu Pond at Ueno Zoo in Tokyo, where it also breeds.

During spring and autumn migration, the area is excellent for shorebirds. The best places are at the mouth of the Takase River and near the ocean at Obuchinuma. The Takase River is a good place to see Garganey in spring.

Time:
If you go in winter, you should allow at least one day for the south, a half day in Ominato (better in the afternoon), and a half day to visit Cape Shiriya if you are doing it by car. You must add travel time to this birding time.

In summer, a minimum would be one day in the south, a half day at Cape Shiriya, and perhaps a half day at Usoriyamako, plus travel time.

Food:
Ominato has restaurants, but you will be better off with a packed lunch. The long narrow part of the peninsula is almost uninhabited on the eastern side, so you should bring drinks, too.

Accommodations:
The Inaho Ryokan (01757-5-2532) is at Tamokinuma, right in the heart of the birding area for the lakes in the south. It is a two-story, greenish-gray building with a green roof. If you are traveling north, it is on the left side of the highway, the second building from the corner before you get to the intersection where the post office is on the far right corner. The owners are accustomed to birdwatchers.

If you visit Ominato in winter, the Hatanaka Ryokan is across the street from Ominato Station. It costs ¥6,000 per person with two meals. It was perfectly satisfactory. Our room was freezing at first, but then they didn't know we were coming. The oil heater got it warmed up, but the fuel ran out during the night. The temperature inside the room without the heater was 6°C. Before breakfast, the maid got it going again. We didn't get out of the *futon* until some of the chill went away. And the halls were freezing. But, with the heater on or inside the *futon*, it was comfortable. This is typical in cold areas in winter, so be prepared.

There are two other *ryokan* across the street from Ominato Station. Other places to stay are the Suzuya Minshuku at Shimokita, Araiya Ryokan at Iwaya, a youth hostel at Shiriya, and the Mutsu Kanko Hotel near the beginning of the road from the Mutsu area to Cape Shiriya. The Yoneda Ryokan is at Chitose Daira.

Maps and Information:
    Champion Maps, Vol. 2, Eastern Japan
    Buyodo Map D-8

    National Maps: 1:50,000 Misawa 三沢

                    Hiranuma 平沼

  Brown, Jan. *Exploring Tohoku.* Tokyo: Weatherhill, 1982.

Useful Kanji:

Misawa	三沢
Lake Ogawara	小川原湖
Tamokinuma	田面木沼
Ichiyanaginuma	市柳沼
Takahokonuma	鷹架沼
Obuchinuma	尾駮沼
Cape Shiriya	尻屋崎
Cape Oma	大間崎
Iwaya	岩屋
Ohata	大畑町
Ominato	大湊
Usoriyamako	宇曽利山湖

HACHIROGATA LAGOON AND OGA PENINSULA

Hachirogata Lagoon was once the second largest lake in Japan. It has been reclaimed and now is 172 sq. km. of farmland. Some of the lake and several waterways remain. Oga Peninsula is noted for its beautiful rocky coast. These two areas should be visited together, even though their best seasons do not always coincide. If you go at a time when birding is not interesting on Oga Peninsula, at least allow time for driving around it to enjoy the scenery.

Transportation:
It is possible to get here by public transportation, but a car will save you a lot of time and trouble and will get you to good birding areas well away from the bus route. From Akita Airport allow one hour to Akita City and another two hours to reach the birding areas on the south coast of Oga Peninsula.

There are direct flights on ANA to Akita from Tokyo (one hour) and Nagoya (1 hour, 10 minutes) and on TDA from Sapporo (1 hour, 15 minutes) and Osaka (1 hour, 35 minutes). By train, Akita is at least five hours from Tokyo. You can go by Shinkansen to either Morioka or to Niigata and change to an express. Tokyo to Morioka is 2 hours, 45 minutes, plus two hours to Akita; Tokyo to Niigata is 1 hour, 53 minutes, plus four hours to Akita. It is possible to a rent a car at either the airport or the train station. There is a large Toyota office at the airport.

Directions:
You will need a good map. Ask for directions when you rent your car. Akita Airport is hard to find, so pay attention to the way if you will be driving back there to leave your car. The direction signs are all in *kanji*. Only after you have made your last turn and are on the correct road will you see a helpful picture of an airplane. If you have come some other way and will go to Akita Airport for the first time on your way out, be sure to get careful directions before you start. Go south from Akita on Hwy. 13 for the airport. Then you must find the road which goes off to your right from Hwy. 13.

Neither Hwy. 13 nor Hwy. 7 goes into the city center. If you are looking for the train station or have other need to go into Akita, look for Akita City Center and Akita Station signs in *kanji*.

Hachirogata & Oga Peninsula

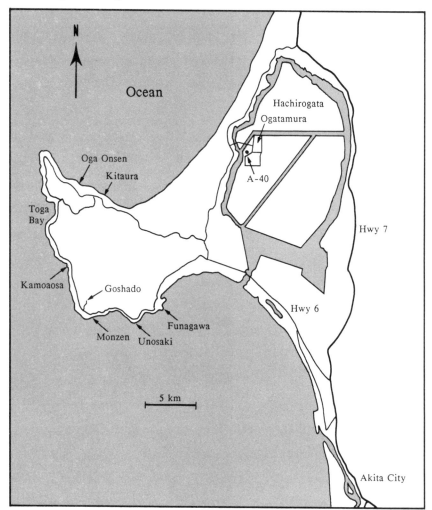

If you are driving to this area from the north, you do not have to go into Akita City. You can turn off Hwy. 7 just north of the Hachirogata area. Otherwise take Hwy. 6 from north of Akita. Just beyond the port you have a choice of roads. Take the one closest to the water.

HACHIROGATA LAGOON

Seasons: migration, all year except late Dec. to early Feb.
Specialties: Chinese Little Bittern, Schrenck's Little Bittern, Brant,
*   Gray-headed Lapwing, Indian Pratincole, Japanese*
*   Marsh Warbler, Japanese Reed Bunting*

Site and Birds:
Hachirogata is flat, open farmland. Look for birds anywhere after
you visit the reserve at A-40 (see map). At A-40 you will see a
sign with a windmill on it. Walk quietly down the path to a small
two-story building. Go in and up to the second floor (after taking
off your shoes). From this vantage point in summer you might see
Chinese Little Bittern, Schrenck's Little Bittern, Marsh Harrier,
Gray-headed Lapwing, Japanese Marsh Warbler, Black-browed
Reed Warbler, Japanese Reed Bunting, and Gray-headed Bunting.
Reed Bunting also is present. There is a small pond in the reserve
where, until it is frozen, there usually are a lot of ducks. Gray-
headed Lapwing is common except in winter. Flocks are often
near the large lake.

In April and May and August and September, there are a lot of
shorebirds on the Akita coast. Fall migration is best. It is the best
time to see a Spoon-billed Sandpiper or the much less rare
Temminck's Stint. Fall also brings flocks of Russet Sparrows. In
the spring, you can see many Spotted Redshanks from Hwy. 6.
Both Chinese Little Bittern and Schrenck's Little Bittern occur in
this same area in summer.

Many waterfowl which winter at Lake Izunuma stop here from
March until mid-May on their way north. Recently flocks of geese
have begun to winter here, but from the end of December until
mid-February this area isn't particularly interesting.

A White Stork has occurred a few times in recent years, but not
even the season can be predicted. Appearances have been in May,
November, and January.

Look around the big lake, the waterways, and in the fields. There
is a lot of territory to cover. In addition, the coastal area good for
shorebirds stretches for about 20 km.

Time:
In a good season, you could easily spend a full day. If you are searching for rare shorebirds, you might want more time. I visited in late December, so I don't know how easy it is to see all the specialties at A-40.

Food:
In Ogatamura (the village in Hachirogata) there is a restaurant called Snack Panda, owned by Kobayashi-san, a birdwatcher. The restaurant is across from the post office. Many birders stop in here for a meal, a snack, or just coffee. Kobayashi-san is most welcoming, and his menu appeals to Westerners. This is a good place to try to get information about the birds in the area.

Accommodations:
See Oga Peninsula. The Doi Ryokan (01854-7-2450 and 2926) is listed by the WBSJ as being in the area, but I do not know where it is or anything about it.

OGA PENINSULA

Season: winter, migration
Specialties: Brant, ducks, gulls, Ancient Murrelet

Site and Birds:
Oga Peninsula is not particularly interesting in summer, and it is full of tourists. In spring and fall it is good for migrating land birds, but its main claim to fame is winter birds. If you go, you should tour the peninsula. Local birders, however, concentrate on the south coast. In winter the wind blowing from the north makes birding even colder and more difficult on the northern coast.

From Ogatamura, take the bridge across the waterway and drive near the northern coast to the village of Kitaura. You will have an opportunity to see gulls and sea ducks and maybe some land birds along this route. At Kitaura, get off the main road and go down to the pier. (Turn at a grocery store with a yellow-orange sign with red-orange writing on it.) This is a good place for gulls. The point at the northwestern tip of the peninsula is also good for gulls, but it can be miserable in winter. If the weather is bad or you don't have much time, beyond Kitaura cut over toward Toga Bay. This is a good place to look for birds. Then you will get on a toll road which goes to the south around the steep, rocky coast.

You may see some birds from Kamoaosa on south, but the best birding is concentrated between Monzen and Funagawa where the road is down near the water.

Along here in winter you can expect to see Eared Grebe, Temminck's Cormorant, Pelagic Cormorant, Mallard, Spot-billed Duck, Greater Scaup, Common Goldeneye, and Red-breasted Merganser as well as Black-headed, Herring, Slaty-backed, Glaucous-winged, Mew, and Black-tailed Gulls. I saw the yellow-faced form of the White Wagtail. Blue Rockthrush is also here.

Sometimes it is possible to see Ancient Murrelet from the shore and a flock of wintering Brant. Look for Brant from Unosaki. Usually an Eastern Reef Heron (dark phase) is around. Horned and Red-necked Grebes, Black Scoter, Harlequin Duck, and Black-legged Kittiwake also occur but can't be counted on. White Stork is a rare visitor, occurring some winters.

A good place to look for land birds is up the 999 steps to Goshado, five small, ancient shrines. From where the road turns off to go down to the waterfront at Monzen, continue toward the north (and uphill) 0.9 km. You will see a sign indicating the entrance to Daisankyo Toll Road, Suizokukan - 13 km., and Nyudozaki - 24 km. Keep going for about 0.2 km. (you don't reach the toll road entrance), and you will see a parking area down to your right. From the parking area, walk up through the forest to the shrines. You could see woodpeckers (Japanese Green), tits, or Rosy Finch. In the dead of winter I saw fresh tracks in the snow which I believe could have been those of a Copper Pheasant.

The list of birds recorded on the south coast of Oga Peninsula since 1973 is long and includes cuckoos, owls, kingfishers (Common and Ruddy), Jungle Nightjar, pipits, shrikes, thrushes, warblers, flycatchers, tits, buntings, and finches. Information on the frequency of their occurrence is unavailable.

Time:
Allow a day for Oga Peninsula if at all possible.

Food:
You will enjoy having your lunch with you, but you can find food in some of the villages and certainly in the resort areas.

Accommodations:

It is most convenient to stay on Oga Peninsula for birding there and at Hachirogata. Due to the large number of tourists, there are many places to stay. Most of the expensive ones are near Oga Onsen on the north coast. Check with the TIC or a travel agent.

The Akita birdwatchers recommend the Isonoya Ryokan in Monzen (0185-27-2011). In winter it costs ¥6,000 per person with two meals. If you are coming from the east, you will recognize Monzen if you will look for a huge flat rock in the water, then a rocky area with a lighthouse at the point. Then the road curves to the north. The village is to your left. Shortly after you pass a big rock monument on your left, a road goes off to the left down to the water. This gets you to the bottom level of Monzen village. Isonoya Ryokan is the third building on your right; the water is on your left. The roof of the *ryokan* is red.

This is a large sprawling *ryokan* on multiple levels with rooms of many sizes. Some hold probably six to ten people, but we had a room just right for two. This was the only place we stayed in Tohoku (northeastern Honshu) in the winter where our stove had enough fuel to last all night. We needed it. The toilet and washing area were nearby; the *ofuro* was on the ground floor. We had dinner in a private room on the second floor and were served more food than I can remember having in such a place. Everything was from the sea. Most of it was delicious, some only interesting. The variety ranged from a whole crab for each person to sea slugs. If you haven't adapted to Japanese seafood, you are in trouble. Since the main industry in this area, besides tourism, is fishing, I expect little else but seafood is offered anywhere.

Although our breakfast would have been appreciated more by a Japanese, it came with a jar of instant coffee and some bread and butter. The people were interested in us and helpful, but showed no sign of knowing any English.

Maps and Information:
Champion Maps, Vol. 2, Eastern Japan
Buyodo Map D-8

National Maps: 1:50,000 Ugohamada 羽後浜田
                         Funakawa   船川
                         Toga   戸賀

JNTO Information Sheet MG-021

Brown, Jan. *Exploring Tohoku.* Tokyo: Weatherhill, 1982.

Useful Kanji:
Akita City	秋田市
Akita Airport	秋田空港
Hachirogata	八郎潟
Ogatamura	大潟村
Snack Panda	スナック パンダ
Kitaura	北浦
Monzen	門前
Unosaki	鵜の崎
Toga Bay	戸賀湾
Kamoaosa	加茂青砂
Goshado	五社堂
Funagawa	船川

LAKE IZUNUMA

Season: October - March
Specialties: geese, swans, ducks

Lake Izunuma is one of the most important wintering areas for geese and ducks in Japan. Birding is also good near the lake. It is easy to get to and should not be missed by a visitor to Japan in the winter.

Transportation:
If you are willing to walk a long way in the cold, you can do this all by public transportation. All the way by train takes four hours from Tokyo, plus time for connections. By a combination of Shinkansen and rental car, it takes 2 hours, 45 minutes. It is certainly possible to bird this area on foot without a car, but it involves spending the entire day walking around the lakes, possibly in cold rain or snow. A car makes birding this area much more pleasant.

Directions:
Take the Tohoku Shinkansen from Tokyo's Ueno Station to Sendai (1 hour, 54 minutes). To go all the way by public transportation, change at Sendai to a local train for Nitta Station (two hours). You cannot rent a car at Nitta. You can get off the Shinkansen at Sendai and rent a car there. It takes 1½ hours to drive the additional 70 km. to Lake Izunuma. It is quicker to go farther on the Shinkansen, another 19 minutes to Furukawa or 38 minutes to Ichinoseki. Lake Izunuma is about halfway between the two, so pick the one where you can most conveniently rent a car. There is a Nippon Rent-a-Car agency in Ichinoseki. It takes about 30 minutes by car from Ichinoseki to Lake Izunuma.

At Ichinoseki, the Nippon Rent-a-Car office is not visible from the station. Go out past the front plaza area to the street in front of the station. Turn right and walk about two minutes. The office is on the right.

Ask directions to Hwy. 4. The main road perpendicular to the front of the station meets the highway. The highway sign is in *kanji*, but the number 4 is evident. You can also take the Tohoku Expressway, a toll road. This isn't necessary because the distance is short. If you do use the expressway, get off at the Tsukidate

Interchange, find your way into Tsukidate, and follow the directions below.

Lake Izunuma

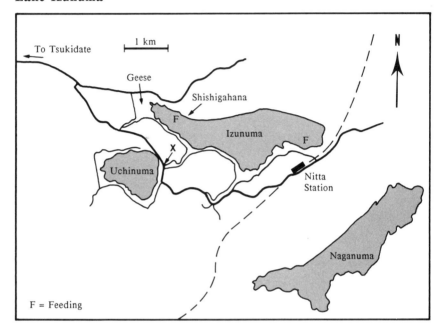

The turnoff from Hwy. 4 to Lake Izunuma is in Tsukidate. If you are coming from Ichinoseki (it is about 28 km.), you will see a sign indicating the intersection with Hwy. 398 just after you cross a bridge. Turn left on Hwy. 398. But when Hwy. 398 veers to the left, take the road that goes straight or slightly to the right. The signs with pictures of birds will give you clues.

From the intersection of Hwy. 4 and Hwy. 398, it is 5.1 km. to the road for the best goose place. See the map. Slightly more than 1 km. before you reach this turn, you will have the option of taking a zigzag to the right onto the road which goes to the south of Lake Izunuma.

You probably can manage with the accompanying map. If you are driving and want to explore farther afield, the Wakayanagi map will be helpful. It is old, however, and does not show the Shinkansen tracks or the Tohoku Expressway.

Site and Birds:

There are three lakes here, but the preferred ones are Izunuma and Uchinuma, which are quite shallow and have large areas of reeds around the edges. These lakes are surrounded by a large area of rather flat land planted mostly in rice, with a few scattered woods and some small villages. Don't neglect the surrounding areas. At the two feeding places on Lake Izunuma (see map) it is possible to get close to the swans and some species of ducks. (There also are toilets at these places.) The geese are often at the east and west ends of Izunuma and the west end of Uchinuma if they haven't flown off to feed. The feeding times and places for the geese vary considerably. You can look for them or just wait until they return. The mudflat near Shishigahana, at the northwest end of Izunuma, is a good place to look for shorebirds. Except for this area, the north side of Izunuma isn't as productive as the rest.

Most of the geese are White-fronted and Bean. Some years a Lesser White-fronted Goose or two appears in the flock of White-fronted Geese, and a Canada Goose, Aleutian subspecies (*B. c. leucopareia*), might be possible. Some years a Snow Goose occurs, an event which causes great excitement among Japanese birders. This is probably the most likely place to see any rare geese wintering in Japan. The geese appear from mid- to late October. During the hunting season (November 15 - February 15), they are sensitive and cannot be approached so easily. Any rare geese will most likely arrive with the regular flocks.

A good number of Smew and Falcated Teal winter on these lakes. Check both lakes to be sure of finding them. Occasionally a Baikal Teal occurs. Garganey comes through on migration. Other ducks to expect are Spot-billed Duck, Green-winged Teal, Gadwall, Wigeon, Pintail, Shoveler, Pochard, Tufted Duck, Greater Scaup, Common Goldeneye, and Common Merganser.

White-tailed Eagle and Steller's Sea-Eagle are rare and usually don't show up before December. They are most likely to be here in January and February and are easiest to find early in the morning. Any rare buntings will not likely come before December. A Caspian Tern, accidental in Japan, was here during the winters of 1983 and 1984. It should be possible to see Long-tailed Rose Finch, Rustic Bunting, Siberian Meadow Bunting, and Reed Bunting. You must search for the Long-tailed Rose Finch, but the other three are common.

If you take the road to the south of Izunuma, the way to get over to the west end of the lake is not obvious. See the map. Coming from Tsukidate, look for a small bell tower on your right, next to a store with a Coke machine in front. Set back from the road on the left is an ancient wooden house. It is so old, it may not be there much longer. Beyond the store, the main road curves to the right, and a paved road branches off at an angle to the left. You do not want either of these roads. Take, instead, the small dirt road to the left before you get to the store. It drops down to the right behind the old building. When you reach a fork, drive up on the levee at the end of the lake. In a few meters you will come to the good goose place.

You can also drive along the levees on the south side of the lake, but be careful. It can be muddy. The levees are narrow. If the farmers are using their wagons or tractors, it is easy for you to be in their way and block the road. You can recognize point X on the map by a cream-colored building with a green roof and "B and G" written in large letters on it. Beyond that, still on the main road, there is a dark green sign at the corner where you turn right to go around Uchinuma. You will become familiar with the area as you explore, and then you can go farther afield to look for more good habitat and birds.

There is a good patch of deciduous forest near the southeast end of Izunuma. You should find tits and Goldcrest here and buntings and finches around the edges.

It can be cold and wet. Especially if you are on foot, you should have some kind of boots for the mud.

Time:
You need a full day. It is pleasant birding, so more time would be fine. For a one-destination outing from Tokyo, two days and one night, including travel time, is about right. Spending the night here allows you to see the geese flying at dawn and at sunset.

Food:
It will be better to have a lunch for birding. There is a grocery store next to Nitta Station as well as the small one where you turn off the southern route to get to the goose place. Probably you can get a snack at the places where the birds are fed. There is a restaurant across the street from Nitta Station.

Accommodations:

The Motoyoshi-ya Ryokan, affiliated with the WBSJ, is across the street from Nitta Station. The telephone number is 02202-8-2010. The cost with the discount is ¥3,800 per person, including two meals. If you stand with your back to Nitta Station, you will be facing a restaurant; the grocery store is on your left. The *ryokan* is across the street from the grocery store, to the left of the restaurant. It has a small sign with a yellow background, a blue map of Japan, a red circle, and the letters AJRA.

This is a typical country *ryokan* where no English is spoken. It is airy to say the least. This is a good opportunity to see what life is like in winter in a traditional Japanese wooden building where the heat can't be kept in and the cold can't be kept out. In December, we entered a freezing room. They turned on an oil heater, but it took some time before we could tell much difference. We were told to turn the heater off before going to sleep. That wasn't necessary: it ran out of fuel. The *futon* was warm and comfortable. Just be sure to have plenty of warm clothes to wear when you aren't in the *futon*. Our dinner was served in our room. We had breakfast in the family living room on the ground floor. The table there, covered with a blanket with a heater underneath, was welcome after our cold room.

The toilets are the non-flush variety. There is a washing area on the stair landing. The bath is out in the garden in a separate building. There are additional toilets behind the bath house. I didn't do much more exploring in the cold and dark.

Things are casual at this *ryokan*. The two times I have stopped here no one was home. The second time we had a reservation. After some time a small child returned home, but he left us standing outside where we stayed another 30 minutes until his mother arrived. On a week-night in December, we were the only guests. It is probably full of birdwatchers on weekends. This is where you will meet Japanese birdwatchers who have come to the area, and it is certainly convenient for birding. You should have no problems here as long as you have warm clothes. If you can't bear the thought of it, stay in Sendai and come for the day.

Maps and Information:
Champion Maps, Vol. 2, Eastern Japan
Buyodo Map D-8

National Map: 1:50,000   Wakayanagi   若柳

Useful Kanji:
  Tsukidate   築館
  Nitta   新田
  Izunuma   伊豆沼
  Uchinuma   内沼

TOKYO

Almost every visitor to Japan will enter the country by way of Tokyo. You must spend some time here to make arrangements if you plan to travel through Japan on your own. You will also find yourself coming back to Tokyo, perhaps several times, in order to get to your next destination. You will have time while taking care of necessary business to do some birding in the Tokyo area.

I have selected the places which I think deserve your attention. There are other birding spots, some of which you may have heard of already. I do not find them worth spending any extra time in Tokyo in order to visit. If you live in Tokyo or will, of necessity, be staying a long time, you will want to find other places. Even so, I think the best are covered in this book.

Shinobazu Pond at Ueno Zoo doesn't merit a section, but it may merit a look. It has a colony of Great Cormorants and occasionally, in winter, will have a rare duck. A pair of Baer's Pochard stayed most of the winter of 1983. Normally the pond is full of hundreds of common ducks. Before you spend much time checking each one of them, you might want to inquire if anything special is there.

Mt. Takao gets a lot of undeserved attention. It is entirely too crowded for birdwatching. If you need more places to go, get instructions to Shinhama Bird Sanctuary and Lake Sayama. But under no circumstances go to Lake Sayama on a weekend.

There are good places to see shorebirds during migration and a few good places for winter birding. Summer is not a good time except for Ukishima Marsh. Every visitor will have time for and should visit Meiji Shrine and Oi. The two places on the Tama River are fine if you have time in Tokyo. For shorebirds, go to Yatsu, the mouth of the Tama River, and the mouth of the Obitsu River. The Mito area can be done in a day trip from Tokyo.

Trips to Miyake Island and the Ogasawara Islands start and finish in Tokyo. There is easy access from Tokyo to Nikko, Karuizawa, and the Mt. Fuji area if you are looking for a two- or three-day trip out of Tokyo.

Accommodations:

If you are new to Japan and your budget allows it, I suggest staying in one of the fine hotels in Tokyo which are accustomed to foreign visitors. The better hotels have people on the staff who speak English well and who will assist you in finding your way. They will either help or advise you where you can get help in making some of the arrangements for your birding trips. It will save you time and trouble if you are staying in central Tokyo near a subway or a train station. The shock to a first-time visitor is great when he learns he can't read anything or communicate with people on the street. You need all the help and comfort you can get to overcome that helpless feeling and get oriented.

Maps and Information:

A visit to the Tourist Information Center (TIC) should be given high priority soon after your arrival. Along with everything else you will need to get from them, be sure to get the Tourist Map of Tokyo and the Map of Tokyo and Vicinity. The Tourist Map of Tokyo has a Transportation Network map of Tokyo and vicinity on the back, which is invaluable. I have never seen another one in English. It also has a subway map, but they are easy to find. The Map of Tokyo and Vicinity is excellent for giving you an idea of the surroundings, for quite some distance, actually. You will find many of your far-away destinations on that map.

MEIJI SHRINE

Season: winter, all year
Specialties: Mandarin Duck, Varied Tit, Azure-winged Magpie

Meiji Shrine should be the first stop for a visiting birder the morning after arriving in Tokyo. It is convenient and easy to find, it is well within the capabilities of even the most exhausted traveler, and it provides a perfect introduction to the common birds. Rarities and birds not expected in the city often appear in winter. The shrine itself is one of the most important in the country and is about 200 meters from the entrance to the garden where most of the birds are to be found.

Transportation:
Both the JNR train and the subway have stations at the entrance of Meiji Shrine. If your hotel is near a station in central Tokyo, you should be able to get here in five to 15 minutes.

Directions:
By the JNR Yamanote Line, get off at Harajuku Station. The main exit (the one where you must walk up stairs and over the tracks rather than down stairs and under the tracks) is near the entrance to the shrine. In either case, when you come out of the station, walk to your right. You can't miss the wide bridge which crosses the railroad tracks.

By subway, get off at Meiji Jingumae Station on the Chiyoda Line. If you are coming from the Hibiya direction (the center of the city), get on the front car of the train or at least use the exit nearest the front end of the train. When you come out onto the street, you will see the entrance to the shrine.

Site and Birds:
The shrine was completed in 1920, at which time most of its 72.4 hectares was planted in trees. These have now grown tall, and the forest is thick. The prime spot for birds is the garden, which had been an imperial garden before the construction of the shrine. This garden is fenced, and there is an admission fee of ¥300. The object is to be first inside. This can be difficult because the opening time varies, maybe not officially, but in practice. It is supposed to open at 9:00 a.m., but sometimes it is open at 8:30. When something special is happening, it may open even earlier.

Get there early, try to determine when you can get inside the
garden, and spend any time you have to wait walking along the
paths around the outside of the garden. The shrine is particularly
nice in the early morning when no one is there.

Throughout the year, you can expect to see Little Grebe, Rufous
Turtle Dove, Brown-eared Bulbul, Varied Tit, Great Tit, Japanese
White-eye, Oriental Greenfinch, Gray Starling, Azure-winged
Magpie, and Jungle Crow. Common Pheasant and Bamboo
Partridge also are resident, but extremely difficult to see. In
winter there are many more birds, and birding is good during
spring and fall migration.

Mandarin Ducks are one of the main winter attractions. Sometimes
nearly 100 are on or behind the pond inside the garden. Most of
the time they hide as soon as people come into the garden. Head
straight for the pond as soon as you get in, making as little
commotion as possible. You should see them out in the middle.
Sometimes they are in the narrow section to your right in the
direction of the iris garden. Walk quietly that way, peeping
through the bushes. They get in the trees and up the bank on the
back of the pond. No one is allowed on the trail which goes
around the back side, so don't climb over the railing. It is
tempting, but the birds need some place to escape from the
visitors. If the Mandarin Ducks have already disappeared by the
time you get there, be patient and look carefully on the far side.
Eventually you should find one or more hidden under the low
overhanging branches at the edge of the water.

In winter you can also expect to see Spot-billed Duck, Green-
winged Teal, Bull-headed Shrike, Dusky Thrush, Bush Warbler,
and Black-faced Bunting. You will have a good chance of seeing
Siberian Bluechat, Daurian Redstart, Brown Thrush, Pale Thrush,
Hawfinch, and Jay. Besides these, anything can appear. Lucky
birders sometimes find White's Ground Thrush. Among the rarities
that spent some time here in the severe winter of 1984 were three
Woodcocks and eight Gray Buntings. There usually are no
woodpeckers. Japanese Pygmy Woodpecker has occurred, but only
rarely.

Be alert during migration. Unexpected birds do appear. In the fall
of 1983 a flock of thirty Gray-faced Buzzard-Eagles turned up.
From mid-September to mid-October, look for Gray-spotted

Flycatchers. They regularly occur in small numbers. Check the tops of tall trees.

Meiji Shrine

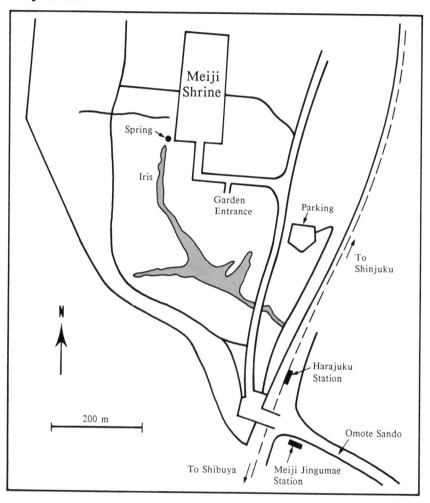

This is the only place in Tokyo to see Varied Tits. The first one I saw was sitting on one of the lanterns along the main path to the shrine between the front gate and the entrance to the garden. They usually aren't that easy to find. I most often find them at the left (east) end of the lake near a small shelter with a thatched roof. If that fails, try the clearing near the toilets across from the iris garden. They sometimes drink from the water fountain there.

One of the best spots is at the far right end of the garden near a small spring. The area around the last part of the path to the spring seems to be a favorite place for unexpected birds.

If your heart is set on seeing a Little Grebe and you can't find one in the garden, try the North Pond near the Treasure House on the opposite end of the shrine grounds. It won't hurt to wander all over the area if you have plenty of time. After a few trips all around, I limited my birding to the garden and near vicinity.

Time:
In a slow season, you can cover the garden in an hour. In winter, you might want to allow two hours or a bit more. Unless it is a weekday or terribly cold, there will probably be too much human activity in the garden to make it worth staying much longer.

Food:
This is not a place for eating. At the parking lot where all the tour buses stop, there are drinks and snacks for sale. Just outside the entrance to the shrine grounds is Harajuku, one of the most fashionable areas in Tokyo. There are at least a hundred restaurants within a ten-minute walk. You can find anything here.

OI

Season: all year
Specialties: water birds

This is a small reserve adjacent to a much larger area of good habitat at Tokyo Bay near Haneda Airport. It is excellent for birding during winter and migration and has a few breeding birds of interest. It, along with Meiji Shrine, is easy to reach and is excellent for the beginning of a birding trip in Japan. By visiting these two places, you can, in a short time, see most of the species in the Tokyo area.

Transportation:
It takes less than ten minutes by Monorail, plus another ten minutes on foot, to reach Oi from the center of Tokyo.

Directions:
Go to Hamamatsucho Station on the JNR Yamanote Line and take the Monorail. This is the end of the line between Tokyo and Haneda Airport, so the Monorail goes only in one direction. There are signs in the Monorail station in English. Get off at Ryutsusenta, the second stop.

Oi

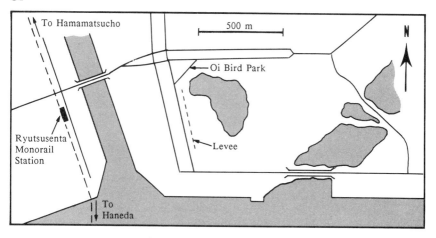

When you get out of the station at Ryutsusenta, cross the road which runs parallel to the track and go right (toward Tokyo Bay)

on the road which runs perpendicular to the track. Some crossing back and forth over this road is required because there is not a sidewalk on both sides. You will cross over a waterway and under a freeway. After you have crossed the feeder road beyond the freeway, you are at the corner of Oi Yacho Koen (Oi Bird Park). There is a sign in Japanese, a fence, and thick shrubbery. Walk to your right to get to the entrance.

The walk from the Monorail station is not pleasant. This road is crowded with large trucks going to and from the harbor. It is noisy and smelly from fumes. If you stay on the sidewalk and obey all the traffic signals, it is safe to walk here. This is another case where it takes far too much time to drive.

After you have finished inside the sanctuary, go back to the sidewalk in front of the entrance and turn left. Either walk down the sidewalk to the next big road and turn left again, or go inside where you see another opening and walk along the levee as far as it goes. When you come down off it, you can take the paths to your left if it isn't too muddy, or you can go to the road and walk down it to the lake and mudflat. The walk along the sidewalk and the road will take at least ten minutes. It is longer if you take the interior route and longer still if you are finding birds.

Site and Birds:
Oi Yacho Koen is a small reserve on reclaimed land belonging to the Tokyo Metropolitan Government. It was set aside as a result of a strong campaign by conservationists. No one can enter the sanctuary area. There is a small observation center with a warden from the WBSJ on duty on weekends. At that time telescopes are provided, but you can go in at any time and look through the openings in the wall to observe the birds in the artificial pond and in the weeds and bushes surrounding it.

It is not the sanctuary itself which makes this area so important, but the land adjacent to it. Now this undeveloped land covers an area many times the size of Oi Yacho Koen. It is grassland with two large ponds which have been attracting more and more birds since its reclamation. Tokyo Bay has been developed to the point that there is almost no place around it which remains suitable for birds. It will be a significant loss when this land is developed.

Unfortunately, a plan has been approved to build an enormous wholesale market on this property. Construction is likely to begin soon, so this area may be greatly changed by the time you see it. Some of the land will remain undeveloped, but the market will be built on top of the two existing ponds. Other ponds will be constructed. It is yet to be determined how this will affect the birds, but nothing more can be done about it.

Start your visit at the observation center. If the warden is around, he will be happy to tell you what birds to look for and where. The blackboard shows recent sightings, but the names of the birds are written in Japanese. Little Grebe, Spot-billed Duck, Coot, Snowy Plover, and Common Sandpiper are there most of the time. In winter there may be other ducks, occasionally a Long-eared Owl that stays well hidden in the trees to the back, Common Kingfisher, and Black-faced Bunting. Look carefully before you leave. Something interesting may be here.

The trip along the levee and through the grassy area is often excellent in winter. But it can be so muddy that sometimes it is not worth the effort. In any season you should see Skylark, White Wagtail, Fan-tailed Warbler, Oriental Greenfinch, and Gray Starling. And in winter, Bull-headed Shrike, Daurian Redstart, Dusky Thrush, Siberian Meadow Bunting, Rustic Bunting, and Reed Bunting are here. If you go in, check the lake to your left when you come down off the end of the levee.

When you get to the bridge on the main road, cross to the other side and look in the mud for shorebirds. This is a fine spot during migration. Usually something is here at any season. After you cross the bridge, you can get down to the lake on the left side. You will be able to see a lot from up high. If you are properly shod, you may want to walk around the edge of the lake.

This is where you will see the most species. Grebes, herons, ducks, shorebirds, and gulls all occur here. Gray Heron is here in winter. It is often possible to find a Smew. Black-tailed Gulls are always here. In winter there are Black-headed and Herring Gulls and occasionally more interesting ones. Especially in winter there is a chance of seeing some birds of prey other than the resident Black Kites.

They should not be expected, but recently Painted Snipe have appeared here with young late in the summer. When I saw them, they were on the far side of this lake almost completely hidden in the reeds. It is always a good idea to ask the warden. Spoon-billed Sandpiper also has appeared here in the fall. It never stays anywhere very long, but ask the warden. He may not realize it is important to you.

Don't ignore Oi in the summer. You should be able to see Chinese Little Bittern, Great Reed Warbler, and Black-browed Reed Warbler.

The list for Oi and the surrounding area is long. Many of these birds are not regulars, but the high incidence of unusual species always makes it worth a trip.

Time:
If you are walking, which I recommend, allow a minimum of an hour and a half from the observation center to the far pond and back again. In the summer, you could shorten this a bit if you were in a hurry. In the winter, with good conditions, you will probably want to stay longer.

Meiji Shrine and Oi make a good combination for your first day in Tokyo. Go to Meiji Shrine first. Catch the Yamanote Line at Harajuku and go to Hamamatsucho to get the Monorail. This takes about 15 minutes. When you are tired, give up and go back to town and do something else.

Food:
There is no food to be found anywhere near Oi. The last drink machines are at the Monorail station at Ryutsusenta. The last time I checked them, they were not stocked with drinks of great appeal to foreigners. It would be a good idea to come already supplied with a box lunch and something to drink.

YATSU MUDFLAT

Season: April - May, August - September
Specialties: shorebirds

This is the best place close to Tokyo to see migrating shorebirds. Don't miss it if you are in the Tokyo area during spring or fall migration. In winter, it is only of moderate interest.

Transportation:
By train, bus, and a short walk, it is about 1 hour, 15 minutes from central Tokyo.

Directions:
Take a JNR Sobu Line train (yellow) bound for either Tsudanuma or Chiba. The destination will be written in Roman letters on the front of the train and on the side of each car. Get off at Tsudanuma Station, just under an hour from Shinjuku. You can follow your progress on the Transportation Network map on the back of the JNTO Tourist Map of Tokyo. If you are on a local train, the station before Tsudanuma is Higashi Funabashi.

When you pass the ticket collector at Tsudanuma, turn right toward the east exit. You can see Takashimaya Department Store across the way if you have chosen the correct exit. Do not take the stairs down to the street, but go to your left and then to your right, staying on the same level. You will then be on an elevated crossing which passes over the street and several rows of bus stops in front of the station. Take the first stairway down to the bus stops nearest the station.

Take the bus at bus stop #10. It goes to Akitsu-kozumi Danchi. After approximately six minutes, get off at Tsudanuma-kokomae. When the road goes down beneath a freeway, push the button for the bus to stop. Your bus stop is a few meters beyond the point where the road returns to ground level.

When you get off the bus you will be across the street from a school. Cross the street at the corner and continue straight ahead alongside the schoolyard. When you reach the end of the schoolyard, you will be facing the mudflat. To return, catch the bus in front of the school. Tsudanuma Station is the end of the line. Get the Sobu Line train going back on track #6.

Site and Birds:
Yatsu mudflat is surrounded by a school, huge apartment blocks, an amusement park with a ferris wheel, a small bridge, a playground, and an expressway. The tide flows in and out through a cemented channel under the road. Don't let that discourage you. There is so little shorebird habitat left around Tokyo (and in Japan) that this unlikely-looking place is a major way station for migrants. In recognition of its vital importance as a place for food and rest for migrating shorebirds, at regular intervals 200 or more WBSJ members go out to spend the day picking up all the trash and debris that is brought in by the tide or thrown in by litterers. This is necessary to clear a place for the birds to stand. It also serves as a way to publicize the importance of this place in an attempt to have it set aside as a protected area.

Yatsu is one of the most easily accessible places for visiting birdwatchers to see shorebirds. You will likely be surprised at the smallness of this place. Despite this, a telescope will add greatly to your enjoyment. There is no need for special footgear unless there has been a lot of rain. In hot weather you will need a hat. There is no shade, and it can be terribly hot in August and September.

From the point where you first reach the mudflat, it is most convenient to check the birds to the right as far as the corner, turn back, and then walk along the long straight side to your left. These two sides have some benches which were put there by the local birders and one small shed which will give you some protection in a downpour. Farther on you can walk along a paved path for bicycles and pedestrians which is between the mudflat and the embankment for the freeway. You can cross over the bridge at the far end and come back down the other side for a little way if you see there are birds over there. Don't go beyond the children's play area. You cannot get back along the mudflat on that side because of the fence around the amusement park, so retrace your steps.

On weekends there will be many cyclists, strollers, and children playing, as well as an army of birdwatchers if there is an outing of one of the WBSJ chapters. All of this commotion doesn't seem to drive the birds away, but they retreat from the edges. You may encounter one of the young birders who frequent the place who will point out some of the birds to you with the aid of the pictures in your field guide.

Yatsu

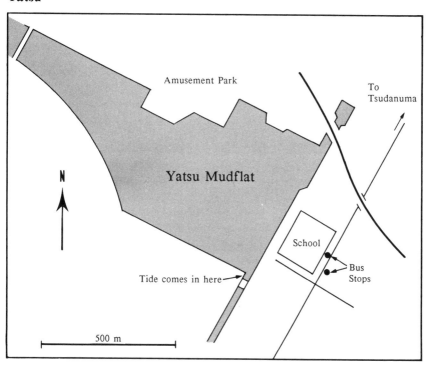

You will have a good chance of seeing many of the common migrants such as Mongolian Plover, Rufous-necked Stint, Dunlin, Great Knot, Greenshank, Gray-tailed Tattler, Common Sandpiper, Terek Sandpiper, Black-tailed Godwit, Bar-tailed Godwit, Curlew, Australian Curlew, and Whimbrel. Broad-billed Sandpiper occurs occasionally as do other not-so-common species. There is always the possibility of seeing something rare. Spoon-billed Sandpiper does occur here, but you will be extremely lucky if you happen to visit Yatsu the same time it does. In winter there is a chance for a few wintering shorebirds, Little Egret, Gray Heron, and several species of ducks. In the field across the side street from the school, you can expect to find Skylarks.

Time:
If the timing is convenient, I prefer to arrive at high tide when the birds are close to the edge. Then I stay at least two or three hours to see what comes in as more mud appears. Tide information is published daily in the *Japan Times*. If you have the time and interest, during the peak of the migration, you could easily stay the better part of a day. Since you can view the mudflat from several sides, the position of the sun is not an important factor.

Food:
There is no food or drink available near Yatsu. Take a lunch or a snack and something to drink. There are many restaurants near Tsudanuma Station.

Useful Kanji:

Tsudanuma Station	津田沼駅
Akitsu-kozumi Danchi	秋津香澄団地
Tsudanuma-kokomae	津田沼高校前

TAMA RIVER

Season: migration, winter
Specialties: Little Ringed Plover, Long-billed Ringed Plover,
Japanese Wagtail

This part of the Tama River, easily reached from central Tokyo, is a bit more than 20 km. inland from the mouth. It is good for ducks in winter, shorebirds during migration, and some of the more common birds which occur in grassy areas along rivers.

Transportation:
It takes about 30 minutes by train from Shinjuku Station, plus five minutes on foot, to reach the river.

Directions:
Find the private Keio Line at Shinjuku Station and take an express or super express train to Seisekisakuragaoka Station. All tickets cost the same, even for the local train. The two faster trains take 26 or 35 minutes, the local takes 50. The train crosses the river just before reaching Seisekisakuragaoka Station. When you pass the ticket collector, turn to your right and walk toward the river. Go past the bus stops and through a small wooded area. When you reach the river, you can walk along the levee or go down nearer to the water.

Tama River

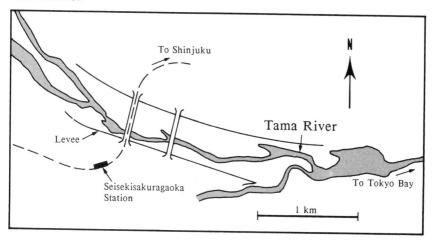

From the point where you get to the river, check to your left for a short distance in case there are some interesting birds. Then head downriver, pass under two bridges, and turn back to your right when you meet a small tributary. The area around the corner is worth exploring for a short distance. You could keep going and get back to town, but the birding is no good and it is easy to get lost. Retrace your steps and either return to the station the way you came or continue on downstream. If you intend to keep going, you will probably need boots.

Site and Birds:
This is a popular recreation area for residents. On weekends there are fishermen, cyclists, strollers, and children playing along the river. This should not be a big problem, but on a weekday there will be fewer people disturbing the birds.

There are mudflats and weedy areas and, on the far side of the small tributary, some trees. Walking is easy in dry weather. Near the river you will be walking over big rocks, so wear suitable shoes. In wet weather, you may encounter a lot of mud.

On a good day, a fair number of species could be present. The endemic Japanese Wagtail should be easy. This is a good place to look for Long-billed Ringed Plover. Other birds to expect include Little Egret, Spot-billed Duck (other ducks in winter including Smew), Black Kite, Common Sandpiper, Black-headed Gull, Little Tern, Rufous Turtle Dove, Skylark, Bull-headed Shrike, Great Reed Warbler, Fan-tailed Warbler, Siberian Meadow Bunting, Rustic Bunting, Gray-headed Bunting, Oriental Greenfinch, Hawfinch, Gray Starling, Carrion Crow, and Jungle Crow. In the grassy area near the point, you might find a Common Pheasant. Common Kingfisher is resident along the small tributary.

Time:
In a good season you could spend four hours checking everything carefully. If time is short, you can cover the area in two hours.

Food:
There is no place to buy food or drink along the birding path, so bring your own and eat along the way. There are many restaurants in and near Seisekisakuragaoka Station.

Useful Kanji:
Keio Line   京王線
Seisekisakuragaoka Station 聖蹟桜が丘駅

MOUTH OF THE TAMA RIVER

Season: shorebird migration, winter
Specialties: ducks, shorebirds

The mouth of the Tama River can be viewed from the Kanagawa Prefecture side, opposite Haneda Airport. This is an excellent place for shorebirds during migration, with easy access from Tokyo. Many ducks winter here.

Transportation:
From Shinagawa Station (on JNR Yamanote Line) it takes less than 30 minutes by train, plus ten minutes on foot, to reach the river.

Directions:
At Shinagawa Station find the Keihin Kyuko (Shinagawa) Line (there are signs in Roman letters) and take an express train to Keihin Kawasaki. Your train will be on track #1. This trip takes about 15 minutes.

Mouth of the Tama River

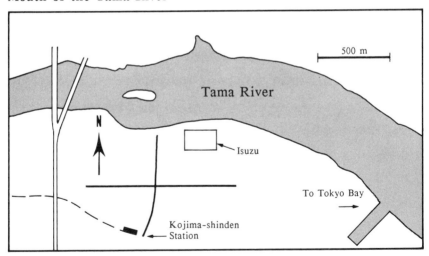

At Kehin Kawasaki Station, go downstairs and take the train on track #3. This is the Keihin Kyuko Daishi Line. Get off at Kojima-shinden, the sixth stop and the other end of the line.

This takes about ten minutes. The ticket all the way from Shinagawa currently costs ¥190.

The Daishi Line runs parallel to the Tama River. As you go toward Kojima-shinden, the river is on your left. When you get off the train, start walking to your left and you will get to the river in about ten minutes. You can walk on the levee from the bridge to the mouth of the river, birding all the way.

Site and Birds:
At low tide a large sandbar emerges in the middle of the river in front of the point where you will come up on the levee (to the left of the Isuzu factory). Some birds should be to your left toward the bridge, but most will be between where you are and the mouth of the river. There will be a large mudflat in front of you and others on down to the right. As you are walking toward the mouth of the river, don't be discouraged when the mudflats disappear. Keep going and you will find more if the tide is low.

People bicycle along this path; others often dig in the mud for shellfish. Although I once saw a man hitting golf balls on the mudflat, there is no room for athletic activities. Most of the visitors are strollers or birdwatchers. There is room to set up a tripod without blocking the path. You can also find a spot to sit to eat your lunch. In dry weather you will not need special footgear, but in wet weather the path can be muddy.

Almost any species of migrating shorebird could occur here. The common species are here, and there is always the chance for a rare one. In the fall of 1983, a Spotted Greenshank stayed several days. A Spoon-billed Sandpiper stayed one day in the fall of 1984 and was followed by a Baird's Sandpiper. As usual, shorebirds cannot be predicted, but this place is well worth a visit. You might see Great Knot, Broad-billed Sandpiper, or Terek Sandpiper. Smew is often here in winter.

Time:
There isn't a lot of territory to cover, so a couple of hours at the site should be enough. You might want to stay as long as half a day. Check the tide schedule in the *Japan Times*. There are few shorebirds around at high tide.

Food:
Bring your own. There is no place to buy food or drinks after you leave the immediate vicinity of Kojima-shinden Station.

Useful Kanji:

Keihin Kyuko Line	京浜急行線
Keihin Kawasaki	京浜川崎
Keihin Kyuko Daishi Line	京浜急行大師線
Kojima-shinden	こじましんでん
Tama River	多摩川

UKISHIMA MARSH

Season: June - August
Specialties: Chinese Little Bittern, Schrenck's Little
Bittern, Japanese Reed Bunting

This is the best place convenient to Tokyo to see Schrenck's Little Bittern and Japanese Reed Bunting. Except in northern Honshu (see Shimokita Peninsula and Hachirogata Lagoon), these birds are difficult to find.

Transportation:
It takes 1 hour, 30 minutes by JNR Limited Express train and 30 minutes by bus to reach the area. You must walk for 2 km. from the bus stop.

Directions:
It is easy to get to Ukishima Marsh, but you must plan your timing carefully. There are few trains and buses. There are local trains, but they take an additional hour from Tokyo. Sometimes it is necessary to transfer. It is well worth the additional expense and careful planning to get the Limited Express.

Take the Limited Express from Tokyo Station to Sawara. This is on the Narita Line and leaves from track #2 in the basement of Tokyo Station. Currently there is a Limited Express every three hours, so don't go without getting the schedule.

At Sawara, take the bus bound for Edosaki and get off at Oppori bus stop. The ticket office for the bus is across the street from Sawara Station and down to your left a bit. It is certainly worth attempting to communicate at the ticket office to find out what time you should catch the return bus in order to be on time for the train you have selected. An even better way is to have someone telephone the bus office for you before you leave Tokyo and get the exact schedules for buses going both ways. The telephone number is 0298-21-5234.

It takes about 30 minutes to get to Oppori bus stop. There are taped announcements on the bus indicating the bus stops. Rather than depending on understanding these announcements, you will be wise to let the bus driver know where you want off and sit up front so he will remember you.

Oppori bus stop comes immediately after the bus crosses a small bridge. When you get off the bus, cross the road the bus is on and take the smaller road which is on your right and which goes alongside the waterway that the bridge spans. Walk along this road, keeping the waterway on your right. Do not go back across the bridge. After half a kilometer this road curves to the left. Keep going.

The bus stop for returning to Sawara is directly across the street from the one where you got off. Both bus stops have a shelter with the bus schedule on a signboard. It will be difficult to figure out these schedules which are in Japanese. If you had no success with other approaches to learning the times, at least have a look at this schedule. Sawara Station is at the end of the line, so you will have no trouble recognizing when you have arrived.

The return train is slightly more complicated. The Limited Express does not go to Tokyo Station. If you want to go to Tokyo Station, get off at Kinshicho and change for Tokyo. If you want to go to Shinjuku or to a station on the way, you can get off at Ryogoku and change to a Sobu Line (yellow) train.

Although Sawara is not shown, the Transportation Network map on the back of the Tourist Map of Tokyo will help you work out how to get back to your starting place. You will find Kinshicho and Ryogoku, so you can better understand where you are if you must change at one of those stations.

Site and Birds:
You will begin to see birds almost as soon as you get off the bus, so the 2-km. hike to the lake is birding all the way. There are houses on your left, but a waterway and some reeds on your right. After the road curves to the left, there are paddy fields on your left and a wider waterway with more reeds on your right. You will be walking on a hard-surfaced road which is raised above ground level. When you get almost to the lake, the reedbed on your right is much more extensive. You will come to a dirt road going off to the right into the reeds. It runs alongside what appears to be foundations for a bridge to be constructed. This road is blocked to traffic. Despite the signs, I walked down it and found fishermen. Apparently pedestrians are allowed.

Ukishima Marsh

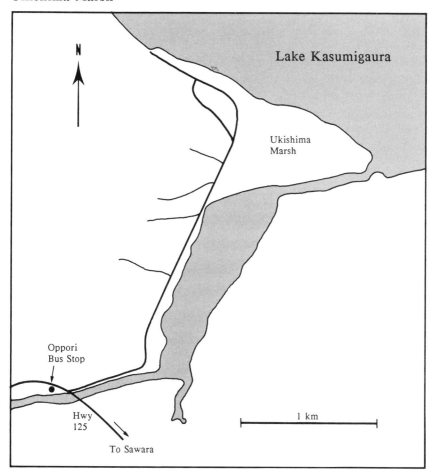

The part of the lakeshore which I saw was cemented. I have been told that the only good site for birds on this enormous lake is this marsh. So don't be sorry if you are on foot and can't explore all around the lake.

Fan-tailed Warbler, Great Reed Warbler, and Black-browed Reed Warbler are common in that order. On an overcast, slightly rainy day, bitterns were flying about a great deal, even at mid-day. They don't necessarily show themselves in such great numbers, but you should be able to see several. Chinese Little Bittern is certainly the most common. You must exercise care in identifying

Schrenck's Little Bittern. It is easy to confuse with Chinese Little Bittern.

Look carefully for Japanese Reed Buntings. They are not abundant, but are present in reeds nearer the lake. Be patient, and you should find them. There may be shorebirds in the paddy fields on the way to the lake. You might see Common Sandpiper or Green Sandpiper. Look for Little Ringed Plover on the dirt road going down beside the bridge foundations.

There are birds here at other seasons, but Ukishima isn't worth a visit except in summer unless you are a resident with plenty of time in the area. Ducks and a few birds of prey are here in winter. There is one record of a Pied Harrier, but don't waste your time looking for that.

Time:
A half day should be ample to see everything. With the long trip to and from Tokyo, this makes it an all-day trip.

Food:
Bring a lunch. There are places to buy food at and near Sawara Station. If you don't know the bus schedule, don't risk missing your bus while you are searching for lunch. Get it before you leave Tokyo. There are a couple of drink machines beside the road near the Oppori bus stop. You will pass one small restaurant shortly after you leave the bus stop, but it appears to be a place where you would have extreme difficulty if you don't speak Japanese. You can better use your time in the area birding. There are restaurants in Sawara if you have spare time before your train leaves.

Useful Kanji:
Ukishima Marsh	浮島草原
Sawara Station	佐原駅
Edosaki	江戸崎
Oppori	押堀

MOUTH OF THE OBITSU RIVER

Season: shorebird migration
Specialties: shorebirds

This is a natural rivermouth, most unusual in Japan, with a vast mudflat, located opposite Tokyo on the far side of Tokyo Bay. It isn't cemented or lined with tetrapods, at least not yet. This is neither a recreational area nor an industrial area. There are smokestacks in the distance, but the nearest buildings are in a farming village about 1 km. away. The only people around will be fishermen and shellfish gatherers. The surrounding area is open and undeveloped with more good birding habitat. It is excellent for shorebirds.

Transportation:
It takes one hour from Tokyo Station by Limited Express train to Kisarazu, 20 minutes by bus, and a little more than 30 minutes on foot to reach the mudflat.

Directions:
The fastest way to get to Kisarazu is by the Limited Express train Sazanami from track #3 in the basement of Tokyo Station. This will cost approximately ¥1,100 one way. An alternate way is to take a train to Chiba and change there to the Uchibo Line for Kisarazu. This takes two hours instead of one.

Go out the west exit of Kisarazu Station and take the Kominato bus bound for Nakajima at bus stop #6. Bus stops 1-5 are on your left as you come out of the exit. Ignore them and walk straight ahead on the street which runs into the train station. Bus stop #6 is toward the far end of the block on the left. Ask the bus driver to let you off at Kuroto-Takasu-Iriguchi bus stop. This trip takes about 20 minutes and costs ¥200.

When you get off the bus, continue in the same direction for a few meters until you come to a road going to the left. Turn left and go to the next road that goes to the left. Turn left here and follow this road until it ends at the riverbank. Then you must walk along a path through tall reeds to reach the mudflat.

To return, catch the bus at the bus stop on the other side of the road. You may be lucky and find a taxi if you don't want to wait for the bus. It is easier to tell a taxi driver to take you to a train station than to some obscure birding spot out in the country.

Some Limited Express trains from Kisarazu do not go to Tokyo Station, but go to Ryogoku or Akihabara instead. These stations are near Tokyo Station. It is easy to connect there to another train going to Tokyo Station or some other destination in the Tokyo area. Consult your Transportation Network map.

Site and Birds:
As you walk from the bus stop, look for birds in the gardens, cultivated fields, and reedbeds. You could see herons, birds of prey, shrikes, and buntings. Look for Fan-tailed Warbler, and, in summer, Great Reed Warbler.

You will need boots. The path to the mudflat can be muddy and is sometimes under two or three inches of water. You cannot walk over this mudflat without getting in water. When the tide comes in, the mudflat disappears quickly, so you are sure to find yourself ankle deep in water before you finish.

On the way out, check the pond to the right (see map). Sometimes in autumn, ducks are here. Falcated Teal has been recorded, but don't count on seeing it. If the tide is out, it is easy to walk to a small woods on the last little island in the rivermouth.

A telescope is an enormous help because the mudflat is so extensive. At low tide, the birds are spread out over a huge area. They become more concentrated as the tide comes in. Go before the tide is on the way in or you won't have time to check all the birds before the water suddenly covers the mud and they fly away. The tide schedule is listed daily in the *Japan Times*.

All the common shorebirds occur here. It is a good place to find Great Knot, a species of interest to most visiting birders. And it is an ideal spot to encounter some of the rarer species. Take all the time necessary to check these flocks carefully. My first trip here was in pursuit of a Spoon-billed Sandpiper which was spotted a day or two earlier. I didn't find it, but when I took a break from searching through all the Rufous-necked Stints, I discovered that the Whimbrel which had been walking back in forth in front of me for some time was really a Little Whimbrel.

Apparently this place is not as popular with Tokyo birders as is Yatsu. It is daunting to look on the map and see how far away it is. Although it costs considerably more to get here than to Yatsu, especially by Limited Express, by that means it requires only a little more travel time. My opinion is undoubtedly colored by my sighting of the Little Whimbrel, but I especially favor birding in such an extensive natural area.

This is one of the few places in the country where you can be quite alone. My Japanese friends have expressed concern that I went by myself. The path goes for some distance through reeds more than two meters high. Along this path I encountered only a couple of women pulling carts full of shellfish. They seemed rather taken aback to see me there, as did the fishermen I met on the mudflat. In Japan I don't expect people to be lurking about waiting for an opportunity to attack an unsuspecting passerby. Still, this is probably a good place to go with a companion.

Mouth of the Obitsu River

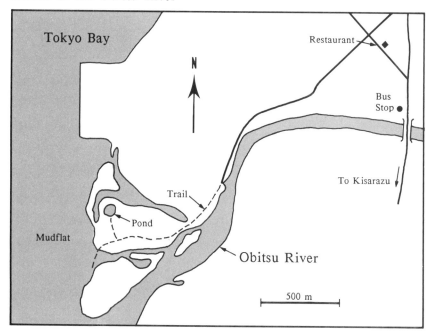

Time:
From bus stop to bus stop, allow three hours for birding. If you don't find birds, you will want to shorten this. If you find thousands of shorebirds and the tide doesn't interfere, you may want to stay longer.

Don't be tempted to go by car from Tokyo. I did once. The trip back took five hours.

Food:
When you are walking from the bus stop, between the first and second left turns you will pass a small restaurant on your right. You can get a bowl of noodles and something to drink here. Otherwise the last food and drink is at Kisarazu Station. It is best to bring what you need with you.

Useful Kanji:
Kisarazu Station	木更津駅
Bus for Nakajima	中島行のバス
Kuroto-Takasu-Iriguchi	畔戸高須入口
Mouth of Obitsu River	小櫃川河口

MIYAKEJIMA

Season: April - June, all year
Specialties: Japanese Murrelet, Japanese Robin, Izu Islands
Thrush, Middendorff's Grasshopper Warbler, Ijima's
Willow Warbler, Varied Tit (P. v. owstoni)

Miyakejima, about 160 km. from Tokyo, is one of the Izu Islands
(part of a national park) and the island of that group with the best
birds. It is a lovely volcanic island which last suffered a serious
eruption in October, 1983. It has two endemic species and is a
place where some otherwise difficult species can be found rather
easily. It is convenient to Tokyo and is small enough that finding
the way is no problem. Miyakejima is an excellent place to include
on your itinerary, especially if you come between mid-April and
mid-June.

Transportation:
NKA has two flights daily from Tokyo taking 50 minutes. Round-
trip fare is ¥15,480. A ferry from Tokyo takes almost seven
hours.   Once on the island, you can travel by bus (time-
consuming) or taxi (expensive to go far). The ideal way is by
rental car.

Directions:
Flights leave Tokyo for Miyakejima every day at 10:30 a.m. and
3:20 p.m. The return flights leave at 11:45 a.m. and 4:35 p.m.
Unlike most flight schedules, this one has not changed in at least
three years. But check well in advance anyway.

The ferry from Tokyo to Miyakejima goes at night. The return
trip is in daylight. If you want to look for seabirds, fly over and
take the ferry back. The ferry leaves Takeshiba dock in Tokyo at
10:10 every night except Tuesday and arrives at Miyakejima at
4:50 a.m. It leaves Miyakejima at 1:20 p.m. every day except
Wednesday and arrives in Tokyo at 7:20 p.m. There are five
classes of tickets, with prices ranging from ¥3,800 to ¥12,630 one
way. The class should only be important during the night when it
determines where and under what conditions you sleep.   The
lowest price is for a place on the floor with everybody else.   The
ferry company's telephone number is 03-432-4551. Tickets can be
purchased at all branches of the JTB (Japan Travel Bureau).

Miyakejima

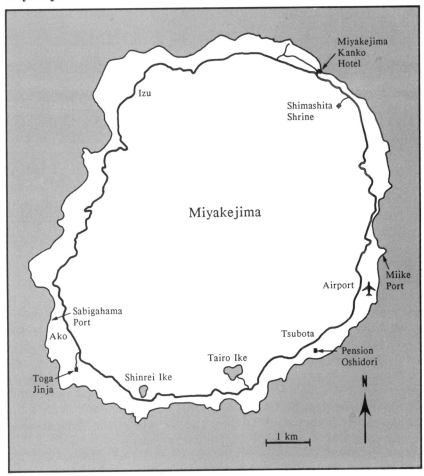

Rental cars are excessively expensive on Miyakejima. I recently was quoted a price of ¥31,000 from both Toyota and Nissan Rent-a-Car for the smallest car from the time of arrival of the morning plane on one day until the time of departure of the afternoon plane on the following day. This was for about 28 hours. The price includes gasoline and insurance.

Some of the *minshuku* and hotels have cars they will rent. Pension Oshidori rented us their car for ¥6,000 per day. They counted calendar days rather than 24-hour periods, but that was all-inclusive. We made arrangements for it before our arrival. When we got there, they handed us the keys without asking for money, driver's license, or anything else. They just told us to be careful.

You can't get lost. One major road circles the island. Everything else branches off from it. You may get temporarily confused, but you can always find your way back to the main road, which is near the shore all the way around the island.

Site and Birds:
Miyakejima is a small, almost round island with a circumference of about 36 km. Its approximately 3,000 residents make a living from fishing and tourism. Besides being of interest ornithologically, the island provides a unique habitat for fish and corals. It has 91 known species of coral, more diversity than any other island at the same latitude. The area is of great importance to marine biologists.

The eruption of 1983 did serious damage to the island. The lava flow covered a large number of homes in the town of Ako as well as Shinrei Ike, a pond which had been good for birds. The ash severely damaged Tairo Ike, probably the best birding spot on Miyakejima. In June of 1984, eight months after the eruption, the trees there were only beginning to get new leaves. In June of 1985, damage to the trees was still evident. Just what all this means to the birds on the island has not yet been determined. It has been estimated, however, that the number of Japanese Robins has declined by two-thirds since the eruption. Until more time has passed after this enormous destruction of habitat and the birds get settled in new territories, it is impossible to say where the best birding places will ultimately be. The island is small enough for you to explore and look for good habitat.

By all means, see what remains at Tairo Ike. You should take the path all the way around the pond and check the woods along the road from the highway to the pond. Izu Islands Thrush and Ijima's Willow Warbler used to be abundant here. It was an excellent place to get good looks at the local subspecies of Varied Tit. In the thickest part of the forest near the northwest edge of the pond, there was a huge tree with a rope around it (a shrine). A Japanese Robin was almost always nearby, though it wasn't particularly easy to find. Even though the forest isn't thick anymore, we found a Japanese Robin in this same area in June of

1985. Before the eruption, Streaked Shearwaters bred at Tairo Ike. They may return.

Japanese Night Heron is on the Miyakejima list, but I do not know for sure that one has been seen in recent years. If the forest recovers at Tairo Ike, it would be worth the effort to go at night and listen. They stay in the deep forest and call after dark.

Japanese Wood Pigeon is common, but not necessarily easy to see. They sit in the tops of large trees, hidden in the leaves. If you don't encounter one elsewhere, go to Tairo Ike just before dusk or in the early morning, when they seem to be more obvious.

On the southwest corner of the island is Toga-jinja, a shrine in thick woods surrounded by lighter woods, open areas, scrub, and rocky shoreline. There have always been many species in this area, and it was untouched by the eruption. This is an excellent place for Collared Scops Owl and Brown Hawk-Owl. Look for them at night. From late July, after the young are out of the nest, until October it is easy to see many owls. They often gather at dusk on the wires near street lights to catch bugs. Beyond the forest past Toga-jinja, look in the shrubbery below the cliffs for Middendorff's Grasshopper Warbler (spring and summer). Another good place for Middendorff's Grasshopper Warbler is in the northwest along the coast west and south of Izu.

Drive on up the west coast of the island. The lava flow crossed this road. A new road has now been completed. It is awesome to stop and look at the lava above and below the highway, remembering that a large part of a town is buried underneath.

Bamboo Partridge is easy to see on Miyakejima. Look around large gardens in Tsubota or other villages, on the edges of cultivated fields near Toga-jinja, or even on the sides of small dirt roads going up the mountain.

Find Shimashita Shrine on the northeast coast. It is just next to and on the north side of the old lava flow from the eruption of 1963, the one before the last one. Birding is good all around here. While you are in the area, walk along the back road from the Miyakejima Kanko Hotel to the west. The habitat is varied, and there are many birds.

Japanese Murrelet breeds on a small island called Sanbondake or Onohara-shima. They are there from January to early May when the nestlings leave. This is about 8 km. to the southwest of Miyakejima. It is possible to charter a fisherman's boat to go out where you can see them.

It is often possible to see Streaked, Sooty, and Short-tailed Shearwaters from the island. Occasionally there is a Brown Booby. Birding is best from the ferry for the first half of the trip from Miyakejima to Tokyo, with plenty of shearwaters and maybe some albatrosses. There is a chance for Japanese Murrelet, but it isn't dependable. This ferry trip is not as good as the one between Tokyo and Hokkaido, but it might be interesting if you have time.

Other birds which you should see are Temminck's Cormorant, Eastern Reef Heron, Gray-faced Buzzard-Eagle (except in winter), Little Cuckoo (spring and summer), Blue Rockthrush, Bush Warbler, Great Tit, Japanese White-eye, and Oriental Greenfinch.

Sanbondake, the nesting site of the Japanese Murrelet, was selected by the US military many years ago as a site for bombing target practice. An American resident of Miyakejima called attention to this and enlisted support which ultimately saved the murrelets. Now the island of Miyakejima itself is facing something potentially more devastating than even its own volcano. The US and Japanese governments jointly are planning to build a military airfield on the island. This would be located at Ako, displacing still again some of the people who have finally moved into new homes after theirs were covered by the lava from the last eruption.

This airfield would completely alter the character of the whole island and destroy a unique natural environment. Apparently the full story about this airfield, how it is to be used and the implications to the residents and the ecology of the island, is not being told in Japan. Those who know it best and oppose the project are in no position to carry on a campaign against the Japanese authorities. The current feeling is that the best hope of getting this stopped is from the US side. Some believe that the laws which keep a military airfield from being built in a national park in the US can prevent US participation in building such an airfield in a national park in another country. For this to happen, the situation on this small island would have to get wide publicity in the US and the support of many people in a position to influence the outcome. It will be much more difficult than getting target practice called off.

Time:
A minimum stay would be from one morning to the following afternoon. It is much better to stay two nights. You need a little time to get oriented, and now it may not be so easy to find the species you are looking for. Even if you arrive on the afternoon plane on the first day, that will give you time to start learning your way about and finding some of the birds. You can devote the next day entirely to birding. Then you will probably be ready to leave by the 11:45 a.m. flight on the third day.

Food:
The restaurants are hard to find, but there are plenty of drink machines along the road. Take your lunch.

Accommodations:
This island is popular with fishermen and swimmers, so there are many places to stay.

Pension Oshidori (04994-6-0346) caters to birdwatchers and gives a discount to WBSJ members. The price is about ¥4,000. It is located in Tsubota village, about five minutes by taxi from the airport. The owners do not speak English, but are extraordinarily kind to foreign visitors. They are happy to play charades to help you understand. The man was so concerned that we might have problems, he not only took us to the airport, but also went inside and looked after us until he was able to send us through the boarding gate. This place is not air-conditioned. In June it is definitely hot and humid. You will be better off if you bring mosquito coils along. Pension Oshidori sometimes provides them, but it is wise to bring you own just in case.

I have also stayed at the Miyakejima Kanko Hotel (04994-20230) on the northeastern coast of the island. Birding is excellent here. Brown Hawk-Owls come to the street lights in front of the hotel. The small road which goes back behind the hotel and then to the west is perfect for an early-morning or late-evening bird walk.

The Miyakejima Onsen Hotel (04994-50131) and the Yamanobe Ryokan (04994-50316) have been recommended. The Yamanobe Ryokan is reported to be the only true Japanese-style place on the island. It is in the woods near Ako.

Maps and Information:

National Map: 1:25,000 Miyakejima 三宅島

Useful Kanji:

Miyakejima	三宅島
Tairo-ike	大路池
Toga-jinja	富賀神社
Izu	伊豆
Shimashita Shrine	島下神社
Tsubota	坪田
Ako	阿古
Sanbondake	三本岳
Onohara-shima	大野原島

OGASAWARA ISLANDS

Season: *summer*
Specialties: *seabirds, Bonin Islands Honeyeater*

Hahajima (Haha Island) is the only place to find the endemic Bonin Islands Honeyeater. Access to the Ogasawara Islands is by boat from Tokyo. The round trip requires a minimum of five or six days, depending on the schedule. The possibilities are good for seeing several seabirds which otherwise are hard to come by. There are no other land birds of special interest.

Transportation:
The ferry from Tokyo to Chichijima takes 30 hours. A boat leaves Chichijima for Hahajima shortly after the ferry arrives. This trip takes about 2½ hours. Usually there are five services each month from Tokyo to Chichijima. On Hahajima, you are on foot.

Directions:
Take the ferry operated by the Ogasawara Kaiun Corporation (03-451-5171) from the Takeshiba Sanbashi dock at Tokyo Bay, a short taxi ride from Hamamatsucho Station (JNR Yamanote Line). It departs about five times each month at 10:00 a.m. and arrives at Chichijima the following afternoon.

There are four classes on this ferry. The prices range from ¥21,500 to ¥53,000 for a one-way ticket. The cheapest ticket gets you only a place on the floor with a blanket, the same as on the Hokkaido ferry. Higher fares get bunks, and the most expensive are for beds in private cabins for two or four people.

After you arrive at Chichijima, take the first boat for Hahajima. You will have either two or three nights on the islands before the next ferry to Tokyo departs. The boat to Hahajima is small and cannot go in particularly rough weather. If you are there during the typhoon season and the weather is uncertain, it is a good idea to see the honeyeater and get back to Chichijima as soon as possible to avoid missing the ferry back to Tokyo.

The ferry leaves Chichijima at noon and arrives in Tokyo at 5:30 p.m. the following day.

Site and Birds:
From the ferry, or in the Ogasawaras, you will have a chance to see Laysan Albatross, Black-footed Albatross, Bonin Petrel, Bulwer's Petrel, Wedge-tailed Shearwater, Audubon's Shearwater, Matsudaira's Storm-Petrel, Brown Booby, Greater Crested Tern, and Brown Noddy. Red-tailed and White-tailed Tropicbirds also are possible. These birds are most likely to occur in summer, but the two albatrosses are here in winter, too.

The Bonin Islands Honeyeater is most often around papaya trees and is easy to find. Katsuodori Island, where you can see Brown Booby, is off the southern tip of Hahajima. Shorebirds are near the Otani River and on the school ground. Notice that the Brown-eared Bulbul, Bush Warbler, and Japanese White-eye on the Ogasawara Islands are different subspecies from those on the mainland.

I have not been to these islands, but I understand that it doesn't take long to find the birds. Most visitors go for fishing or swimming. If necessary, you can find something else to do while waiting for the ferry back to Tokyo.

Time:
Here you have no choice. There is no need to stay beyond the next departure of the ferry for Tokyo. The entire trip will take either five or six days, with two or three nights on the islands.

Food:
There will be food on the ferry and on both islands. You have the option of eating in restaurants or carrying a packed lunch.

Accommodations:
Two *minshuku* on Hahajima are Asakaze (04998-3-2131) and Kinsho (04998-3-2141).

Useful Kanji:
Chichijima	父島
Hahajima	母島
Otani River	大谷川
Katsuodori Island	鰹鳥島

MITO AREA

Mito is close enough to Tokyo for a day trip. Within a short distance of the city there are three areas which are good for birding, especially in winter. These are (1) Kotokunuma, the woods behind it, and the neighboring Ibaraki Prefecture Park (Kenminomori), (2) Lake Hinuma, and (3) the coast around Ooarai. This is a good trip for a Tokyo resident, a birder who must spend a lot of time in Tokyo, and those who expect to have little opportunity to travel extensively in Japan and who, consequently, will not be sure of seeing some of these species elsewhere. Since Falcated Teal are certain at Kotokunuma, many people will find it worthwhile to allot a day for this trip.

Transportation:
By express train it takes 1½ hours from Tokyo to Mito. Rent a car at Mito Station. It is feasible to go to Kotokunuma and possible to reach the other areas by public transportation. If you intend to travel by public transportation, I suggest devoting the whole day to the Kotokunuma area. It is too time-consuming and complicated to attempt to reach the other destinations. A car would permit you to visit all three areas if you rationed your time carefully.

Directions:
From Ueno Station in Tokyo, take the express train Tokiwa for Mito on the JNR Joban Line. It will cost approximately ¥3,000. There is a Limited Express which costs considerably more and gets there in 1 hour, 20 minutes, saving only ten minutes over the regular express. The frequency of these trains varies depending on the time of day. Check the schedules when you plan your trip.

There is a Nippon Rent-a-Car agency near the station. When you come out of the station, look to the right side of the plaza area. Where the overhead pedestrian crossing farthest to your right crosses the street, you should see a tall building with a large neon sign advertising Toshiba. From that point go a few steps to the right until you reach the corner. Without crossing that street, turn to your left. On the corner opposite where you should walk to the left is the Terrace Cafe. As you walk down this long block, you will pass the Seiyu parking lot on your left and a long stone wall on your right. It takes two or three minutes to walk from the station to the car rental office. Since you will not be doing any

long-distance driving, this is a good time to take advantage of the
special prices on the smallest cars, if your group will fit into one.

Mito Area

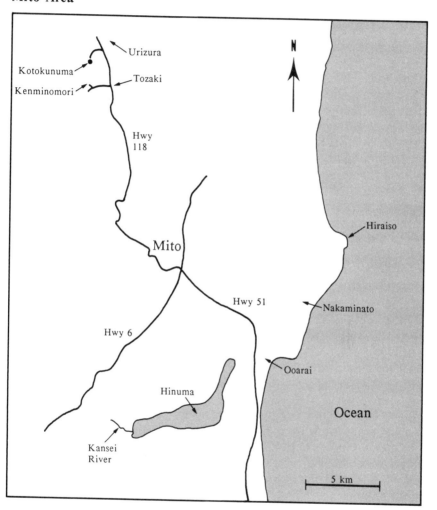

Accommodations:
The area to the west of Kotokunuma is picturesque with small
farms, some traditional architecture, and narrow roads winding
through the hills. There are accommodations in Mito for those
who wish to stay longer and explore. Check with the TIC or the
local tourist office if you want a *minshuku* or *ryokan* in the
countryside.

KOTOKUNUMA

Season: winter
Specialties: Whooper Swan, Whistling Swan, Falcated Teal,
    Yellow-throated Bunting, Gray Bunting

Kotokunuma is a small lake which serves as the water supply for the neighboring town. More than 20 years ago, some swans appeared on the lake, and the owner of the small restaurant across the street began putting out bread crusts for them. This had the desired effect. Now a large number of waterfowl of many species regularly winter here. There is a slight zoo-like atmosphere, especially at feeding time, but you can be sure of seeing many species at close range. Besides the small flock of Falcated Teal which comes every year, some years there are one or two Baikal Teal. Occasionally even rarer ducks are reported. There is a forest behind the lake where there is a good possibility of finding some species which are usually difficult to find in this part of Japan.

Directions:
From the Nippon Rent-a-Car office go to your left as you drive out, continuing in the same direction you were headed before you got there. Distances are measured from this point. At the second signal light, turn left. After approximately 4.8 km. you will reach the intersection with Hwy. 118. Turn right and stay on Hwy. 118 until you see a small sign with a picture of a swan on it, about 16.7 km. from the starting point. Turn left here, and in 1 km. you will be at the lake.

By public transportation, take the train for Urizura from Mito on the Suigun Line. From there take a taxi to the lake. To return, if you can't find a better solution while at the lake, walk back to Hwy. 118 and wait for a taxi to come by. Otherwise it is said to be a 40-minute walk from the station, with little opportunity for birdwatching and plenty of opportunity to get lost. (This would be a good time to have notes in Japanese asking for a taxi and giving the name of your destination.) There is also a bus from Mito to Urizura. I suspect the train is much faster.

Kotokunuma and Kenminomori

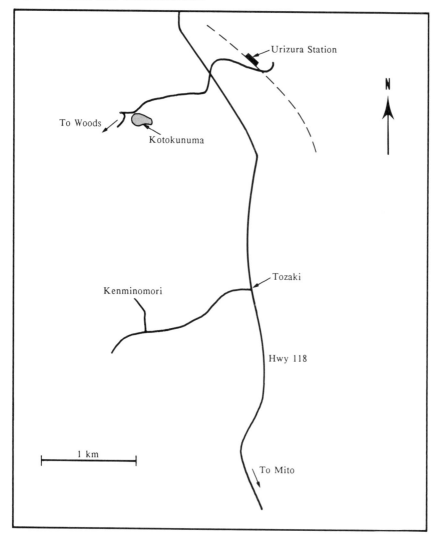

Site and Birds:

On the side where you first reach the lake, the bank is concrete, and there is a tall chain-link fence. This is the place where the birds are fed, once early in the morning and again around 11:00 a.m., and where you can get closest to them. You can walk down the road along the side of the lake to get good views of the birds which don't participate in the dash for the bread crusts. Any rare

ducks will most likely be far away from this activity. On
weekends, photographers line the bank next to the road. The other
three sides of the lake are off limits. If you can't read the sign in
Japanese saying so, the photographers will see that you don't get
where you shouldn't go, especially if you are carrying a camera.
Everybody should have an equal chance at photographs.

The largest concentration of birds is here in January and
February. My latest visit was on March 12. Although most species
were still represented and a few Falcated Teal remained, the
number of birds was far less than I have seen earlier. There
should be several dozen Whooper Swans and a few Whistling
Swans. There also should be Mallard, Spot-billed Duck, Green-
winged Teal, Wigeon (always look for an American Wigeon, rare
but seen from time to time in Japan), Pintail, Shoveler, Pochard,
Tufted Duck, and, of course, the flock of Falcated Teal, the
prime attraction. Examine the birds carefully, and inquire, if you
are able, so you will be sure not to miss Baikal Teal or other rare
ducks which may be there.

Be sure to look for passerines in the trees and bushes between the
road and the lake. This is a good place for Daurian Redstart.

The Japanese birders stay at the lake with the photographers. This
makes it possible for you to be almost alone in a fine forest, no
matter how many visitors are at Kotokunuma. Walk down to the
far end of the lake and turn in, away from the road. Here you
must be careful not to walk near that end of the lake or to go into
the forest on the side of the lake opposite the road. Instead, angle
off to your right, through some paddy fields and toward the
wooded hills away from the lake. The fallow paddy fields are
good for birds. The mixed forest on the hills behind has roads and
trails leading through it. Some areas have been cut. In other places
the undergrowth has been cut, but much has been left
undisturbed. This variety of dense and open areas makes it most
attractive for birds. The only people I've seen in here have been
some people carting away logs.

I have seen as many as 20 Yellow-throated Buntings along a
narrow road through this forest. This bird is said to be
uncommon, except in western Japan. In the same area I have also
seen two or three Gray Buntings, a most difficult bird to see.
Gray Buntings aren't rare, but actually seeing one is an

accomplishment. There are pheasants in the area. The ones I saw were Common, but Copper Pheasants have been reported. Also look for owls. Among the birds you can expect in this area are hawks, woodpeckers, White Wagtail, Japanese Wagtail, Indian Tree Pipit, Dusky Thrush, Bush Warbler, Goldcrest, Long-tailed Tit, Great Tit, Japanese White-eye, Siberian Meadow Bunting, Rustic Bunting, Black-faced Bunting, and Jay.

Time:

If you are in a hurry, you can probably see everything you need to at Kotokunuma in 30 minutes. This does not allow time for photography. You will seldom have an opportunity to get so close to a Falcated Teal. The woods is worth a couple of hours -- several hours if many birds are present.

Food:

The little restaurant across the street is a good place to warm up in the winter. You can get a hot lunch of noodles or stop in for a cup of tea. The owner welcomes birdwatchers and is especially kind to foreign visitors. If you come when the bank is not lined with birders, you can get information in the restaurant about the rarer birds you should be looking for. Otherwise, carry your lunch and picnic in the woods.

KENMINOMORI (IBARAKI PREFECTURE PARK)

The emphasis at this park is on the Wildlife Center to which I had a negative reaction. There is a small museum containing many birds and a few animals, few of which received the attention of a skilled taxidermist. A larger part of the center is devoted to cages containing live birds. Many of them are in cages which are much too small, and the birds appeared to me to be in poor condition. It was one of those places where I had the urge to open all the cages and turn everything loose. There is, however, a large collection of pheasants of many species. These birds are in better cages and seem to be well cared for. I was told that the prefecture government is raising them to sell to shooters.

Ignore the Wildlife Center and find the extensive park behind it. This is a lovely, wooded, hilly area with many paths. If you can go there on a winter day when few people are around, you should find good birds. It is, however, a popular area in spring, summer, and autumn and on nice weekends in winter.

Both Common and Copper Pheasants are resident. Gray Buntings
occur in winter. Other typical woodland birds, as well as assorted
buntings, undoubtedly are around. I have only been here once. If
there is not time to do both, choose the woods behind
Kotokunuma because there are fewer people to disturb the birds.

Directions:
From Kotokunuma, go to Hwy. 118 and turn to the right, back
toward Mito. Go approximately 2.5 km. to an intersection where
there is a bus stop. This is Tozaki or Kozaki. Turn right and go
another 1.5 km. You will cross one large intersection before you
reach the place where you turn right toward the park. It should
take less than ten minutes to get here from Kotokunuma.

If you do not have a car, try to find a taxi to take you. Otherwise
the bus from Mito headed for Oomiya gets to the Tozaki (Kozaki)
bus stop in 35 minutes. From there it is said to take 20 minutes to
walk to the park. The maps I have are all contradictory, and I
have not been to this place on my own under circumstances when
I could work out the distances and directions. If you get lost, the
phone number of the Wildlife Center is 02929-8-0259.

Time:
One hour should be sufficient if you don't visit the Wildlife
Center.

HINUMA

Season: winter, shorebird migration
Specialties: Smew, Gray-headed Bunting

This lake of more than 800 hectares is surrounded by a variety of
good habitat, so with time and some effort you could find a large
number of species. There are cultivated fields and a few
farmhouses near the lake, but for Japan, this area has escaped
extensive development. It is probably a good area in all seasons,
but most Japanese birders from Tokyo make the trip in winter to
search for rare visitors.

Transportation:
Although buses go to this area, I think for a foreigner who doesn't
speak the language and who doesn't have unlimited time, a car
from Mito Station is the only way to visit this place. Anyway,

trying to cover such a large area without a car would take all the pleasure out of the experience.

Hinuma

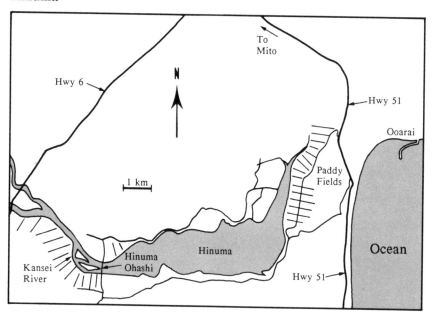

Directions:
From Mito, take Hwy. 51 toward the ocean. Approximately 10.5 km. from the intersection in Mito of Hwy. 6 and Hwy. 51, you will reach a place where Hwy. 51 becomes a freeway. Before that happens, get off to the right and follow the road to the right to reach the lake. It is also possible to get off of Hwy. 51 about 2 km. sooner, just after the highway crosses the river. There, get off to the right, then turn left on a road which angles toward the lake, passing through paddy fields on the way. You will need a good map to see where you are trying to go throughout your exploration of the area.

Site and Birds:
Explore the east end of the lake (see map), looking for birds not only on the water, but also in the grassy areas and fields surrounding it. Then take the road to the south of the lake over to the west side. Turn right when you reach the T-junction. That road will take you to the west end of the lake and the Kansei River. Explore this area to the right and to the left (see map). The

lake is so large, a telescope is necessary if you are to identify any but the ducks close to shore.

Hinuma gained in popularity with Japanese birders when a small flock of Canvasbacks wintered here in 1983. Of more interest to American birdwatchers are the Smew which occur regularly. There usually are many ducks on the lake. Look for Falcated Teal on the east end. This is a good area for birds of prey. Occasionally a White-tailed Eagle appears.

During spring and fall migration, it is possible to see a number of shorebirds including Long-toed Stint, Sharp-tailed Sandpiper, Ruff, Spotted Redshank, Greenshank, and Wood Sandpiper. In September, you can expect to see Honey Buzzard and Gray-faced Buzzard-Eagle.

From May through August, Gray-headed Bunting is common. Check at Hinuma Ohashi and along the Kansei River. Also look for Chinese Little Bittern, Ruddy Crake, Little Ringed Plover, Common Sandpiper, Fan-tailed Warbler, and Black-browed Reed Warbler. Painted Snipe is listed for the area, but I don't know if it can be expected. Finding one in such a vast area would be a feat, but you should certainly be aware that it is a possibility.

Time:
In a good season you could spend several hours here. If you are rushed, you could have a look around in two hours.

Food:
I have seen no places to get food or drink near Hinuma. Bring it with you.

COAST FROM OOARAI TO HIRAISO

If you visit Hinuma in the winter, it is worth taking time to drive along the coast for at least a quick look. First try to get where you can have a good view of the beach and the water immediately south of the point where Hwy. 51 becomes a freeway. Depending on the road situation when you come, this could be difficult. Then follow the road north along the coast to the port at Ooarai. Try to get a look out beyond the breakwater. You should be able to see a lot of gulls if the fishing boats are in port processing their catch. Then continue north along the coast, across a large river to

Nakaminato, and again up the coast road until you reach Hiraiso. There, go out on the point. Gulls are often present in great numbers.

Ancient Murrelets have been seen from the coast. Look for Red-throated Loon, Temminck's Cormorant, Pelagic Cormorant, White-winged Scoter, and Harlequin Duck. Among the Herring, Mew, and Black-tailed Gulls, there is a good chance of finding Slaty-backed and Glaucous.

Maps and Information:
Champion Maps, Vol. 2, Eastern Japan
Buyodo Map D-6

National Maps: 1:50,000   Isohama   磯浜

Ishioka   石岡

Useful Kanji:

Mito	水戸
Kotokunuma	古徳沼
Urizura Station	瓜連駅
Kenminomori	県民の森
Tozaki	戸崎
Hinuma	涸沼
Ooarai	大洗
Nakaminato	那珂湊
Hiraiso	平磯町

NIKKO NATIONAL PARK

Season: *May - June, October - November*
Specialties: *Ural Owl, Japanese Robin, Arctic Warbler, Japanese Yellow Bunting*

This is a large national park with a variety of habitat, beautiful scenery, convenient public transportation, plenty of hiking trails, many hotels, and interesting birds and wildflowers. It is relatively easy for a foreign visitor to manage alone here. Unfortunately, from the birdwatcher's standpoint, it is one of the most popular destinations for Japanese tourists. The usual mountain species are here in spring and early summer. Nikko is a good place to look for unusual visitors in late fall. In winter, most of the birds are gone, but occasional rarities occur.

Warning: Do not go to Nikko between mid-July and the beginning of September and expect to see birds. The same may apply when the fall colors are at their peak. Birding is impossible with so many people around.

Transportation:
It takes 1 hour, 45 minutes by train from Tokyo to Nikko Station. From there go by bus or rental car. A car is more convenient, but not necessary if you plan to stay in the area between Nikko and Yumoto Onsen. Regular bus service will get you to many hiking trails. Buses may not be available for early morning birdwatching. In summer it is light by 4:15, and the birds are much easier to see then that even at 6:00. If you wish to go some distance from where you are staying, try to arrange for a taxi or someone at your hotel to deliver you early in the morning.

Directions:
JNR trains go from Ueno Station (in Tokyo) to Nikko, but the Tobu Railway is cheaper and quicker. Get the train from Tobu Asakusa Station (it can be reached by subway). I strongly recommend the Limited Express. It costs ¥1,800. All seats are reserved, it is air-conditioned and comfortable, and you can order food served at your seat. It takes 1 hour, 45 minutes from Tokyo to Tobu-Nikko Station. Many of these trains terminate at Shimo-Imaichi Station, about nine minutes from Tobu-Nikko. Take the local train on the next track. There will be an announcement in English directing you to the proper train.

Nikko

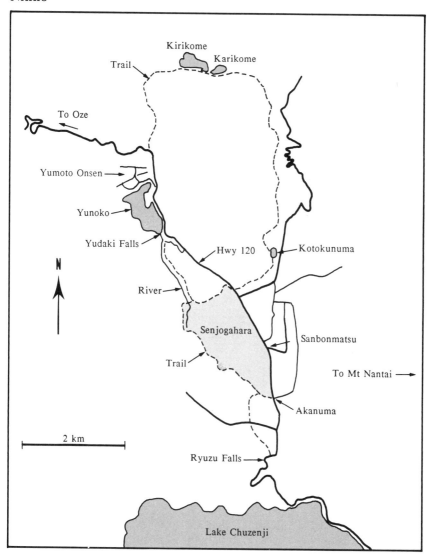

If you do not book your return journey in Tokyo, take special care to learn the schedule of the returning Limited Express trains and make certain you get a ticket and a reserved seat for the proper train. Again, you may have to leave Tobu-Nikko on the local train and change to the Limited Express at Shimo-Imaichi Station. The ordinary trains are often filled to overflowing, so you could stand for two hours. They are hot and generally miserable in summer.

I have gone to Nikko by car from Tokyo and do not recommend it. It takes much more time and is complicated. You can rent a car at the Tobu-Nikko Station. A Nippon Rent-a-Car office (0288-54-0821) is in the station. Go through the gate and turn left. The office is on your right, next to the side entrance to the station. They charge extra for air-conditioning in the summer.

You may want to stop in Nikko to look at the Toshogu Shrine, a famous shrine popular with tourists. It is a short way past the station. Then you will drive up the mountain on a winding toll road (Hwy. 120) to the birding areas. This drive may take 45 minutes from Nikko.

Site and Birds:
Yumoto Onsen, 30 km. from Nikko Station, is an ideal place for birdwatchers to stay. It is much smaller and less commercial than the other centers. It is located on the shores of the small and beautiful lake Yunoko. There is good birding even in the village itself, and it is near the most important birding areas. You can visit the hot spring at the back of the village for a bath after birding.

Senjogahara, between Yudaki Falls and Ryuzu Falls, is a marshy area with scattered trees. It is an excellent place for birds and is famous for its wildflowers. If you start from the parking lot at Yudaki Falls, you will first go alongside a stream through a forest. Then the path leads into the marsh where you will often be walking on a boardwalk. The path which runs mostly parallel to the highway and nearest to it is the best one if you haven't time to explore them all. It closely follows the stream. You can turn off before Ryuzu Falls and meet the highway at Akanuma. You can catch a bus there which will take you back to your car. You could easily spend half a day on this trail if the birds are good, so you may not have time to walk all the way back. It is a good place to take a picnic lunch and something to drink in case you find things so good you don't want to leave. You can get a snack at Akanuma, where there are also plenty of cold drink machines.

Kotokunuma is a tiny pond in lovely habitat. The path from Hwy. 120 leading to the pond is not long and is an ideal route for dawn-to-breakfast birding. At that hour, you can park your car on the highway where a side road joins it. This is only a few steps from the entrance to the trail beside the stream. In summer, birds are even here by the road. The trail goes through a fairly thick forest for a little more than half the distance from the highway to the pond before it reaches an open marshy area and then the pond. You will also find a small farm with fruit trees close to the pond. This area is good for Brown Dipper and Japanese Yellow Bunting. In the fall and winter this is the place to look for Solitary Snipe.

Yunoko has good birds in winter. Smew is usually among the ducks on the lake. In summer the trail through the forest along the west side of the lake is good early in the morning before the people appear. Thrushes and warblers (Pale-legged and Crowned Willow) are often here. There is a fork in the trail toward the south end of the lake. The path to the right leads downhill into a more open forest, a good place for woodpeckers.

Lakes Karikomi and Kirikomi are up the mountain behind Yumoto Onsen. To make the complete loop to the lakes, down the trail to Kotokunuma, and back up to Yumoto Onsen would take all day. But you can go to the lakes and return the same way in half a day. Don't go when Nikko is crowded. Everyone likes this trail. It goes through dense, dark woods all the way to these lakes. It is a good spot for Japanese Robin and Arctic Warbler, but there are few birds.

Sanbonmatsu is a place beside the highway with souvenir shops and restaurants. From here walk to the east down the narrow road which goes through a small woods and to some cultivated fields. Both times I walked through this woods I saw a Ural Owl. The fields are good for buntings in the fall and winter. You can walk on beyond these fields and take a trail up toward Mt. Nantai. This is one of the best areas for fall and winter birding. The road to the west, south of Akanuma also is worth exploring.

Other birds to look for at Nikko are Latham's Snipe, Common Cuckoo, Little Cuckoo, Great Spotted Woodpecker, White-backed Woodpecker, House Martin, White Wagtail, Japanese Wagtail, Northern Shrike, Brown Dipper, Winter Wren, Japanese Accentor, Siberian Blue Robin, Siberian Bluechat, Stonechat, Siberian Thrush, Brown Thrush, Gray-headed Thrush, Dusky Thrush,

Short-tailed Bush Warbler, Bush Warbler, Goldcrest, Narcissus Flycatcher, Blue-and-White Flycatcher, Brown Flycatcher, Long-tailed Tit, Willow Tit, Coal Tit, Varied Tit, Great Tit, Nuthatch, Brown Creeper, Japanese White-eye, Siberian Meadow Bunting, Rustic Bunting, Black-faced Bunting, Brambling, Hawfinch, and Russet Sparrow.

Time:
You can easily spend two full days here in the seasons when you have access to the trails. More time would permit you to explore other trails or to go back to some of the best spots. In winter, cross-country skis would open up a lot of territory. (See Oze.)

Food:
Because there are so many tourists, food is available everywhere. You will have breakfast and dinner where you stay. It is most convenient to take a packed lunch or buy some snacks to carry with you birdwatching.

Accommodations:
There are many places to stay in the Nikko area, including some fine Western-style hotels. Most are more expensive than similar accommodations elsewhere, and from July through October, the rates are increased, sometimes by as much as 50%. You can get information about places to stay from the TIC, the Nikko Tourist Association (0288-4-2496), or a travel agent.

I have stayed in three places at Yumoto Onsen and recommend two of them. The least expensive is Hotel Sangetsu (0288-62-2424). It is small and exceptionally clean. It is Japanese style, but has small rooms for two or three people. We ate dinner in our room, but had breakfast in the breakfast room. There are toilets and wash basins on each floor and an *ofuro* on the ground floor connected to the local hot spring. You will have to manage in Japanese here and be satisfied with a pure Japanese breakfast likely to contain most of the items a foreigner will like the least. In November it cost ¥7,000 per person with two meals. It is in the center of the village, easy to find.

The Nikko Grand is a first-rate hotel, fairly small despite its name, set back against the hillside with an enormous colony of House Martins nesting under its eaves. In the high season it cost ¥20,000 per person with two meals. I think the price was high relative to similar places elsewhere in Japan, but it was the cheapest of the top hotels in the area at that time.

The staff was helpful and accommodating to our party of four foreigners, the only non-Japanese guests. The rooms were Japanese style with private baths. I still recommend the *ofuro*. We had a maid who looked after us and served dinner in our rooms. Breakfast is served at either 7:30 or 8:30 (you decide the night before) in the breakfast room. They will serve a Japanese version of a Western breakfast. They broke with custom and gave us all the coffee we could drink. Some English is spoken and understood at this hotel, so you aren't completely on your own. Anyone would be comfortable here, and it is a suitable place for a group. During the best season for birds it should be cheaper.

Maps and Information:

National Map: 1:25,000 Nantaisan 男体山

Nikko Kanko Chizu - map showing all bus stops with some
      names in English
JNTO Information Sheet MG-031
JNTO brochure - Nikko

Useful Kanji:

Yumoto Onsen	湯元温泉
Yunoko	湯の湖
Yudaki Falls	湯滝
Kotokunuma	光徳沼
Senjogahara	戦場が原
Sanbonmatsu	三本松
Akanuma	赤沼
Kirikome	切込
Karikome	刈込

OZE

Season: late May - June
Specialties: mountain birds, wildflowers

Lake Ozenuma and Ozegahara are part of Nikko National Park, but they cannot be reached easily or quickly. Ozegahara is a vast marshy plain at 1400 meters, noted for its rare vegetation and 40 species of dragonflies. Lake Ozenuma, several kilometers to the east, is in a wooded area. All of Oze is surrounded by mountains. Both areas are noted for birds, but they are essentially the same species as occur in the more easily accessible parts of Nikko National Park.

Transportation:
The only way into this area is on foot. It can be approached from several directions by car and bus. The most direct way takes one hour to drive from Yumoto Onsen and an additional three hours to walk to the lake. You can take a train from Tokyo to Numata Station (2 hours, 20 minutes) and after almost three more hours on more than one bus, get to where you can begin walking. This way you can have the choice of several entrances.

Directions:
If you plan to use public transportation to reach this area, it is possible to walk in one way and out by another route. There are a number of possibilities. Since it is all quite complicated, work it out well in advance with the TIC. You will need bus and train schedules, reservations, good maps, and detailed directions.

The straightforward way is to drive from Yumoto Onsen to the end of the road at Oshimizu and walk in from there. Continue on Hwy. 120 from Yumoto Onsen. There is another toll road (¥600) just past Yumoto. After about 16 km., you will get to Katashina (see Champion Maps, page 35), where a road turns off toward the right to Tokura. This is Hwy. 401. At Tokura take the main fork to the right which goes to Oshimizu. It is 16 to 18 km. from Hwy. 120 to the end of the road at Oshimizu. The entire drive should take an hour. The road actually goes beyond Oshimizu, but it is blocked to traffic at all times. Apparently it is used only by park officials and for getting supplies to the lodges.

Oze

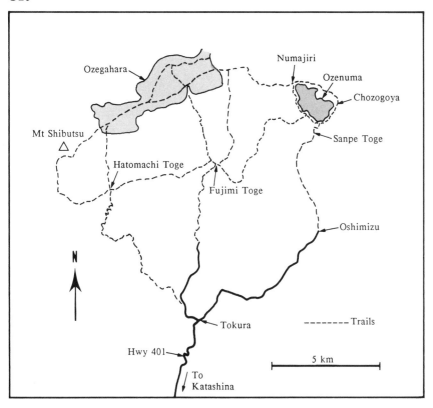

Site and Birds:

To my great disappointment, I have not yet been able to walk all the way to Oze. Therefore, most of this information is secondhand. The best birdwatching is around Ozenuma and Ozegahara. You will want to walk around the lake and then to the marsh. To protect the vegetation, you must walk on a boardwalk through the marsh. If it is crowded, this can be a problem.

From Oshimizu to Ozenuma you will walk via Sanpe Toge (pass). This is a breeding place for Gray Bunting. You might also see Siberian Blue Robin, Arctic Warbler, Goldcrest, and Blue-and-White Flycatcher in this area. Near the northeast corner of the lake, look for Latham's Snipe, Stonechat, and Gray-headed Bunting. Lanceolated Grasshopper Warbler is rare, but occurs here. Around the northwest corner of the lake, at Numajiri, look for Japanese Robin. It is also in the forest around the wetland. In the

Mt. Shibutsu area, southeast of Ozegahara, look for Hodgson's Hawk-Eagle, White-throated Needle-tailed Swift, White-rumped Swift, Alpine Accentor, and Japanese Accentor.

The best season for birds is a good time to see the wildflowers, so be prepared to share the area with others. It is also beautiful in the fall. At the end of October, probably after the peak of the fall colors, there are often big flocks of migrating thrushes and Bramblings.

Some resident birds of interest are Mandarin Duck, Common Buzzard, Copper Pheasant, Ural Owl, Japanese Green Woodpecker, Gray Wagtail, Indian Tree Pipit, Brown Dipper, Siberian Bluechat, Siberian Meadow Bunting, Bullfinch, Japanese Grosbeak, and Nutcracker.

Spring and summer visitors include Horsfield's Hawk-Cuckoo, Common Cuckoo, Oriental Cuckoo, Little Cuckoo, Jungle Nightjar, Siberian Thrush, Short-tailed Bush Warbler, Crowned Willow Warbler, Narcissus Flycatcher, and Sooty Flycatcher.

Time:
It is impossible to get to the end of the road, walk in, have time for birding, and get out in one day. Certainly it would not be possible to see both the lake and the marsh. Allow a minimum of two days and one night.

Food:
Bring it. After you begin walking, there is no food until you reach the lodges. You can get a packed lunch for the next day at your lodge.

Accommodations:
Tokura is a ski resort and so has many places to stay. There are two lodges at Oshimizu. Your real need is for lodging after you begin your hike. Camping is allowed. Inquire at the TIC. Mrs. Hirano, a well-known naturalist, runs Lodge Chozogoya at the east end of Ozenuma. I understand that this is much nicer than the typical mountain lodges. The telephone number is 027858-7443. Reservations can be made at Dinichozogoya, 027858-7100 and 7388, from 8:00 a.m. to 6:00 p.m. Lodges are also at both ends of the marsh and at the passes Hatomachi Toge and Fujimi Toge. It is essential to have reservations before going in.

Mountain lodges typically have large sleeping areas where everyone is put, but with sexes segregated. A *futon* is provided, as are meals, but the accommodations are basic. According to my source, Lodge Chozogoya has a number of smaller rooms, so you won't be sharing with too many people.

Maps and Information:
Champion Maps, Vol. 2, Eastern Japan
Buyodo Map D-6

National Maps: 1:50,000   Hiuchigatake 燧ヶ岳

Fujiwara 藤原

Useful Kanji:

Katashina	片品
Tokura	戸倉
Oshimizu	大清水
Sanpe Toge	三平峠
Ozenuma	尾瀬沼
Chozogoya	長蔵小屋
Numajiri	沼尻
Ozegahara	尾瀬が原
Hatomachi Toge	鳩待峠
Fujimi Toge	富士見峠

TOGAKUSHI

Season: *late April - late June*
Specialties: *Ashy Minivet, Jungle Nightjar, Siberian Thrush, Arctic*
Warbler, Japanese Yellow Bunting, Gray Bunting,
Russet Sparrow

The Togakushi Highland, at the foot of Mt. Togakushi, is a scenic area in the Joshinetsu Kogen (Plateau) National Park. It is well known among Japanese birders for the large number of forest and highland species which breed here. Some birders consider it the best area for mountain birds in Japan. All the same species should occur in Karuizawa, Kamikochi, and Nikko too. Since each area has a different character and there are many variables involved in determining exactly how many birds can be seen with what degree of ease, it is probably more a matter of personal choice.

Transportation:
From Tokyo (Ueno Station), it takes three hours by Limited Express to reach Nagano. It is possible to get from Nagano to Togakushi by bus in about 1 hour, 30 minutes. The best and most convenient way to get there and to see the birds in the area is to go by rented car from Nagano. Do not drive from Tokyo. It will more than double your travel time.

Directions:
At Ueno Station take the Limited Express on the JNR Shinetsu Main Line. These trains leave hourly. At Nagano, if you are driving, get directions for finding the Togakushi Bird Line, a 17-km. toll road (Hwy. 128). Page 32 of the Champion Maps should help. Before you get on the toll road, you may pass Zenkoji Temple. I have not seen this, but it is supposed to be one of the most popular Buddhist temples.

Shortly after the end of the toll road, take the highway to the right toward Chusha. This area should be your base for birding around Togakushi. There are many places to stay. You can walk from Chusha if you wish. The birding is good off the paved road. Or drive to Shinrin Shokubutsu-en, the Forestry Botanical Garden. The word garden doesn't describe this very well. Forest is better.

Site and Birds:
My experience with Togakushi is limited. I went there with the staff from the WBSJ for the annual meeting of the WBSJ at the beginning of June in 1982. All my birding was done between our inn and the Shinrin Shokubutsu-en. The most memorable part of this trip for me was when all 252 people at this meeting went birding in one body in this forest.

Togakushi

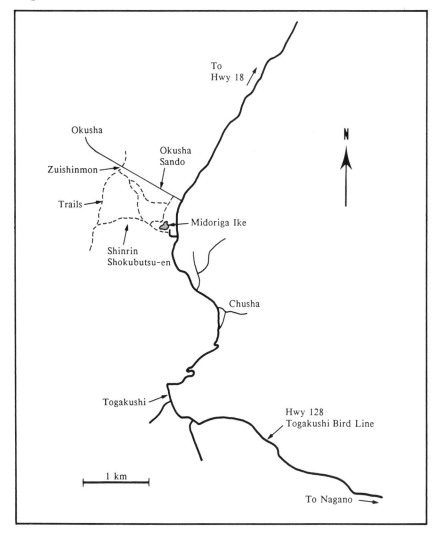

The last part of the journey coming from Tokyo is lovely with the road winding through the mountains. The Joshinetsu Kogen National Park is filled with volcanos and countless hot springs. The landscape is varied, often with deep valleys and sharply eroded rocky cliffs. Around Togakushi the highlands are rolling with open meadows, forests, some small lakes, and a couple of streams. The Togakushi Mountains, rising to the west, are rugged and steep and are popular with skilled mountaineers. It is a pleasant place.

Go first to the Shinrin Shokubutsu-en. It is a short walk from Chusha, and there are birds to be seen if you stay off the main road. Look near the *torii* (gate) at the shrine at Chusha for Red-cheeked Myna. Common and Little Cuckoos were abundant in the nearby fields when I was there. You can drive to the forest and park near the entrance.

Near the entrance is Midoriga Ike, a pond which should be checked for birds. Russet Sparrows usually nest in the trees beside it. Besides an enormous variety of trees, including black alder, cedar, and beech, there are many kinds of wildflowers. Numerous paths go through the forest. For some distance you can walk on a boardwalk over a swampy area filled with ferns and skunk cabbage. The vegetation changes, so be sure to cover the whole territory to find all the different habitats.

Look for White-backed Woodpecker and Indian Tree Pipit in the black alders, Siberian Thrush, Gray Thrush, Narcissus Flycatcher, and Japanese Yellow Bunting near the river, and Gray Bunting in the larch and maple trees. After thoroughly checking this area, walk to Zuishinmon and Okusha. On the way, look for Siberian Blue Robin, Goldcrest, and Brown Creeper. Then go back by way of Okusha Sando (the road to the shrine) where you may see Arctic Warbler, Crowned Willow Warbler, Blue-and-White Flycatcher, and Gray Bunting.

Try to visit Shinrin Shokubutsu-en at dawn. It is a beautiful place with plenty of birds under the right conditions. After the WBSJ crowd dispersed, I was able to go back there and see it almost empty of people. But as I was leaving (this was a Sunday morning in early June, well before the school holidays), 17 enormous tour buses arrived full of school children who charged into the forest.

Shades of Mt. Fuji. Up until then I thought I was in a remote area which was crowded only because of the WBSJ annual meeting. It is hard to realize, but there are people everywhere in Japan. Try to avoid weekends as well as holidays for visiting such places.

From your hotel or a local tourist information office, you can get a map of the area showing hiking trails. There are many other walks you can take from here, both across the plateau and into the mountains. Although the Japanese birders emphasize Shinrin Shokubutsu-en, I suspect some exploration would turn up many more good birding areas. Trails go off in both directions from the main road.

According to my map, if you will continue down this road for 19.3 km. from the end of the Bird Line Toll Road, you will run into Hwy. 18. Go north on Hwy. 18 for 3.5 km., and you will see Lake Nojori. This is a summer resort which first became popular when foreign missionaries discovered it. It is probably worth checking for birds.

Besides the birds already mentioned, in spring and summer look for Japanese Lesser Sparrow Hawk, Sparrow Hawk, Gray-faced Buzzard-Eagle, Latham's Snipe, Japanese Green Pigeon, Horsfield's Hawk-Cuckoo, Oriental Cuckoo, Scops Owl, Collared Scops Owl, Brown Hawk-Owl, Ural Owl, White-throated Needle-tailed Swift, White-rumped Swift, Brown Thrush, Great Reed Warbler, and Pale-legged Willow Warbler. Ruddy Kingfisher and Black Paradise Flycatcher are on the list, but I'd be surprised if they can be expected. Resident birds include Copper and Common Pheasant, Japanese Green Woodpecker, Brown Dipper, five species of tits, Jay, and Nutcracker.

If you should come here in winter, look for Bohemian and Japanese Waxwings, Pale Thrush, Gray-headed Thrush, Rosy Finch, Pallas's Rosy Finch, Red Crossbill, and Hawfinch. Pallas's Rosy Finch is always difficult to find. Many winters it goes unreported in Japan.

Time:
Again, my bias is to stay a couple of days if you go to the trouble to come at all. Shinrin Shokubutsu-en is worth two to three hours, probably longer if you go to Okusha. So in one day you can see a lot, though it won't give you time to cover many of the trails or to

hike up to higher elevations. Nagano is on the same train line and an hour beyond Karuizawa, so visits to these places could be combined. The birds are similar, so a short-time visitor to Japan must consider the time available.

Food:
There are restaurants in the town, but no food near the forest park. Eat at your hotel and take a box lunch. This area is famous for homemade *soba* (buckwheat noodles). Have at least one meal in a good restaurant to try this local specialty.

Accommodations:
There are many hotels, *ryokan*, and *minshuku*. Koshimizu Lodge (02625-4-2124) is near the forest park and gives a 10% discount to WBSJ members. It is large enough to handle a group.

Maps and Information:
Champion Maps, Vol. 2, Eastern Japan
Buyodo Map D-6

National Maps: 1:50,000 Togakushi 戸隠

Useful Kanji:
Togakushi   戸隠
Chusha   中社
Okusha   奥社
Shinrin Shokubutsu-en 森林植物園
Zuishinmon   随神門
Midoriga Ike   緑が池
Lake Nojori   野尻湖

KARUIZAWA

Season: late April - June, mid-December to mid-March
Specialties: Copper Pheasant, Horsfield's Hawk-Cuckoo, Thick-billed Shrike, Siberian Thrush, Short-tailed Bush Warbler, Japanese Yellow Bunting, Red-cheeked Myna.

Karuizawa is an excellent place for birding and shouldn't be missed. It is easy to reach from Tokyo. A foreign visitor should have no trouble finding his way and otherwise functioning in Karuizawa. It is a small town in a lovely mountain setting, extremely popular as a summer resort. During July and August its population increases from 14,000 to more than 200,000, so come some other time. In both winter and spring there are many birds of special interest to foreign birders. The area is pleasant for birdwatching, and most of the birds are not difficult to find.

Transportation:
The train from Tokyo to Karuizawa takes 2 hours, 10 minutes. A rental car is certainly advantageous but not absolutely essential. Buses and taxis are available, and bicycles are for rent.

Directions:
At Ueno Station (Tokyo) take the JNR Shinetsu Main Line train. The Limited Express leaves every hour on the hour from 7:00 a.m. to 8:00 p.m. All seats on this train are reserved, and the fare is ¥3,900. The Express does not run as often, it takes 20 minutes longer, and the fare is ¥2,800.

All trains stop at Karuizawa. Some will also stop at Naka-Karuizawa, about 4 km. beyond. This station is closer to Hoshino Onsen, but the rental car offices are near Karuizawa Station. If you are going by taxi to Hoshino Onsen and your train does not stop at Naka-Karuizawa, it is not worth waiting for another train to Naka-Karuizawa.

At Karuizawa Station there is an Eki Rent-a-Car office to your right after you pass through the exit. The Nippon Rent-a-Car office is nearby, but impossible to see from the front of the station. To get to it, walk straight out the front of the station, cross the highway, and keep going straight until you reach the next corner. The office is across that street on your right, next to the building on the corner.

Karuizawa

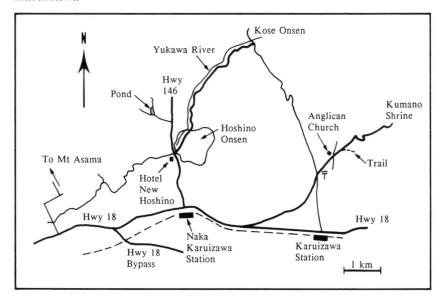

To get to Hoshino Onsen, go west on Hwy. 18, the main road in front of the station. As you get near the turn, you will see signs in English on the right indicating the Historical Museum, Karuizawa Gymnasium, Welfare Center, and Public Hall. You will cross a bridge and soon come to an intersection where a highway sign in *kanji* indicates two places are 35 km. and 18 km. to the right. Naka-Karuizawa Station is to the left, but not easy to recognize immediately. Turn right. You will go under a green sign which reaches across the road. From here it is 1.4 km. to the Hotel New Hoshino on the left (past the Volcano Coffee Shop). The Hoshino Onsen Hotel and the main part of the forest are across the road on the right.

Site and Birds:
Birding is good almost anywhere in Karuizawa. For many years the residents of Karuizawa have attempted to maintain an environment attractive to birds. There are strict rules for building requiring a minimum of 30 square meters of land before any kind of building can be built and limiting the building to only 30 percent of the area of the building site. Recently, all the mercury street lights were replaced when it was determined that they were having a detrimental effect on the birds. Because of the enlightened attitude toward development in this town, it is an

attractive place for both people and wildlife. By simply wandering up and down the streets in the residential areas you will find good birds.

HOSHINO ONSEN

Hoshino Onsen is a good starting place for Karuizawa birding. The father of the present Mr. Hoshino established this as a sanctuary in 1934, the first bird sanctuary in Japan. Now Hoshino-san, who is the chairman of the Karuizawa chapter of the WBSJ, continues to do everything possible to attract birds to this large forested area. All over Karuizawa the residents are encouraged to feed the birds throughout the severe winter, but birds are especially abundant in Hoshino Onsen because of the vast quantities of food Hoshino-san supplies for them. He welcomes and encourages birdwatchers provided they obey his strict rule that the birds are not to be disturbed. From April through October a ranger is present, who, for no charge, takes any interested visitors on bird walks.

It will take some time to walk along all the roads and trails in the *onsen*. As always, the earlier you are out, the better. In spring and early summer be sure to get out at dawn. Walk behind the old hotel on the side away from the Yukawa River. There is a small stream on the left and then a little farther on an even smaller one coming downhill from the left, more or less perpendicular to the river. Here, early in the morning while everything is quiet, you will have a good chance of seeing Copper Pheasants. I saw two males and a female here together in the winter. I had the good fortune also to see a Ural Owl from the road which leads uphill just beyond the bridge over the main stream near the old hotel. In winter, keep on the lookout for mistletoe. Flocks of waxwings, both Japanese and Bohemian, frequent the area, eating mistletoe berries.

YUKAWA RIVER

The road beside the river continues for four kilometers. Birding is excellent along this road even after you leave the area belonging to Hoshino Onsen. It is almost level, so it is an easy walk or bicycle ride. If your time is limited, you can drive along here, but stop often or you will miss something. Copper Pheasants often come to the river to drink. With patience and care, you should be able to find one of these elusive birds in this area. In summer, watch along the banks of the tiny streams which feed this main stream, as well as along any stream no more than a meter wide, for Short-tailed Bush Warblers.

From the end of this road, Kyu-Karuizawa is 2.9 km. to the right. Kose Onsen is 0.1 km. to the left. The signs are in *kanji*.

POND AND WOODS

From the entrance to the New Hoshino Hotel, go north on the highway for 1.1 km., keeping to the right at the fork. Take the road to the left which goes between tennis courts and the Seibu Department Store. From the turn, go another 0.6 km., again keeping to the right. At this point, find a place to park, and walk to the small pond on the right. This is an excellent spot in any season. The pond, fed by a small stream, does not freeze in winter. Even in the coldest season, cress grows in the water. There are weeds around the pond and a muddy place clear of snow on the far side where birds come to drink. The mixed woods behind the pond is good in any season, but difficult to get into in winter due to deep snow.

In winter this is a good place to see Japanese Accentor, Yellow-throated Bunting, and Long-tailed Rose Finch. Pallas's Rosy Finch is never easy; in fact it doesn't occur every year. But look for it here around the cress and the weeds, as well as around the cress in the shallow stream behind the old Hoshino Hotel.

"FORIST" ROAD

A road and hiking trail leading up to Mt. Asama, an active volcano, is good both in summer and in winter. Begin measuring from the highway at the entrance to the Hotel New Hoshino. Go north and take the first road to the left. After 3.1 km., turn left again at an intersection where there is a sign indicating Asamadai and "Forist" Road to the left. Continue on this road, going straight at a stop sign where another sign indicates Forist Road and Oiwake straight ahead. At 5.2 km. there is an intersection where two parallel roads go to the right. On the left side of the intersection there is a sign in English, "Nagano Prefecture Office, Oiwake Water Supply, no trespassing". Take the right-hand road of the two parallel roads on the right and follow it around to the right. Approximately 6.2 km. from your starting point, turn left. In summer, a pole blocks the road at this point, so you must continue from here on foot. In winter it is possible to drive a bit farther.

In winter, look for Pallas's Rosy Finch in the weeds beside this road. It is a good place to find Long-tailed Rose Finch and Red Crossbill. In summer, Latham's Snipe is common here and easy to find. Also look here for cuckoos, Stonechat, Arctic Warbler, and Gray-headed Bunting. Horsfield's Hawk-Cuckoo occurs more often in the deep forest, but sometimes it is along here nearer the ground so it is easier to see. Japanese Grosbeak is resident.

When you leave this area, you can go straight at the intersection by the Oiwake Water Supply for 0.3 km. to reach Hwy. 18. Turn left and you will soon be back in front of Naka-Karuizawa Station (3.8 km.). Hwy. 18 divides into the main business route and the bypass. Stay to the left to get back to Karuizawa.

TRAIL TO USUI OBSERVATION PLATFORM

The trail to the Usui Observation Platform near Kumano Shrine is excellent in summer. From Karuizawa Station, go north 1.8 km. and turn right at a big intersection. This is a major shopping street. The main post office will be on your right, 0.2 km. from the turn. You will see the Anglican Church and a sign "Asaji Villa" 0.8 km. from the turn. Continue going straight another 0.3 km. past the church until you see a small tan sign on the right of the road. This is the entrance to a trail which will take you up the hill to the observation area. From here it is 3.2 km. to the top. You can return by the road. This is a good place to look for Ruddy Kingfisher and other summer visitors. On the way to this trail, you will pass a small stream just past the Anglican Church. Check for birds along this stream too.

After you have explored these areas, you will have gotten your bearings and will be ready to strike out on your own to look for other good places. In winter your choice of destinations will be limited by snow on the roads. Since Karuizawa is hilly, without chains you are likely to get in trouble if you take roads which haven't been cleared. In summer it is worthwhile to drive around south of Hwy. 18 and the railroad track. Lately there has been a lot of development here, including a golf course which has ruined some good birding habitat. But look here for Great Reed Warblers if you haven't found them elsewhere. Japanese Yellow Buntings occur in the lower elevations to the south and southwest.

A publication of the Karuizawa Wild Bird Society, *Birding Guide in Karuizawa*, which is for sale at Hoshino Onsen, contains a full-page map of the forest of Hoshino Onsen with various locations numbered. Hoshino-san shared the following hints with me: look for Collared Scops Owl around 12, 13, and 14; Brown Hawk-Owl at 13, 14, and 15; Siberian Blue Robin and Blue-and-White Flycatcher at 5, 6, and 7 and 21, 22, and 23; and Japanese Yellow Bunting at 1, 2, 3, and 4.

Lately Hoopoes, which are rare in Japan, have occurred in Karuizawa in summer. Inquire at Hoshino Onsen.

Resident birds you should find include Spot-billed Duck, Black Kite, Common Buzzard, Copper Pheasant, Common Pheasant, Rufous Turtle Dove, Japanese Green Woodpecker, Great Spotted Woodpecker, Japanese Pygmy Woodpecker, Gray Wagtail, Japanese Wagtail, Indian Tree Pipit, Brown-eared Bulbul, Bull-headed Shrike, Brown Dipper, Winter Wren, Japanese Accentor (easier in winter), Siberian Bluechat, Bush Warbler, Long-tailed Tit, Willow Tit, Coal Tit, Nuthatch, Siberian Meadow Bunting, Black-faced Bunting, Oriental Greenfinch, Bullfinch, Japanese Grosbeak, Jay, and Azure-winged Magpie.

Summer visitors include Latham's Snipe, Japanese Green Pigeon (few, but look in Hoshino woods), Horsfield's Hawk-Cuckoo, Common Cuckoo, Oriental Cuckoo, Little Cuckoo, Jungle Nightjar, White-rumped Swift, Skylark, House Martin, Ashy Minivet, Brown Shrike, Siberian Blue Robin, Siberian Thrush, White's Ground Thrush, Gray Thrush, Brown Thrush, Short-tailed Bush Warbler, Great Reed Warbler, Arctic Warbler, Crowned Willow Warbler, Narcissus Flycatcher, Blue-and-White Flycatcher, Brown Flycatcher, and Red-cheeked Myna.

Look for Thick-billed Shrike and Black Paradise Flycatcher. Neither is easy to find, but they do occur. Two or three Greater Pied Kingfishers are recorded each year. Look for them near small streams in Hoshino woods.

Time:
An absolute minimum is two days and one night in Karuizawa. Two nights, giving you two dawns, would be much better. If you can afford the time, it is a good place to stay even longer. I stayed 48 hours in winter and did not have enough time to cover all the areas accessible in that season. It is a fine place to stay several days, but, as always, there are other places and other birds to see.

Food:
There are plenty of restaurants, so getting something to eat is no problem. Especially in spring and summer when you won't need to come indoors to get some relief from the cold, a packed lunch would be most enjoyable. Kagimoto-ya, a famous *soba* restaurant, is an interesting place to have lunch. It is between Hwy. 18 and Naka-Karuizawa Station, on the left if you are facing the station. The phone number is 02674-5-5208.

Accommodations:
Hotel New Hoshino (2133, Oaza Nagakura, Karuizawa-machi, Kitasaku-gun, 389-01, Japan, telephone 02674-5-6081) is an ideal place for birdwatchers. This hotel is on the opposite side of the highway from the old hotel and the main part of the *onsen*, but Hoshino-san recommends this for birdwatchers.

Let them know you are there for birdwatching, and ask for one of the cabins so you can birdwatch from your window. In the winter they will be sure the feeders on your windows are full of nuts, suet, seeds, and other treats. You will be hard put to leave the show at your window to go see what else you can find.

If you stay in one of these cabins, they will, without disturbing you, deliver a Western breakfast in a big basket to a little compartment in your wall which can be opened from the outside and inside. The cabins have Western-style bathrooms with hot water coming from the *onsen*. The rate is ¥20,000 per person per day double occupancy, including breakfast and dinner. Rooms in the hotel may be cheaper than the cabins. You can write directly to them in English for reservations.

If Hoshino Onsen is too rich for your budget, there are countless other places to stay in the area. Two places where you can get a 10% discount with your WBSJ membership card are Lodge Ariake (02674-5-3096) and Ryokan Asami-so (02674-5-6118).

Maps and Information:
Champion Maps, Vol. 2, Eastern Japan
Buyodo Map D-6

National Maps: 1:50,000 Karuizawa 軽井沢

                       Miyota   御代田

JNTO Information Sheet - Karuizawa Kogen
Birding Guide in Karuizawa, Japan Wild Bird Society

Useful Kanji:
Karuizawa   軽井沢
Naka-Karuizawa   中軽井沢
Hoshino Onsen   星野温泉
Yukawa River   湯川
Usui Observation Platform 碓氷峠見晴台
Kumano Shrine   熊野神社

MT. FUJI AREA

Season: *fall through spring*
Specialties: *Alpine Accentor, Japanese Accentor, Nutcracker,*
species common at elevations of 900 to 2500 meters

The main attraction of this area is Mt. Fuji itself. This brings countless visitors, detracting from the birding, which otherwise would be excellent. A variety of habitat, a breathtakingly beautiful mountain (from a distance), many kinds of wildflowers, and a good number of species of birds are here for your enjoyment if you can escape the crowds.

Transportation:
There are at least two direct express trains each day from Tokyo's Shinjuku Station to Kawaguchiko. These take 2 hours, 10 minutes. Other trains require a change at Otsuki, thus taking longer. From Kawaguchiko it is most convenient to have a rented car.

It is easy to drive from Tokyo at a time of day when the traffic is not too heavy, provided you rent your car from a location as close as possible to an entrance to the Chuo Expressway. This will minimize the time spent driving in Tokyo and the risk of getting lost. Driving is for the brave, but only because of the problems involved in finding and getting on the proper freeway in Tokyo. The travel time will be about the same as by train. It is about 120 km. from Tokyo.

Directions:
The easiest way is to take the direct JNR express train from Shinjuku Station to Kawaguchiko. One leaves early in the morning and another in early afternoon. Arrange for a rental car before you leave. Find a company which is at the station or which will meet you there.

The Chuo Expressway from Tokyo goes all the way to Kawaguchiko. The last part of the journey is on an expressway which branches off from the main one. There are highway signs in English. The toll from Tokyo is about ¥2,300.

Site and Birds:
Every visitor to Japan wants to see Mt. Fuji. It is not overrated if you can see it on a clear day from a distance or if you get a good

view from an airplane. Unfortunately most foreign visitors are disappointed when they actually get to the mountain. The traffic congestion, the unbelievable number of visitors, the extensive tourist development, and the trash thoughtlessly abandoned in some areas have seriously scarred the beauty of this magnificent mountain.

Mt. Fuji Area

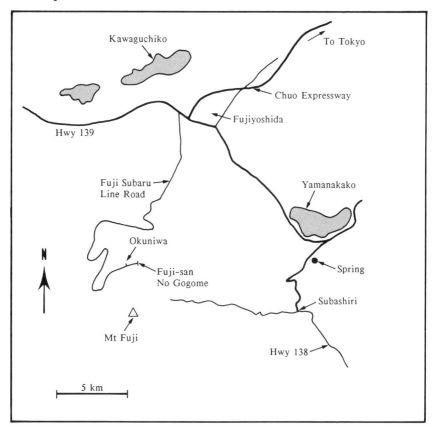

If you are prepared for this and take careful precautions to avoid crowds, a birding trip to Fuji-san (in this case *san* is not honorific, but a word which means mountain) can be most enjoyable. Stay away in the summer. The mountain is open for climbing during July and August. Besides the usual visitors, more than 20,000 people climb Fuji-san every day. There are countless vacation cottages in the area, so I suspect that weekends are crowded throughout the year. There is beauty to be found here at any season. More birds are here in the spring, but in winter there is at least a chance of finding something special like Pallas's Rosy Finch.

YAMANAKAKO

Five large lakes are at the base of Fuji-san. The most popular one for birdwatching is Yamanakako (Lake Yamanaka) at 982 meters. To get there, go to the left on Hwy. 138 from Kawaguchiko. From the toll booth at the end of the expressway, it is about 10 km. to Yamanakako. The lake itself usually has few birds. In winter, however, check it for a possible Falcated Teal or Smew. The east and northeast edges of the lake are best. Also check the woods there.

A more productive place is south of the lake in a residential area. There are many cottages in the forest, some on large lots. By walking up and down the roads, you can usually see many birds. There is a spring near here which is a good place to start.

Take Hwy. 138 around the south side of Yamanakako. From the intersection where Hwy. 138 goes to the right and another road continues around the south shore of the lake, go right on Hwy. 138 approximately 0.7 km. until you see a pedestrian crossing and a restaurant on the left called "Cafe de White Tree". Turn left at that corner. There should also be a small sign with "Cannon" and "Pension Zoo" written on it. Go 0.4 km. on this road until you reach a large wooden sign hanging from stone posts on your right. This appears to be a map of all the lots in the area. Take the road on the right side of the sign and go a short distance until you see a sign on the right which shows a lake painted blue and has some red and yellow writing on it. Just here is a stone tablet and a small shrine. Park and walk down the hill past the shrine until you reach the spring.

When I visited this spring in early summer, it was already occupied by about 150 Boy Scouts. But it did look like a fine place for birds if too many people aren't around. After you climb back up, walk on down the road for a few minutes. You will have a fine view of treetops across the gulley where you might see something interesting. After that, spend some time walking or driving through this residential area. Undoubtedly at dawn, long before the visitors arrive, this is an excellent spot.

SUBASHIRI

Find your way back to the highway at the Cafe de White Tree and continue south on Hwy. 138 for 7.7 km. to Subashiri. There you will find a road to the right leading up Mt. Fuji. Take this road and start birding again. It is paved for a little way. On weekends and in summer that section is likely to have a lot of motorcyclists racing on it. After the pavement stops, the motorcyclists find it less interesting. You can drive up as far as road conditions allow, and you should be bothered by few other visitors.

Beyond the end of the pavement, many tracks lead into the forest. It appears that this area is being prepared for development, most likely more vacation cottages. These tracks will enable you to walk into the forest at many different levels as you make your way up the mountain. With enough time for wandering about, you should find a lot of birds along here. Among the birds I saw in early summer were Indian Tree Pipit, Japanese Accentor, Japanese Robin, Siberian Bluechat, Gray Thrush, Brown Thrush, Bush Warbler, Arctic Warbler, Brown Flycatcher, and Nutcracker.

FUJI-SAN NO GOGOME

The next area to visit is the Fifth Stage of Mount Fuji (Fuji-san no Gogome). Go back to Kawaguchiko via Hwy. 138 and then to the Fuji Subaru Line Road, the toll road (¥1,200) going to the Fifth Stage. This is beyond where you got off the freeway. The end of the toll road is as far up Fuji-san as you can go by car. Gogome is about at the tree line (2,500 meters), so there is little of ornithological interest above that.

If you can find places to park and trails to explore on the way up, you should see birds. It is difficult to spot ways to get into the forest along here. You should find it easier to investigate the different vegetation zones along the road up from Subashiri.

At Gogome there are the usual souvenir shops and a huge parking area normally filled with tour buses and cars. Stop about 1 km. before that at Okuniwa. You will see a small parking area on the left side of the road as you go up the mountain. From here, walk downhill along the trail for about ten minutes to Okuniwa-so, a souvenir shop and restaurant.

The best place for birds is the tiny spring about two meters from the right side of the building. But this is at its best only at dawn and late in the evening after everyone has gone. I saw Japanese Accentor, numerous Siberian Bluechats, Brown Thrush, several Arctic Warblers, Bullfinch, and Nutcracker here. It is an excellent place for taking photographs because you can sit just inside the building and the birds will come close. There is more about Okuniwa-so under Accommodations.

The trail continues on downhill from this spring. There usually are good birds in the woods a little way below the spring. Another trail goes to the left from Okuniwa-so. This has a stone path and was probably designed by the owners to attract visitors. It does, by the bus load, during the day. If you are there either early or late, it is worth the 15 minutes it takes to cover it.

If you want to do more walking on the mountain, you should have a good map showing the trails. Across the highway from the parking lot at Okuniwa, you can get on a trail which probably circles the mountain at that level. Such a trip is not to be undertaken lightly, but the trail is a fine place to walk as far as you wish before turning back to your car. After the people begin to arrive on the mountain, the trail in the direction away from the end of toll road (west) is much less crowded. The birds are best from this level down. Up above you can see White-rumped Swift and Alpine Accentor, but you can also find them near the Fifth Level.

We spent the night up here in early summer and enjoyed birding around Okuniwa-so, especially at the spring, from dawn until 8:00 a.m. Then we went to explore the trail leading around the mountain. People began arriving about 9:00. By 10:00, the mountain was so covered with people we gave up.

They came in countless buses, at that season mostly school groups, children of all ages. The children from each school were dressed alike. Most were identical from head to toe with hats, sweatsuits, backpacks, and shoes exactly the same. Some, perhaps less prosperous, would have only caps, or caps and backpacks alike. By 10:00 a.m., from where we stood, we could look down on several

thousand people. It was a colorful sight. The path to the left of
Okuniwa-so looked like a commercial flower garden, with two or
three hundred people of each color all together in a tightly-knit
group, never getting mixed up with the neighboring color scheme.
This is a typical Japanese phenomenon and one which foreigners
find fascinating. But the crowds and the noise ruin birdwatching.

If you spend time checking different kinds of habitat at a variety
of elevations, you should be able to find 40 to 50 species in the
spring. The list of birds which have been recorded in the Mt. Fuji
area is long, but undoubtedly the pressures from development
have brought about a decrease in the number of species and in the
number of birds which occur here. There are no birds that are
sure to be seen here that can't also be found in other similar areas.

Rumor has it that a Japanese Night Heron (a most elusive species)
nested for two or three years recently in the woods behind the
Fuji View Hotel at Kawaguchiko. It was not there in 1984. I
understand that this is a good woods nevertheless.

Despite my negative comments, Fuji-san is a good area for birds.
Visiting birders can have a trip to Japan's most famous landmark
and a good birding expedition at the same time. This can be
important for those whose time is limited.

Time:
Stay at least one night, leaving Tokyo early one morning and
returning the following afternoon. You could spend several days in
the area exploring trails around the base of the mountain and at
several levels between the base and the Fifth Stage. This will be
pleasant, but not the best way for a short-time visitor to build up
a long list of Japanese birds.

It takes about 45 minutes to drive from Kawaguchiko up to
Gogome. It is not far from Kawaguchiko to Yamanakako, but
there can be enormous traffic jams on that road. If you are not
there at a quiet time, don't be surprised if this drive takes more
than 30 minutes.

Food:
There is no scarcity of restaurants and grocery stores at the base
of the mountain. Food is available at the end of the toll road at

Gogome and at Okuniwa-so. It is best to take your lunch and eat while birding.

Accommodations:

There are plenty of places to stay. The problem may be to find something suitable which doesn't cost too much. The famous hotels are the Fuji View Hotel at Kawaguchiko (05558-3-2211) and Hotel Mt. Fuji at Yamanakako (05556-2-2111). Both these hotels have Tokyo offices which will make reservations.

Minshuku Fujitaka-mura near Yamanakako gives a discount to WBSJ members. The price is about ¥4,200.

It is possible to spend the night at Okuniwa-so (05558-2-2910). This is primarily a souvenir shop which serves lunches to visitors. After the day's visitors have gone, if you have made prior arrangements, they will let you sleep in one of the small *tatami* rooms which serve as dining rooms in the daytime. When the table is removed and the *futon* brought in, it is little different from a room in any *minshuku*. The toilet is outdoors, and washing is also done outdoors. Large containers of water, dippers, and small basins are provided. I suggest you find all this before it gets dark. Take a flashlight. The cost is ¥4,500 per person with dinner and breakfast. If you make your request well in advance, you may be able to have the room on the end next to the spring. By staying here, you can most conveniently see the birds at the best time of day.

Maps and Information:

JNTO Map of Tokyo and Vicinity
Buyodo Map D-6
JNTO Information Sheet MG-035

Useful Kanji:

Yamanakako	山中湖
Subashiri	須走
Fuji-san no Gogome	富士山の五合目
Okuniwa-so	奥庭荘

KAMIKOCHI AND THE JAPAN ALPS

Season: late May to mid-June
Specialties: mountain birds

Kamikochi is without doubt one of the most beautiful spots in all of Japan. It is a favorite place for alpinists and is excellent for birdwatching. Because of the time required to get there, not many Japanese birders regularly visit the area. Trails lead from Kamikochi into the high mountains, where it is possible to camp or stay in mountain huts. For birdwatchers, there is plenty to do without climbing.

Transportation:
From Tokyo it takes 3 hours, 15 minutes by train to Matsumoto and another two hours by a combination of train and bus, or about one hour by car, to Kamikochi.

Directions:
From Tokyo's Shinjuku Station, take the Limited Express train Azusa for Matsumoto on the JNR Chuo Main Line. If you are not traveling on a JNR Pass, the ordinary car reserved seats are comfortable, only two seats on each side of the aisle. There are at least ten of these trains daily.

Japan Alps

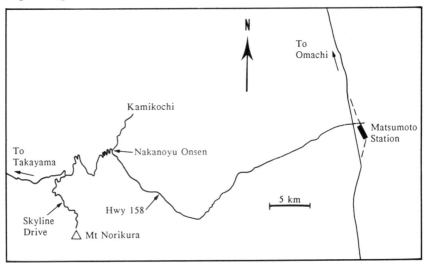

If you do not wish to make the entire trip in one day, Matsumoto is a good stopping place. It is an interesting town with a famous castle.

By public transportation, take the Matsumoto Dentetsu (electric railway) from Matsumoto Station to Shin-Shimashima (30 minutes). There, get the Matsumoto Dentetsu Bus to Kamikochi (1 hour, 30 minutes).

Kamikochi

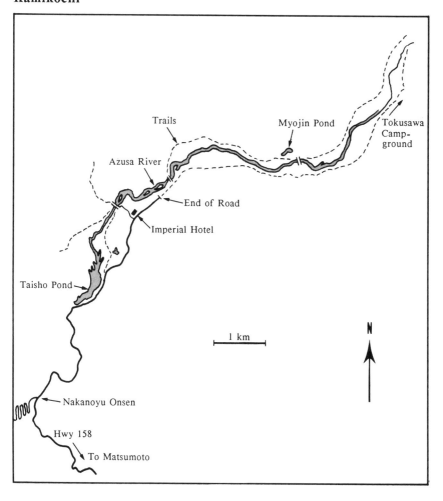

There are several rental car offices to the right as you leave
Matsumoto Station. You want to get on Hwy. 158, near the
station, to the left as you come out. Get exact directions when you
pick up your car. This road is easy to find and easy to follow.
There are many signs along the way in Roman letters, but it is
still best to learn to recognize the *kanji* for Kamikochi.

During the peak season and on weekends from July through
October, private cars are not allowed to drive all the way into
Kamikochi. If you are intending to drive, no matter when you are
going, it is best to double check to make sure it is possible. There
is no need for a car in Kamikochi, but a car will allow you to go
up Mt. Norikura conveniently and take a day trip to Takayama if
you wish.

The route is picturesque, but there are no real birding
opportunities on the way. The road is narrow with few places to
pull off and stop. I do not recommend driving through these
mountains in the dark. In many places there is little or no
protection if you should go off the side of the road.

The last 6 km. from Nakanoyu Onsen to Kamikochi (the part that
is closed to private cars during the busy season) is especially
narrow and further congested by construction of new tunnels.
Driving is not difficult in daylight and good weather, but be
cautious.

If the place you choose to stay is beyond the bus terminal (end of
the road), you will have to park your car in the lot at the terminal
and pay.

Site and Birds:
Kamikochi is situated in a basin at 1500 meters. It is one of those
rare places in Japan where you can look in any direction without
finding an eyesore. On the way up to Kamikochi you will see
dams and concrete abutments, but in Kamikochi the river is
almost in its natural condition. The mountains rise steeply around
this small basin. The Azusa River flows through the middle of
Kamikochi. Taisho Pond resulted from the natural damming of
this river in 1915 during the last eruption of Mt. Yake. In this
vicinity there are subalpine mixed forests, ponds, and marshy
areas.

Kamikochi is not a town, but a place at the end of the road. It has a bus terminal, a noodle shop, several hotels, *ryokan*, and *minshuku*. It is a starting place for climbing in the alps. It is open only from late April to November. Most accommodations close early in November. The best season in Kamikochi is short, but it is possible to see birds there over a much longer period if you are willing to put up with inconveniences. In May it is still quite cold, with snow on the ground in Kamikochi itself. The first two weeks in June are ideal, with snow still on the mountain peaks, adding to the beauty of the place. The rainy season is from mid-June to mid-July. As soon as that is over, the crowds come.

From dawn to breakfast, look for birds in the forest and along the river near your accommodations. Then set out on a long hike toward Tokusawa Campground. That round trip will take at least four hours. Take your lunch and go farther if you are so inclined. This path goes along the river. It is easy walking and almost level. You will soon leave the crowd behind.

Those who are interested in serious climbing can take tents and camp or stay in mountain huts. Get more information from the TIC. If you wish to climb a little and come back the same day, the mountains on the same side of the river as the road are less steep. You can get to the alpine species quicker and easier by driving up Mt. Norikura and hiking a short distance from the parking lot.

Birds to look for include Horsfield's Hawk-Cuckoo, Oriental Cuckoo, Little Cuckoo, Japanese Wagtail, Ashy Minivet, Winter Wren, Japanese Robin, Siberian Blue Robin, Siberian Bluechat, Siberian Thrush, Gray Thrush, Brown Thrush, Arctic Warbler, Goldcrest, Narcissus Flycatcher, Blue-and-White Flycatcher, Brown Flycatcher, Nuthatch, Brown Creeper, Black-faced Bunting, Bullfinch, and Japanese Grosbeak.

I once visited Kamikochi at the end of October when the summer birds had gone. Dippers were abundant in the river, and there were plenty of tits (Long-tailed, Willow, Coal, Varied, and Great) as well as Japanese Pygmy Woodpeckers and Goldcrests. I saw a Greater Pied Kingfisher, probably resident, a Goshawk, and a Golden Eagle. It is a good time to visit if you can't go in the spring. Migrants and early winter visitors are likely.

Time:
Kamikochi cannot be reached quickly, but it is well worth the time and effort required to get here. Allow yourself enough time to make the trip worthwhile. The more time you can spend, the more species you will see. And it is so pleasant. Allow at least one full day for a long hike up the river and another full day if you intend to do any climbing. On one day, drive to the top of Mt. Norikura and look for the Rock Ptarmigan. If you have your own transportation, there will be time left for further birding at Kamikochi. Or you could visit Mt. Norikura on the way back to Matsumoto.

Food:
There is a basic restaurant on the second floor at the bus terminal. Here you pay when you enter and then fetch your own food, exchanging a plastic disk for your bowl of noodles. The Gosenjaku Ryokan, near the Kappa Bridge, serves Western food at lunchtime to non-residents. The Kamikochi Imperial Hotel has the Alpenrose Restaurant which serves light lunches a la carte. It is expensive. It is probably best to have your meals where you are staying and order a packed lunch to take birding.

Accommodations:
There is a wide range of accommodations in Kamikochi, from the Konashidaira Campground, near the bus terminal, to fine hotels and *ryokan*. As is often the case in lovely, remote places, they are not cheap. If your budget will allow it, however, I strongly recommend the Kamikochi Imperial Hotel (0263-95-2001), a branch of the Imperial Hotel in Tokyo. It is a small hotel, accommodating only 150 guests. It is quiet and lovely, in the best of taste, all Western style, even the food. Although almost all the guests are Japanese, it has an English-speaking staff. The views from the hotel are magnificent. Best of all, you can watch birds from your window. It is in the woods with plenty of birds, away from the other hotels.

Fortunately, the best season for birds is the off-season in Kamikochi, so the prices are lower. A double room at the Imperial Hotel starts from ¥19,000. Guests are not required to eat at the hotel, but a full-course set dinner is ¥5,000. The price for rooms is higher on Saturday nights and nights before national holidays, even in the off-season. This hotel will accept small groups only in the off-season and never on Saturdays.

The prices are about the same as at the better *ryokan* in Kamikochi. This is the one exception to my usual advice to do things the Japanese way. This hotel is the class of Kamikochi and one of the most famous hotels in Japan. Here you will want to wear something other than birding gear for dinner. Dress is casual. A nice sweater and slacks for men and a skirt for women, or at least slacks far more elegant than those worn for birding, would be appropriate.

If you stay in Matsumoto, there are two Tokyu Inns across from the station. Daini Tokyu Inn (0263-36-0109) is newer and is slightly more expensive. A twin room is ¥11,000 before the Hertz discount. This is probably a good place to find a *ryokan* if you prefer that style.

MT. NORIKURA

Season: June - September
Specialties: Rock Ptarmigan, Alpine Accentor, Japanese Accentor,
*   Nutcracker*

From Kamikochi, it is 26 km. and about 45 minutes by car to the entrance to the 14.5-km. Skyline Drive up Mt. Norikura. This toll road is open only from June to October. Nature lovers are not pleased about this road and the scar it left on the mountain or about the great number of tour buses which go up it. Nevertheless, it is there, and it provides the easiest way to see Rock Ptarmigan in Japan. Hike a short distance from the parking lot at the end of the road, and you should be able to find all the specialties except the Nutcracker, which is more likely lower down. This shouldn't take much more than an hour. You should be able to get quite near both accentors. A telescope may be useful for finding the ptarmigans, though they, too, could be close by.

Driving is slow on the Skyline Drive and on the mountain roads leading to it. Allow plenty of time.

It is possible to take a bus from Kamikochi to Mt. Norikura. In the off-season, a change of bus is required. You can go early, stay awhile, and catch another bus to return when you are ready.

TAKAYAMA

Takayama, west of the mountains from Kamikochi, is a town of considerable interest to tourists. It can be reached in 1 hour, 30 minutes by car from Kamikochi. Don't leave Kamikochi to go there to look for birds. But if you are going anyway, there is a good birding spot.

Shiroyama Park, a small forest-covered "mountain" in the center of town, is worth a visit. It is easy to find because you can see the hill from anywhere in town. It is also marked on the map in the JNTO Information Sheet MG-044. You can get a good map (in Japanese) at the tourist office in front of Takayama Station.

Go up the hill from the playground, and you will find many trails through the forest. Look at the edge of the forest near the Miyagawa River, which runs through the town, for breeding Mandarin Ducks. Early in the spring they use nest boxes which have been put up in the park.

Birds you might see in the proper season include Japanese Green Woodpecker, Varied Tit, Siskin, Gray Thrush, Pale Thrush, Narcissus Flycatcher, Blue-and-White Flycatcher, Long-tailed Rose Finch, Rosy Finch, Brambling, Yellow-throated Bunting, Rustic Bunting, Japanese Grosbeak, and Bullfinch.

MT. TATEYAMA

This is a place to go for the Rock Ptarmigan and other alpine specialties if you have plenty of time and a desire for greater adventure than is offered by driving up Mt. Norikura to see these birds. I've not yet had the opportunity to visit Mt. Tateyama, but from all reports it is a good place. Again, try to avoid it on weekends and holidays.

Mt. Tateyama can be approached from Toyama, near the Japan Sea coast, and from Matsumoto, the most likely direction for a visitor to Japan. From Matsumoto, take Hwy. 147 to Omachi and then the Omachi Toll Road. From the end of that road you must continue by cable car to reach Murodo Plateau (2,440 meters). Tateyama Hotel (0764-65-3333) is at the top. This is a good place from which to set out to find the ptarmigan and other birds. The Champion Maps, pages 24, 31, and 32, will help.

If you wish, you can take a bus to Midagahara (35 minutes) and
Bijodaira (one hour from Murodo) for further birdwatching.
Midagahara (1,900 meters) is a plateau with an abundance of
wildflowers from the middle of July. At Bijodaira, the Bijodaira
Hotel (0764-82-1718) is convenient for birdwatching.

From Toyama, take the Dentetsu Toyama train to Tateyama (one
hour). From there it is ten minutes by cable car to Bijodaira. Then
there is the same bus service from there to Murodo.

Maps and Information:
Champion Maps, Vol. 2, Eastern Japan

National Maps: 1:50,000 Kamikochi   上高地

Tateyama   立山

Gohyakukoku 五百石

JNTO Information Sheets MG-042 and MG-044

Useful Kanji:

Matsumoto	松本
Kamikochi	上高地
Mt. Norikura	乗鞍岳
Nakanoyu Onsen	中ノ湯温泉
Takayama	高山
Shiroyama Park	白山公園
Tateyama	立山
Omachi	大町
Murodo Plateau	室堂
Midagahara	弥陀が原
Bijodaira	美女平

KATANOKAMO-IKE

Season: winter
Specialties: *Bean Goose, Baikal Teal, Falcated Teal*

Katanokamo-ike, which became a sanctuary in 1984, has long been an important wintering place for geese and ducks. (See also Lake Izunuma.) Just at the coast on the Sea of Japan, it is far away from the usual routes which most foreign visitors take through Japan. It is near Kanazawa, a city worth your attention. For birders visiting this part of Japan, Katanokamo-ike should not be missed.

Transportation:
It takes one hour by train, plus ten minutes by taxi from Kanazawa. Using the Hokuriku Expressway, it takes about one hour from Kanazawa by car. Komatsu Airport, serving this area, is about halfway between Kanazawa and Katanokamo-ike. ANA has flights to Komatsu from Tokyo (one hour), Sapporo (1 hour, 35 minutes), and Fukuoka (1 hour, 15 minutes). Rental cars are available at the airport. A car is not essential, but it will permit you to explore farther afield and also to visit Eiheiji Temple. Eiheiji is about 30 minutes in the other direction and is a must for anyone in the area. (Eiheiji Temple is near the Fukui Kita Interchange #25 on the Hokuriku Expressway.)

Directions:
By train, take the JNR Hokuriku Line from Kanazawa to Daishoji. Only the local train stops at Daishoji. At the station, get a taxi for Katanokamo-ike. You can easily walk from the sanctuary to the seacoast for birdwatching. More exploration will depend on your energy and the severity of the weather. If someone is at the sanctuary, perhaps you can ask them to call a taxi to take you back to the station.

By car, get off the Hokuriku Expressway at the Kaga Interchange (#23). After the toll booth, turn right and go a short distance until you reach Hwy. 8. Turn left and go about 1.1 km. to the first signal. There is a Caltex station at that corner. The road doesn't look promising, but turn left at the signal. You will soon come up behind the Sunroute Hotel (the sign is not in English, but the building is noticeable). Make your way around to the front, and you will be at Daishoji Station.

With your back to the station, go straight ahead (0.4 km.) to the second signal and turn left. Go about 0.5 km., through one signal. Turn right just before the second signal. Don't cross the bridge over the small gulley. Now go 0.5 km. and turn left past the school, crossing over the last bridge over the gulley. (This doesn't count the small red bridge leading to the shrine.) After you have turned left, the schoolyard will be on your left. Beyond the school take the road to the right.

Katanokamo-ike

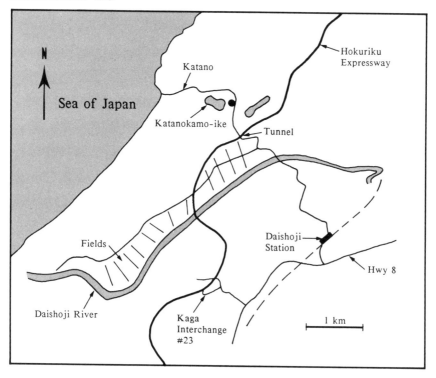

About 0.3 km. from the bridge by the school you should make a right turn over another small bridge. Just after this bridge (0.1 km.) turn left on the narrow road going between houses. Follow this road, cross a bigger river on a bigger bridge, and go straight on the main road. Soon you will be able to see a tunnel going through a hill far to your right. You will come to a road to the right which will take you to that tunnel. At the road where you should turn right there has been, at least, a sign with green on it and another sign shaped like an arrow with red on it. From this

turn go 1.1 km. to Katanokamo-ike, on the far side of the hill through the tunnel. The pond will be on your left.

Site and Birds:

Katanokamo-ike (Katano = name of the village between the sanctuary and the ocean, kamo = duck, ike = pond) is a good-sized pond which you can see only from the nature center. From all other points, the view of the pond is blocked by fences or trees. A telescope is essential. As usual, the rare species can be depended upon to be at the far end. There is a telescope in the nature center, but yours will probably be superior. If you walk down to the ocean, you will be tempted to try to make your way through the woods to the back side of the pond. Don't do it. That is absolutely off limits.

This is a sure place to see Bean Geese and an almost sure place to see Baikal Teal and Falcated Teal, though in small numbers. White-fronted Geese are here every winter. There is a chance of seeing a Lesser White-fronted Goose. You can never be sure of seeing this bird anywhere in Japan, but always check flocks of White-fronted Geese. The official checklist of Katanokamo-ike has it recorded only in December and January. The common ducks are all here. Spot-billed Duck is a resident. Expect to see Mallard, Green-winged Teal, Gadwall, Wigeon, Pintail, Shoveler, Pochard, and Tufted Duck. Garganey is a transient in the fall from September through November. The geese and ducks sometimes go off to feed, but usually are back at the pond by 10:00 a.m. White-tailed Eagle can be seen occasionally, and Steller's Sea-Eagle has occurred. Goshawk, Sparrow Hawk, and Common Buzzard are here in winter. Gray Heron is a resident.

Across the road from the nature center is another pond which serves as a reservoir. Sometimes ducks are on that pond as well. After checking these two ponds, walk on beyond the nature center and follow the road to the left to the ocean. This will take you past fields and eventually through the little village of Katano. In the village, take the road to the left. Look for thrushes and buntings along here. Both pheasants are resident. From the nature center, it is less than 2 km. to the ocean.

At the ocean you may see grebes, Eastern Reef Heron, sea ducks, Mew Gull, Ancient Murrelet, and Blue Rockthrush. To the right at the seashore is a small pine forest. Check this for birds. In winter there is at least a chance of finding Common Redpoll, Red Crossbill, and Chinese Grosbeak.

If you have a car, from the nature center go back to the turn from the main road (where the arrow-shaped sign was) and go to your right, again toward the ocean. Don't cross the Daishoji River, but continue toward the ocean. Geese are often in the fields along here.

Time:
Two or three hours should be ample if you are in a car.

Food:
There is no food or drink available after you leave Daishoji. There are some restaurants in the town. If you can manage, it is more convenient to bring your lunch.

Accommodations:
You may want to spend the night in Kanazawa or at one of the *onsen* in the other direction from Daishoji. In Daishoji, the Tokugetsu-so Ryokan (07617-2-1138) is associated with the WBSJ and gives a discount to members. Others are Katano-so Ryokan (07617-3-2500) and Hashimoto Ryokan (07617-2-0606), which is in front of Daishoji Station.

Maps and Information:
Champion Maps, Vol. 3, Western Japan
Buyodo Map D-3

National Map: 1:25,000 Daishoji 大聖寺

Useful Kanji:
Katanokamo-ike   片野鴨池
Daishoji   大聖寺
Kaga Interchange   加賀インターチェンジ
Hokuriku Expressway   北陸自動車道
Sunroute Hotel   サンルートホテル

KAHOKUGATA

Season: winter, all year
Specialties: Whistling Swan, Baikal Teal, Smew, White-tailed Eagle

Kahokugata is a lagoon with a large area of reclaimed land. I have not visited this area, but it is reputed to be excellent in winter and a good place to find birds throughout the year. It is near Kanazawa, a city with much of interest for a visitor who wants to see more of the traditional culture of Japan. Kanazawa is one of those special places not yet overrun with tourists. A birdwatcher visiting Kanazawa should take the time to go to Kahokugata.

Transportation:
From Kanazawa, it takes 20 minutes by train, plus ten minutes by taxi to reach Kahokugata. By car, it probably takes about the same amount of time, depending on the traffic.

Directions:
From Kanazawa Station, take either the Nanao Line or the Hokuriku Line to Tsubata Station. There, get a taxi to take you to Konanohashi Bridge, a good starting place for a walk through Kahokugata.

By car, from the Kanazawa Higashi Interchange on the Hokuriku Expressway go north on Hwy. 8 and then take Hwy. 159 where it branches off to the left. From Hwy. 159 you should be able to find a road to the left which will take you to Konanohashi Bridge. The location of Kahokugata should be clear on your highway map. Then use the accompanying map to find your way around to look for birds.

Site and Birds:
From what I have heard, this is a large area, possibly a far walk in severe weather in winter, but with many places to find good birds. The best birding is in winter, when you can expect to see Whistling Swan and several kinds of ducks. White-tailed Eagle is regularly here, but I don't know to what degree you can count on seeing it. Other birds which could be here include Rough-legged Buzzard, Common Buzzard, Northern Harrier, Marsh Harrier, Peregrine Falcon, Hobby, Merlin, Kestrel, and Short-eared Owl. Sometimes Jackdaw and Rook occur. And there is a chance you could see a Bittern if you are lucky.

Kahokugata

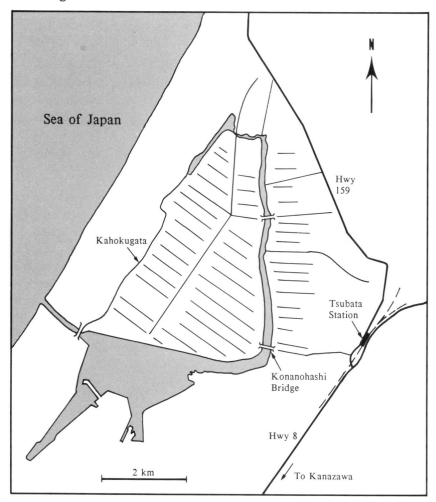

There are shorebirds in spring and fall, including Rufous-necked Stint, Sharp-tailed Sandpiper, and Ruff. Garganey is a fall migrant. In summer you can expect to see Chinese Little Bittern, Marsh Harrier, Gray-headed Lapwing, Common Cuckoo, Black-browed Reed Warbler, Great Reed Warbler, and Fan-tailed Warbler.

Time:
I cannot give you a good estimate of the time required here. You should find enough good habitat to keep you occupied for some time. If your time is limited, start on the east side where the birding is said to be best.

Food:
Bring food and drink with you.

Accommodations:
Stay in Kanazawa. This is a good place to try an elegant *ryokan* if your budget allows. Ruth Steven's book discusses several, as well as many other places which are less expensive. I had a once-in-a-lifetime experience staying at Kincharyo Ryokan. The prices are higher than those given in the guidebook and are the reason why most of us can't be regular visitors. It was nothing short of perfection, and I am grateful I could do it. The judgment of whether it is worth it must be an individual one. I would suggest saving this kind of experience until you have tried all other types of Japanese accommodations and have familiarized yourself as best you can with Japanese style and tradition. Otherwise you may not appreciate some of the beauties and subtleties of your surroundings and the service.

Maps and Information:
   Champion Maps, Vol. 3, Western Japan
   Buyodo Map D-3

   National Maps: 1:50,000 Kanazawa 金沢

                        Tsubata   津幡

   Stevens, Ruth P. *Kanazawa: The Other Side of Japan.*
      Kanazawa: The Society to Introduce Kanazawa to the
         World, 1979.
   JNTO Information Sheet MG-043

Useful Kanji:

Kahokugata	河北潟
Tsubata	津幡
Konanohashi Bridge	湖南大橋

HEGURA-JIMA

Season: late April to mid-May, late September to mid-October
Specialties: rare migrants

Hegura-jima is an island in the Sea of Japan off the Noto Peninsula. At most, it is about 1.5 km. long and 0.5 km. wide. This is a place for only the hardiest of the hard-core birders. It is difficult to get to, accommodations are meager, you could be stranded for days because of rough seas, and it could get boring. You could see anything here, or nothing. But the birds that are recorded during migration make it worth the risk to many birders. Hegura-jima is to Japan what Attu is to North America.

Transportation:
The daily boat from Wajima to Hegura-jima takes 1 hour, 15 minutes. Wajima is 2 hours, 30 minutes from Kanazawa by train or approximately two hours by car. You are on foot on the island.

Directions:
The ship to Hegura-jima leaves Wajima port at 8:30 a.m. and leaves Hegura-jima for the return trip at 2:30 p.m. (This schedule is likely to change.) It is not a ferry, but it is, nevertheless, a good-sized ship with two decks of enclosed seating. The sea in this area can be extremely rough, and the weather creates havoc with this run, especially in the fall. If the boat cannot leave Wajima on time, the day's trip is cancelled. It is best to check with both the weather bureau and the ship office, telephone 0768-22-4381.

To get to Wajima from Kanazawa, take the JNR Nanao Line. Kanazawa is on a major railroad line, but getting there from Tokyo is rather complicated and time-consuming. There are several routes you can choose. It is best to get professional help in determining which is most convenient for you. At the time of this writing, there is an overnight train with sleeping cars which goes all the way from Kanazawa to Ueno Station in Tokyo, but no similar train in the other direction.

The nearest airport to Kanazawa is Komatsu. There is an airport on the other side of Kanazawa at Toyama, not much farther away. You could fly to whichever one had the most convenient schedule and then either go to Kanazawa to get the train or rent a car and drive straight to Wajima. Toyama can be reached by air only from Tokyo. Flights to Komatsu come from Tokyo, Sapporo, and Fukuoka. Both of these airports are presently served only by ANA.

Wajima is a small town. It is a short taxi ride from the station to the port. On Hegura-jima you are on your own. Ask directions to your *minshuku*. You will soon know your way around the island.

If you get stranded in Wajima, the morning market is a special one, worth some of your time. Wajima is also where the finest Japanese lacquerware is made.

Site and Birds:
To begin with the boat, which is an important factor in considering a trip to Hegura-jima, don't expect to see any particularly interesting seabirds on the voyage. The usual possibilities are Streaked Shearwater, Temminck's and Pelagic Cormorants, Northern Phalarope, and Black-tailed Gull.

The boat is modern and fast. The morning I boarded it, instead of the typical loud announcements and commercial messages coming from the loudspeaker and the game shows on the TV at the front of the cabin, we were treated to lovely, sedate strains of Mozart. As the boat left the harbor I began to suspect this was not an accident, but was intended to soothe the nerves of the passengers. Although the sky was clear, the waves were enormous, and the majority of the passengers were seasick. So far I've never been seasick, but I found this trip far from pleasant. I had to hang on the whole way to keep from being thrown out of my seat. The return trip was much better and caused no undue discomfort for my more susceptible companions. Be prepared for the worst on this trip. I strongly recommend seasick medicine and any other precautions you find effective.

Hegura-jima is flat, with sandy beaches, rocky areas, some ponds, grassy places, and some small woods. At least 274 species have been recorded. The list would make you want to head straight to Hegura-jima and forget about the rest of the country. But you can't depend on anything actually being here. And some of these rarities have occurred only a few times. Your chances of seeing many rare species depend on pure luck and the amount of time you can stay and wait to see what turns up.

It should be easy to find the birds and get close enough for good looks. There aren't any impenetrable areas where the birds can hide, and the island is so small you can get to any point quickly. During the migration, Japanese birders will probably be around and will share news of any important finds.

Hegura-jima and Tsushima are both excellent places during spring migration, but Hegura-jima is said to be far better than Tsushima during the fall migration. The problem to bear in mind is that the sea is rougher in the fall. Consequently there are more cancellations of the boat service.

I visited this island once in mid-October and stayed only four hours, due to problems with the boat. I spent 24 hours in Wajima because the boat did not make the trip the day I intended to go. Once I got to Hegura-jima, I didn't have the courage to stay, because of the weather forecast. It turned out to be a wise decision rather than a cowardly one because the next boat came five days later. My day was considered a dead day, but the birds included Scops Owl, Red-throated Pipit, Northern Shrike, Japanese Waxwing, 30 Daurian Redstarts, Pale Thrush, six Goldcrests, Pine Bunting, ten Yellow-throated Buntings, 25 Siskins, and eight Common Redpolls.

According to a report covering the records for a three-year period, Black-capped Kingfisher, Ruddy Kingfisher, Forest Wagtail, Thick-billed Shrike, and Tri-colored Flycatcher occurred only in the spring; Red-breasted Flycatcher and Pine Bunting occurred only in the fall. This probably isn't absolute, but it does indicate when you have the best chance of seeing these birds.

Time:
The Japanese, because of their inability to get time off from work, think nothing of going to Hegura-jima for the four hours between the time the boat arrives in the morning and leaves in the afternoon. You can circle the island two or three times in that period. I did this myself, though unintentionally. Unless I lived in Wajima, I would never under any circumstances consider doing it again. Getting there requires the investment of too much time and money for so little birding.

It is a great place for two or three compatible birding enthusiasts who are not upset by spartan conditions and who understand that seeing rare birds depends entirely on the weather and fate. Don't forget to bring something to read and a deck of cards. And most important, you must be prepared to stay a few days longer than you intend if the sea is too rough for the boat to come.

Food:
You can eat at your *minshuku*. My Japanese friends warned me that I would not be happy with the food available so I should bring extra snacks. Since we took a packed lunch from Wajima, I didn't have a chance to try the local food. It is difficult to tell how the food is without sampling it because Japanese always expect foreigners to dislike Japanese food. For your information, I noticed that my Japanese friends all brought food with them. I did not see a restaurant or a grocery store during my brief stay. The locals obviously get food somewhere, but I recommend eating what is provided at your *minshuku* and bringing anything you might want to supplement that. With something that would do for lunch, you could avoid having to go indoors to eat.

Accommodations:
There are two *minshuku*. Hakutoen (0768-22-2178) gives a 10% discount to WBSJ members. The other one, Tsukasa (0768-22-4961), is near the port. During the peak of migration, especially on weekends, these places can be crowded. If there is the demand, they keep adding people until all the floor space is taken. You will have privacy only if you are there when few others are.

I went inside one of these *minshuku*, which I believe to be Hakutoen. It looked perfectly acceptable. Birders who are accustomed to this type of birdwatching will not find the accommodations an undue hardship.

One university birdwatching club was camping on the island when I was there. I don't know what the rules are concerning this, if there are any, but I think bringing camping equipment all the way to Japan for the rare instances when you can use it is not worth the effort.

This island is not suitable for a tour group because of the facilities, the size of the island, and the uncertainties related to getting there and back again. I understand that the locals are not enamored by the numbers of Japanese birdwatchers who come, so more than a small handful of foreigners might not be received

with favor. Tour groups seeking this kind of birding should visit
Tsushima in the spring.

Useful Kanji:
  Wajima   輪島
  Hegura-jima   舳倉島
  Hakutoen   白塔園
  Tsukasa   つかさ

MIKATAGOKO

Season: winter
Specialties: White-tailed Eagle, ducks

The scenery around Mikatagoko (Mikata Five Lakes) is lovely, and there are good birds in winter, including an occasional rarity. For a short-time visitor to Japan it isn't worth making a special trip solely for Mikatagoko. If you are driving between Kanazawa and Kyoto or between Kanazawa and Matsue, you should definitely see this place. It is near enough to Eiheiji Temple to be added to that itinerary, but it is not one of Japan's musts at any cost.

Transportation:
It takes at least 2 hours, 10 minutes by train from Fukui. It is much more convenient by car on the Hokuriku Expressway. Even in winter with a lot of snow, the trip takes about an hour and a half. Birding here will be much more pleasant with a car.

Directions:
By train from Fukui, take the Hokuriku Line to Tsuruga (1 hour, 40 minutes). Change to the Obama Line and go to Kiyama (30 minutes).

By car from Fukui or Kyoto, take the Hokuriku Expressway and get off at the Tsuruga Interchange. Make your way to Hwy. 27 and go south to Kiyama (between Mihama and Mikata).

If you are coming from Matsue or Miyazu, take Hwy. 27 to Kiyama. Hwy. 162 goes along the coast between Obama and Mikata. It is a beautiful area, but dangerous in winter. The road is narrow, often with no barriers, and in winter there is a great deal of snow. When I tried to drive from Obama the first week in March, the road was closed about halfway to Mikata.

With the help of a good map, follow the roads around the lakes. The Rainbow Line, a toll road (blue on the Buyodo map), was closed because of snow in early March. Follow as many of the roads as are open. The roads on the sides of the lakes nearest the main highway are most likely to be open in winter. This area normally has heavy snow.

Mikatagoko

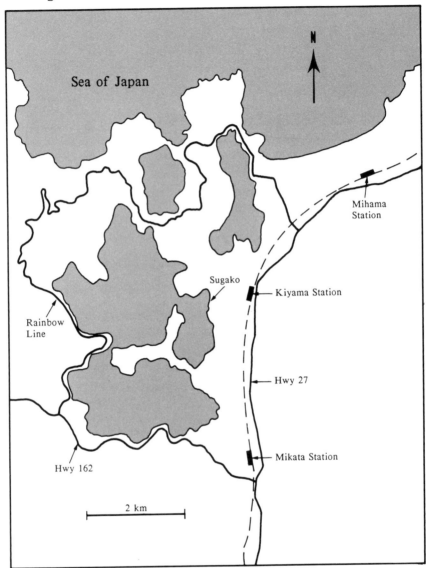

Site and Birds:
Off the main roads there are unspoiled villages. You will see many
kura (old storehouses) and buildings with thatched roofs. Steep,
wooded hills surround the lakes, which, in March, were partially
frozen. It is a fine area to visit to enjoy traditional Japanese

architecture. I can imagine that in early spring after the snow is gone and before the summer tourists arrive, it is a delightful place. I have no information, however, about birding in that season. This seems to be almost exclusively a winter place as far as Japanese birders are concerned.

The small lake (Sugako) directly west of Kiyama Station is good for ducks. The one to the northeast of it should have ducks in the southeast corner. And there are rice fields south of that lake where you should find shorebirds during migration.

You will most likely see Little Grebe, Eared Grebe, Great Crested Grebe, Gray Heron, White-fronted Goose, Mandarin. Duck, Mallard, Spot-billed Duck, Green-winged Teal, Wigeon, Pochard, Tufted Duck, and Smew. White-tailed Eagle winters here, and sometimes, too, Steller's Sea-Eagle and Golden Eagle. Look also for thrushes and buntings. This place became famous when Red-crested Pochard occurred, but this bird is accidental in Japan.

Time:
It would be easy to spend a day here if conditions were right. You can, just as well, drive around and see a great deal in two or three hours.

Food:
There are some restaurants along Hwy. 27 between Mikata and Mihama. In winter you will probably welcome getting in out of the cold for lunch, but it would be pleasant to have lunch in your car while you watch the ducks on a lake.

Accommodations:
Hirose Ryokan (07703-2-1123) was the best-looking place I saw that was open in the winter. Many *ryokan* were closed. At ¥15,000 per person, I did not think it was good value for money. The food was ordinary at best, the room was the same, the large *ofuro* was not functioning though there was a tiny bath in the room, and it is the only place I've seen in Japan at that price where the TV was coin-operated. This isn't important to a foreigner who doesn't understand Japanese, but it does indicate to me that something is out of line. I felt it cost considerably more than it was worth, and it lists even higher prices during the season.

Another *ryokan* which I did not see is Nishikinami Ryokan (07703-2-1123). Its prices are listed at ¥13,000 - ¥15,000 per person.

Kogetsuso (07704-5-0241) is a *minshuku* in Mikata which is associated with the WBSJ, so gives discounts to members. There should be other places to stay which are open in winter. Inquire locally.

Maps and Information:
Champion Maps, Vol. 3, Western Japan
Buyodo Map D-3

National Map: 1:50,000 Nishizu 西津

Useful Kanji:
Mikatagoko	三方五湖
Kiyama	気山
Mikata	三方
Mihama	美浜
Tsuruga	敦賀

Note:
If you are driving between Mikatagoko and Matsue, you will pass Miyazu Bay and the famous scenic site, Amanohashidate. I don't think this is worth a special trip. If you are going by anyway in winter, take a walk down the long narrow spit of land to check ducks on each side and see what else is around.

NABETA YATOMI AND THE KISO RIVER

Season: winter
Specialties: Baikal Teal, birds of prey, shorebirds, Gray-headed Lapwing

Birders who live in Nagoya and visitors who must spend some time there will find birding excellent in the Nabeta area. It is not worth a special trip to Nagoya by visitors to Japan unless a wintering rare bird should make it so. This is land reclaimed from the bay. Nabeta Yatomi is a bird park with an observatory overlooking a lake. The rice fields to the west and north are often better than the park itself.

Transportation:
The bus from Nagoya to Nabeta takes 50 minutes. From the park, you will probably walk about 4 or 5 km. while checking the neighboring fields.

With a car, you will be warmer in winter and can visit the surrounding area with ease. It will also enable you to go to two areas on the Kiso River, not too far away, and have a full day of birding. The problem is in finding the way through Nagoya. The drive should take about an hour.

It takes two hours to get to Nagoya from Tokyo by Shinkansen.

Directions:
At the Metetsu Bus Terminal in Nagoya, take the Miekotsu bus for Nabeta Yatomi Bird Park. There are only three a day, so check the schedule carefully (telephone 0592-27-3131).

To drive, it is essential to start with a good map and clear instructions. I made the trip with Japanese birders and was not driving. They had a detailed map and, unlike me, could read it and all the signs on the road. They got lost several times between Nagoya Station and Nabeta. I can't be sure from that experience how difficult it really is to find the way. The city is crowded and congested, but on my map the route looks straightforward. My map, however, shows no number at all for the first highway you must take.

Go south from the station about 7 km. to meet Hwy. 23. Go right

(west) on Hwy. 23 roughly 11 or 12 km. and turn left (south) to
Nabeta. Use the accompanying map to find where you want to go
on your map. If you should be coming through this area on the
Tomei Expressway, get off at Yatomi Interchange. From there you
are on your own.

Nabeta Yatomi & the Kiso River Area

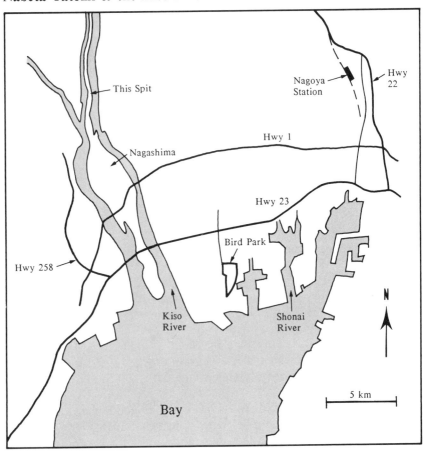

Site and Birds:
The park itself attracts a lot of visitors on weekends. It has a large
parking area, a play area, and a two-story observation center from
which you can view the birds on the lake. Stop here first to find
out what birds are in the area. The telephone number at the bird
park is 05676-8-2338.

The neighboring area is flat, mostly cultivated fields. There are roads crisscrossing it, making birding easy. If you have a car, check the Shonai River, to the east, for ducks and shorebirds.

Assorted ducks, such as Wigeon, Pochard, and Tufted, winter on the lake. Occasionally a more interesting one will be there too. Garganey passes through on migration. This is also a good area for migrant shorebirds. Indian Pratincole comes through in spring and fall.

The whole area is good for birds of prey in winter. Short-eared Owls are reasonably easy to see. Gray-headed Lapwing and Lapwing are in the fields. Look also for thrushes and assorted buntings.

Nabeta Yatomi

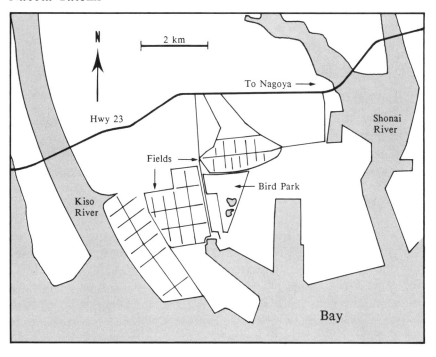

The Nabeta area occasionally attracts rare species in winter. A Chinese Great Gray Shrike spent the winter here in 1984. It is worth inquiring about unusual birds. Have someone telephone for you in Japanese.

Chinese Little Bittern and Great Reed Warbler are here in summer. The brochure from the bird park lists Painted Snipe as a resident. This is not considered by most to be a sure thing, but maybe the people at Nabeta know better.

Time:
This will depend on whether you are on foot or in a car. By car, you should be able to see a great deal in two hours. On foot it is a good idea to allow at least a half day, probably more.

Food:
Bring it. There may be drinks for sale at the bird park.

Accommodations:
You will probably want to spend the night in Nagoya.

Maps and Information:
    Champion Maps, Vol. 3, Western Japan
    Buyodo Map D-3

    National Map: 1:50,000 Nagoya Nanbu 名古屋南部

Useful Kanji:
    Nabeta Yatomi Bird Park   鍋田弥富野鳥園
    Metetsu Bus Terminal   名鉄バスターミナル
    Miekotsu Bus   三重交通バス
    Yatomi Interchange   弥富インターチエンジ

KISO RIVER

If you go to Nabeta by car, you may want to find the Kiso River and look for Baikal Teal. They do not come here every winter, but they come in great numbers when they do. The area is good for other birds too, so it should be worth taking a look.

I have not been here. Once you get to Nabeta, one place on the Kiso River looks easy to find. The way to the other place is clear on the Buyodo Map D-3, but the ease in getting there will depend on how well the highways are marked.

From Nabeta, find roads which will take you to the western edge of the reclaimed land. At the southwest end you will be at the bay, but drive on toward the north up the western edge of this area, and you will soon be overlooking the Kiso River. This is supposed to be a good area for ducks, and Baikal Teal could be here.

There are three rivers which come together near the bay. The Kiso River is the easternmost. The next good area is several kilometers to the north. Getting there may be a bit tricky. If you came on the Tomei Expressway, got off at Yatomi Interchange, and can find your way back, the place you want to be is near the next interchange to the west of Yatomi. This is the Nagashima Interchange. Nagashima is the island in the middle of these rivers. The name is written in Roman letters on the D-3 map.

You want to start looking for birds just north of the Nagashima Interchange. Take the road (or path) up the narrow spit of land between the Kiso River and the one next to it (to the west). Apparently it is possible to travel along this spit for about 6 km. If the Baikal Teal are really around, you will find them in one of these two areas.

From the map, it looks as if you could work your way up the western edge of the reclaimed land near Nabeta to Hwy. 23. Then go west on Hwy. 23 across the rivers and turn right onto Hwy. 258. Go only as far as the next major intersection and turn right on Hwy. 1. You can turn left on a small road after you have reached Nagashima and make your way north to this spit of land.

Maps and Information:
  National Maps: 1:50,000 Kuwana 桑名
                           Tsushima 津島

Useful Kanji:
  Kiso River 木曽川
  Nagashima 長島

ATSUMI PENINSULA

Season: late September - early October, shorebird migration
Specialties: hawk migration, shorebirds

Cape Irago, at the tip of the Atsumi Peninsula, is a prime location for hawk watching during the fall migration. The Shiokawa tidal flat is on the way and is an excellent place for shorebirds and other migrants during the same season. It is good for shorebirds in the spring, too, but it may not be worth going so far for only one purpose. It depends on where you start from.

Atsumi Peninsula

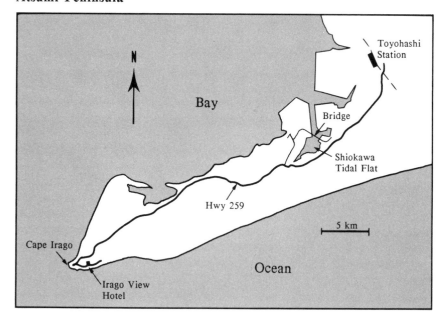

Transportation:
The total time from Tokyo to Cape Irago is about four hours. It takes 2 hours, 23 minutes by Shinkansen to Toyohashi and 1 hour, 30 minutes by rental car from there to the cape. The trip from Toyohashi can also be made by bus.

Directions:
Take the Shinkansen from Tokyo Station to Toyohashi. Be sure to take a Kodama train, since the Hikari does not stop at Toyohashi. You will arrive at Toyohashi on track #13. Go out the east exit,

which is in the direction of the lower numbered tracks. When you come out of the station, you will find the Eki Rent-a-Car office to your right and the Nippon Rent-a-Car office to your left across the side street.

Take Hwy. 259 all the way to Cape Irago. You want to get on the main street which runs into the station (it has streetcar tracks on it). From the corner near the front of the station and directly in front of the Seibu Department Store, go away from the station approximately 0.3 km. and turn right at a large intersection. The main post office is on that corner on the right, but the sign is difficult to see. The large microwave tower on a building on the left of that intersection is another clue. Also, you may notice that the streetcar tracks turn left where you should turn right. Now, you are on Hwy. 259. This highway is relatively well marked. Although it twists and turns, you should have no trouble if you pay close attention.

If you are going by bus, catch it outside the station at bus stop #4. Get off at Toshima and walk 15 minutes to Shiokawa. For Cape Irago, get back on the same bus and go to the Iragomisaki bus stop, which is the end of the line.

SHIOKAWA

To get to the first area, look for the Coffee Brake Shop, a restaurant in the shape of a windmill, on the left of the highway about 13.4 km. from Toyohashi Station. From there, continue another 0.6 km. and turn right onto a small, hard-surfaced road which is immediately past a bridge over a small stream. All this is difficult to see (road, bridge, and stream), so pay close attention. At this turn, a traditional building with a tile roof is on the left of the highway. Home Center Sawa is a little way beyond the turn on the right of the highway. Just beyond the turnoff, a blue sign with a lot of *kanji* and "Tahara T" is over the highway. You may get past the turn before you see it and notice all the landmarks, but it is easy to turn back. Drive down this small road about 0.5 km. and straight onto the seawall.

For the second area, go back to Hwy. 259 and continue for another 1.5 km. Just before a Caltex sign on the right, you can see a small, unpaved road angling off to the right. It has a sign indicating no entry. A few meters past there, you can turn right onto a paved road. Go down it for 0.7 km. to the second crossroad (the first one which is paved). Turn right and go 0.3 km. to an embankment. When you get up the embankment, there is a wide area where, if you are careful, you can park your car so that it is out of the way. From here to the right, the road is overgrown with weeds. There is no need to attempt to drive on it. The concrete top of the seawall is to the left. A sign in Japanese says not to go there, but it is ok to walk. At the bend in the seawall, 100 meters or so away, you will be looking over a good sandbar.

Shiokawa

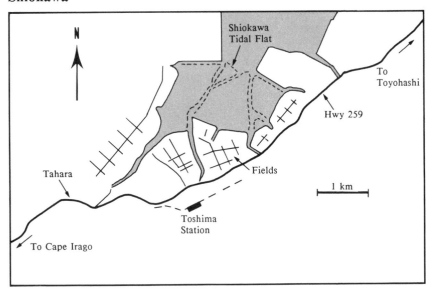

Site and Birds:

Probably the best time to see the shorebirds is a couple of hours after high tide, as the flats are becoming exposed. Close to high tide, there is little place for the shorebirds to stand. You will see all the usual migrants. This is a good place for Spotted Redshank, Greenshank, Green Sandpiper, and Wood Sandpiper. Spoon-billed Sandpiper is recorded here almost every year.

There are open fields between the seawall and the highway and many roads going through them. This is an excellent area which should be checked thoroughly. Many migrants stop here. You will have a reasonably good chance of seeing flocks of Indian Pratincoles during migration. Lately they have also been breeding here. Large numbers of Gray-headed Lapwings are usually about. You could see anything. In 1981, a Dotterel spent several days in a cabbage patch.

If you have time after you have carefully covered the tidal flats and the reclaimed land, you may want to explore other areas. The large bridge that you will be looking at from here was built recently. That brought about many changes in the topography of the area. You can get on the other side of the river, look along those seawalls, and continue out to the point near the bridge. Once this area was good for migrating Gray-spotted Flycatchers, but there isn't good information on the birds here since the construction of the bridge.

Time:
Look for the tide schedule for Nagoya in the *Japan Times* and plan your arrival at Shiokawa according to that. If there are birds on the mudflats and a lot to look at in the reclaimed land, you would be happy here at least half a day. Usually, the length of stay is determined by when you must get to Cape Irago.

Food:
There are some restaurants on the highway nearby, and a town is not more than 2 km. ahead. You could bring a box lunch from Toyohashi Station, get a cold drink from a vending machine along the highway near the turnoff, and eat while birding.

CAPE IRAGO

Get back on the highway and go 31 km. to Cape Irago (Iragomisaki). This will take about 55 minutes. Near the end of the road, there is a turn to the right which leads to the ferry. Ignore this area for now, and stay on the highway as it curves to the left. At the next intersection, you can turn right and go to the parking lot at the end of the road, or you can turn left and go 1.3 km. to the road leading uphill to the Irago View Hotel.

Site and Birds:
This is a lovely cape, wooded and hilly, with a beach. The purpose for going here is to see the hawk migration, so find a good vantage point. There are two main areas from which you can view this phenomenon. You can choose the parking lot near the end of the cape or the parking lot at the Irago View Hotel, about

1.5 km. away, on the top of a hill.

The hawks are supposed to pass in the greatest numbers between dawn and 10:00 a.m. When I arrived in the late afternoon, there were still many hawks coming by; when I left at noon the following day, they were still passing at the same rate they had been all morning. The hawks usually fly along a route which passes over or near both these parking lots. If you see that more are nearer the area where you aren't, you can move.

October 8-10 is considered the peak time for the hawk migration. Even on October 1 and 2, when I went, there were plenty of hawks and plenty of birdwatchers, too. Gray-faced Buzzard-Eagles and Honey Buzzards are by far the most numerous, passing in large flocks. It is also possible to see Osprey, Goshawk, Japanese Lesser Sparrow Hawk, Sparrow Hawk, Common Buzzard, Peregrine Falcon, Hobby, and Kestrel. Hodgson's Hawk-Eagle and Merlin are rare.

Don't forget to look for land birds. In the early morning or late afternoon, preferably after most of the tourists have gone, walk from the lower parking lot to the end of the cape, either on the path or in the woods if you want to scramble up the hill. You can't miss the flocks of migrating Brown-eared Bulbuls. It should be easy to find Gray-spotted Flycatchers only a little way beyond the parking lot. There is nothing else you can be sure of, but it is possible to have some pleasant surprises. Look in the trees for perched hawks. A good place to look for seabirds is on the other side of the hill at the end of the cape.

The hawk migration also coincides with the migration of the migrant skipper butterfly *Parnara guttata*. Butterfly-watchers will be mixed in with the birdwatchers at the cape.

Time:
One night at Cape Irago is enough, but you will have a chance to see some more species if you stay two. I arrived in the late afternoon and watched the hawks until dark. The next morning, I was up birding at first light and then left the area by noon. I wanted time to check the birds at Shiokawa again on my way back to Toyohashi to get the train. I thought it was ample time, though I would have enjoyed an extra day. You should spend at least one night in order to see the birds in early morning. It doesn't take

long to check the small woods at the end of the cape, so most of the time you will be staring into the sky, waiting to see what will fly over.

Food:
Stands selling local melons and snacks and some places to buy a hot meal (all Japanese food) are at the lower parking lot.

Accomodations:
Since this is a popular tourist area, there are many places to stay. For birdwatchers, I recommend either one of the *minshuku* next to the lower parking lot or the Irago View Hotel. In this season, Izutsuya Minshuku (05313-5-6178) and Takonoya Minshuku (05313-5-6864) are full of birdwatchers, who are permitted to set up telescopes and watch from the roof. I made a quick trip through Izutsuya Minshuku to get to the roof to visit with my friends. It looked typical. The owners were friendly, inviting me in and showing me the way to the top.

If a fine hotel fits your mood or your budget, I highly recommend the Irago View Hotel (05313-5-6111). It is a high-class resort hotel with a magnificent view. Every room looks out on the ocean. I prefer the west view, but the view from our room facing east was lovely, too. On Saturday night in the off-season (when you will want to go), it costs ¥18,000 per person if there are only two people, ¥16,000 per person every other night of the week. For groups of three or more, the price is reduced. This includes dinner and breakfast.

At dinner, you can choose the Seaview Restaurant which serves French and Chinese food, the Japanese restaurant, or dinner with a Hawaiian floor show. We had a delicious, well-prepared, and beautifully presented meal in the Japanese restaurant. An enormous platter of *sashimi* was the main feature. If you don't appreciate that, try one of the other eating places. A breakfast buffet is served from 7:00 to 10:00 a.m., convenient for birdwatchers. Besides the array of Japanese breakfast items, it included a variety of breads, fruit, coffee, and juice, as well as Chinese dumplings.

If you are interested in learning about Japanese culture, this will give you a good view of another type of holiday popular with those who can afford it. This hotel has 159 rooms and caters mostly to groups. The scene is a little different from that in the run-of-the-mill tourist hotels and interesting to observe. The rooms are large and comfortable, the food is good, and you can stand outside the front door to watch migrating hawks. The migration does not coincide with the tourist season, so you shouldn't have any problem getting a room. But, of course, call ahead if possible.

Maps and Information:
Champion Maps, Vol. 3, Western Japan
Buyodo Map D-3

Useful Kanji:
Toyohashi   豊橋
Iragomisaki 伊良湖岬

KYOTO

All visitors to Japan should see Kyoto. Concentrate on Japanese culture, and save birdwatching for someplace else. But do carry your binoculars. You will see some birds while visiting temples, shrines, and gardens.

People who have little time in Japan may want to make an effort to find birds in Kyoto if they will not have an opportunity for a serious birding expedition. Since Kyoto has many foreign visitors, there are ample signs in Roman letters, good maps in English, and much information and assistance available. You can easily find your way about, so detailed instructions will not be given here.

Daimonjiyama (Mt. Daimonji) usually has many birds. Take the trails behind Kinkakuji Temple (Golden Pavilion) to get up the mountain. Bamboo Partridge, Japanese Green Woodpecker, Long-tailed Tit, Varied Tit, and Japanese Grosbeak are resident. In winter, look for Pale Thrush, Yellow-throated Bunting, Gray Bunting, and Long-tailed Rose Finch. In summer, you might see Brown Hawk-Owl, Ashy Minivet, Siberian Blue Robin, and Blue-and-White Flycatcher. Baikal Teal has been seen on the pond at Kinkakuji.

You could see something any time of the year in the Botanical Garden, next to the Kamo River, north of the center of Kyoto. Look for Japanese Green Pigeon, Common Kingfisher, White's Ground Thrush, Pale Thrush, and Brambling.

Midoroga-ike (pond), northeast of the Botanical Garden, has breeding Little Grebe, Mallard, Spot-billed Duck, Ruddy Crake, and Common Kingfisher. There are ducks in winter. In the same season, Wryneck, Japanese Accentor, and Yellow-throated Bunting have been reported. Gray-spotted Flycatcher is sometimes here during migration. Baikal Teal also has occurred here. Don't expect this bird in Kyoto, but look for it if you have a chance.

Mt. Kurama, well to the north of the city, is said to be good in spring and early summer. Look for Brown Dipper, Crowned Willow Warbler, Narcissus Flycatcher, Blue-and-White Flycatcher, and tits.

Along Kamogawa (Kamo River), which runs through Kyoto, you

might see Black-headed Gull and Japanese Wagtail. Long-billed Ringed Plover occurs, but is rare.

Mt. Hiei used to be popular for birding, but the Japanese birdwatchers say it isn't so good anymore. On the basis of my one brief trip there, I would not recommend it for birding.

Most visitors to Kyoto will also visit Nara. Mt. Kasuga, behind the Kasuga Shrine, is said to be good in winter.

I have made many trips to Kyoto, but have never been willing to give up looking at other things in order to check out these sites. I cannot make any statement about the likelihood of finding any of these birds.

Maps and Information:
    JNTO Information Sheets MG-052 and MG-053
    JNTO - Tourist Map of Kyoto and Nara

UJI

Baikal Teal occur most winters on the lake behind Kisenyama Dam near Uji. The number fluctuates from perhaps ten to several hundred. The problem is in gaining access to enough of this large lake to have a chance of finding them. If you are desperate to see this bird, you might want to try here. You will need a car.

From Kyoto you can take the Keihan Line to Keihan Uji Station. I doubt that you can rent a car in Uji, but you could make this trip by taxi. You can keep the taxi while you look for the birds. The walk back is at least 6 km.

From the Keihan Uji Station take the road on the north side of the Uji River and go to the southeast (your left with your back to Kyoto). Before you reach the Amagose Dam, take a road going to your left and uphill. After about a kilometer you have the choice of going left to a village or right on a road going uphill. Go to the right. This road should lead you to the north end of the lake formed by the Kisenyama Dam.

When I tried to do it, I got almost there and hit the end of the road. The road was under construction. The people in the construction office told me the road had never gone beyond that point, though it is shown on the map and I have talked to people who claim they have been there. It may be that you will have to walk the last bit. The dam and the road along the west side of the lake are off limits. I have tried to approach this lake from all directions and have failed. You may have better luck. Try from the north side. It may be that the Baikal Teal have chosen this place because nobody can get near it. If they have found an inaccessible place in Japan, they deserve to remain there undisturbed.

Uji

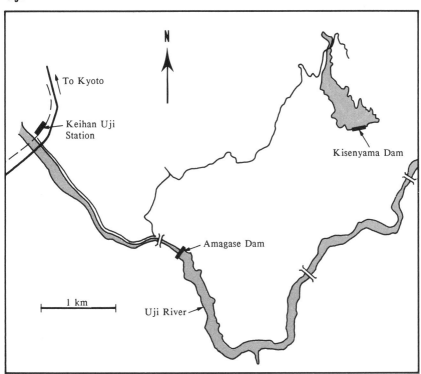

While you are in Uji, have a look at the local points of interest. Byodoin Temple and Koshoji Temple are certainly worth visiting.

OSAKA

Osaka should not be on your itinerary for birdwatching. Since Osaka is a business center, some birdwatchers may go there for other purposes. If you find yourself in that situation, there are four places you can go in search of birds. Ask for directions at your hotel.

Along the Yodogawa River you can see ducks in winter. There is also the possibility of Marsh Harrier, Long-eared Owl, and Short-eared Owl.

Nanko Yacho Koen is a man-made tidal flat which is good for shorebirds during migration. In the winter you can expect to see common ducks. Public transportation is convenient for this. From Nishiumeda, take the Yotsuhashisen subway line to Suminoekoen (22 minutes). Change there to the new tram, and go to Nakafuto, the end of the line. This will take 15 minutes. Walk the rest of the way.

Mt. Minoo, a quasi-national park, is north of the Osaka Airport. In spring and early summer, it is good for passerines. In winter, look for Japanese Green Pigeon, Japanese Accentor, Red Crossbill, and Bullfinch.

Koya-ike Pond in Itami City, also near Osaka Airport, has ducks in winter. It also has many domestic Mute Swans.

Maps and Information:
    Map of Osaka and Vicinity - JNTO
        This gives public transportation information on one side
        and has a fine map of a large area on the other. You
        will find this helpful for Osaka, Kyoto, Nagoya,
        Mikatagoko, Eiheiji Temple, and points in between.

    Osaka - Osaka Tourist Association

MATSUE - MT. DAISEN AREA

Season: winter, migration, spring on Mt. Daisen
Specialties: exceptionally large number of species

The Matsue area is one of the jewels of Japan, both for birds and for cultural interest. There are many fine birding spots with enough variety of habitat for 232 species to be on the local list. Almost any bird which can be expected to appear on Honshu has been recorded here. Relatively few tourists, not only foreign but also Japanese, come here. This part of Japan looks like the Japan foreigners expect, with much of the traditional architecture remaining. You will find many unspoiled villages off the main roads in Shimane and Tottori prefectures.

Transportation:
Matsue is served by two airports, Izumo and Yonago. ANA has flights from Tokyo to Yonago (1 hour, 20 minutes), and TDA has flights from Osaka to Yonago (55 minutes), Tokyo to Izumo (1 hour, 20 minutes), and Osaka to Izumo (one hour).

There is train service to Matsue. Since it is far from a Shinkansen line, the trip takes a long time.

A car is essential for birding. Long-distance driving from Matsue will be slow, even slower in winter. If you have plenty of time, it is an interesting part of Japan to explore.

Directions:
You will need some good maps. The Buyodo map D-2 gives a good view of the entire area. With the aid of the accompanying map, you can locate the places you want to go. More detailed maps will be useful for finding small roads. The most popular places are discussed under Site and Birds. With your maps, they will not be difficult to find.

Site and Birds:
With Matsue as a base, it is possible to visit many birding spots all the way from Jinsai-ko and Hinomisaki (Cape Hino), west of Izumo Airport, to Hikona and the Hino River, east of Yonago Airport. It is also possible to visit Mt. Daisen in a day from Matsue, but you may want to consider spending the night somewhere closer.

Matsue Area

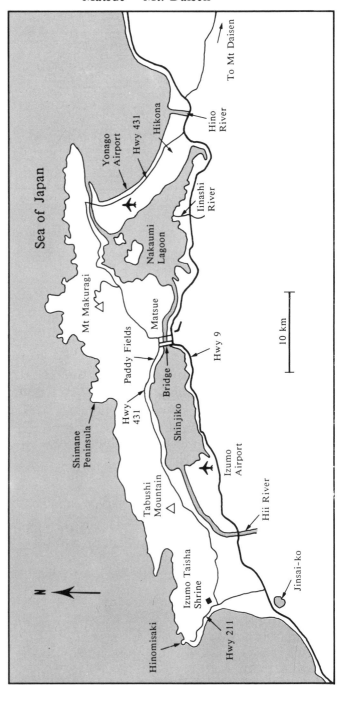

Matsue, a small town by Japanese standards, has a population of about 140,000. It lies between Shinjiko (Lake Shinji) and the Nakaumi Lagoon, both excellent areas for birding. Parts of the Shimane Peninsula, just to the north, are included in the Daisen-Oki National Park. There is scenic beauty and much of interest for those who wish to learn more about the traditions and culture of the country. It is especially suited for a long, relaxed visit, combining birding with other activities.

The bird list is long and includes many species a foreign birder would be delighted to see. Unfortunately it gives no information as to the abundance of each species. Nevertheless, because of its location on the western side of Japan near the Korean peninsula and its fine and varied habitat, this area should have many interesting birds at any season.

Winter is perhaps the best season, but it is cold with much snow. It is possible to drive up the toll road to Mt. Daisen if you have chains. Birding there then is limited to looking in the forest around the parking lot for woodpeckers and tits. The rest of the area is accessible, but be sure to dress appropriately. You can do a lot of birding from a car if the weather is particularly severe.

Mt. Daisen (1713 meters) comes into its own in spring and early summer. I visited this part of Japan in late winter, so I missed Mt. Daisen. Many Japanese consider it as fine as any mountain birding area in the country. Even though there aren't as many tourists here as in some other parts of Japan, there will be many more than you want to see in the summer. Come early, or at least before the end of June. All the usual mountain species (including cuckoos, thrushes, warblers, and flycatchers) are on the list. Brown Dipper is here and Nutcracker too, though not so many. You will have a chance of seeing Hodgson's Hawk-Eagle. Japanese Accentor is up high. In spring there are flocks of Rosy Finches.

The entire area is excellent during migration. April-May and September-October are best. There should be plenty of shorebirds.

To make it easier to follow on the map, the birding sites are described starting at the west end and working east. They will not necessarily be in the most convenient order for visiting.

HINOMISAKI (CAPE HINO)

From Izumo Taisha Shrine, take Hwy. 211 to the cape. To the
west of the cape is a small island, Fumishima, where Temminck's
and Pelagic Cormorants and Black-tailed Gulls breed. There are
not many Pelagic Cormorants. At the end you can drive along
several narrow roads and check the birds in the small coves.

IZUMO-TAISHA SHRINE

This is one of the three most important Shinto shrines in Japan. It
is an older style of architecture than the others. I find it the most
interesting of the three. By all means, take the time for a visit.
The forest behind the shrine is also good for birds.

JINSAI-KO

Jinsai-ko (Lake Jinsai) is to the south of Hwy. 9, west of where it
intersects the highway going south from Izumo Shrine (which may
be Hwy. 431). You will see the lake from Hwy. 9. At the far end
of the lake you will be able to turn off the highway and find
small roads which will take you all the way around it. There are
some good views of the lake and a lot of open agricultural land
good for birds too. This is a good place to find a White-tailed
Eagle.

The east side of the lake and the neighboring stream and fields
may be the best area. It is hard to spot the turn from the highway,
so make your way back from the other side of the lake. An island
with a small shrine is near the eastern shore. Baikal Teal may be
nearby. Many ducks winter on this lake. Always look for
Penduline Tit and the rare Pallas's Reed Bunting. Greater Pied
Kingfisher occurs.

TABUSHI MOUNTAIN

Tabushi Mountain (Tabushiyama) is to the west of Hirata, north
of Hwy. 431, and west of Shinjiko. Birds to expect here are
Japanese Green Woodpecker, Japanese Pygmy Woodpecker, Bull-
headed Shrike, Winter Wren, White's Ground Thrush, Pale Thrush,
Dusky Thrush, Goldcrest, tits, Japanese White-eye, and buntings.
Sometimes Goshawk and Sparrow Hawk occur.

HII RIVER

This area, just north of the Izumo Airport at the west end of Shinjiko, should not be missed. Birding is excellent along the river from the mouth back about 2 or 3 km. and in all the surrounding agricultural land.

A detailed map will be useful but is not essential. Roads crisscross the area. You will enjoy wandering all over it. The river has a number of sandbars near the mouth. The road on the north side of the Hii River is on top of a high bank, from which you have an excellent view of the river and the sandbars on one side and the paddy fields on the other. You can drive along the seawall at the west end of Shinjiko. Allow plenty of time to look carefully through the fields.

The birds here are similar to those found at Hikona on the east end of Nakaumi Lagoon. Shinjiko is a freshwater lake though, while Nakaumi Lagoon has sea water coming in through a channel at the northeast end. You should have a good chance of finding Penduline Tit in the weeds along the Hii River in winter. This bird is not easy to find in Japan. Look in the same area for Pallas's Reed Bunting. You could see four species of grebes, White-fronted Goose, Bean Goose, Whooper and Whistling Swans, ducks (including Baikal Teal, Falcated Teal, and Smew), several gulls, Japanese Wagtail, thrushes, Fan-tailed Warbler, and buntings. Among the birds of prey in the area in winter are White-tailed Eagle, Northern Harrier, Marsh Harrier, Peregrine Falcon, and Kestrel. In the fields between Izumo Airport and the Hii River, look for Rook and Jackdaw. Yellow Wagtail and Red-throated Pipit pass through on migration. This is an excellent place for shorebirds. In summer, look for Chinese Little Bittern and Great Reed Warbler.

PADDY FIELDS

The nameless paddy fields just to the west of Matsue on the north side of Shinjiko are excellent for migrating waders. These fields are north of Hwy. 431, approximately 2 to 3 km. from the bridge at the east end of Shinjiko which connects the two parts of Matsue.

MT. MAKURAGI

Mt. Makuragi, on the Shimane Peninsula north of Nakaumi Lagoon, has good birds. Kezaji, a temple, is on this mountain, which has an elevation of 456 meters. Hwy. 212, which intersects Hwy. 431 at the northwest corner of Nakaumi Lagoon, goes up the mountain. It is worth a try in winter if the snow doesn't prevent your driving up.

IINASHI RIVER

The Iinashi River is about 20 km. to the east of Matsue on the south side of Nakaumi Lagoon. In heavy traffic and heavy snow, it takes about 30 minutes to get here from Matsue. Most of the traffic through this area uses Hwy. 9, so you can expect slow driving. If you are traveling east, turn left from the highway and follow the road alongside the river to the mouth. There is a road on the top of the embankment on the east side and possibly one on the west side as well. There are sandbars in the river, plenty of reeds, and open fields nearby.

This area has many of the same birds in winter as the Hii River and Hikona. This is a good place for buntings and Brambling. Check all Reed Buntings carefully for Pallas's Reed Bunting. This is a good place, so don't pass it up when you drive down Hwy. 9.

HIKONA RECLAIMED LAND

Hikona Reclaimed Land is an important place for birding on the east side of Nakaumi Lagoon, south of Yonago Airport and about 5 km. northwest of Yonago. Take the main road which is nearest the lagoon on the east side. You will have to search a bit for Hikona because there is no direct route. Depending on the way you choose, somewhere between 5 and 7 km. after you leave Hwy. 9, you should find a gate into the reclaimed land. You must leave your car here and walk the rest of the way. This is a big place, so be prepared to spend some time if it isn't so bitterly cold you can't stand it. It is a good idea to wear boots. You need to walk a lot, and it could be wet and boggy.

If you can't find this gate, ask directions to Awashima Jinja (shrine). It is about 2 km. closer to Yonago than the entrance to the reclaimed land. You can walk along the water's edge toward

Hikona Reclaimed Land

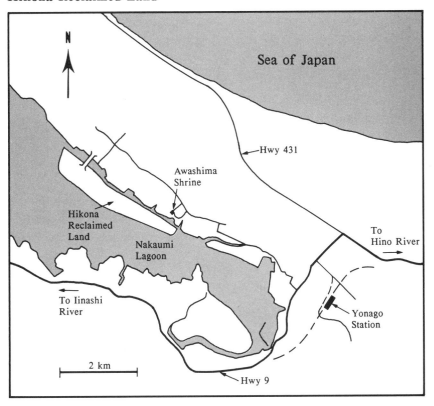

the entrance, looking across at the reclaimed land. If you cannot enter the reclaimed land, this path is the best substitute.

Most of the birds you can expect are the same as those around the Hii River, but the numbers of Whistling Swans, geese, and ducks are usually greater. In addition, Common Shelduck sometimes occurs here. More than 15 species of birds of prey have been recorded. There is an excellent chance of seeing White-tailed Eagle, Rough-legged Buzzard, Common Buzzard, Northern Harrier, Marsh Harrier, Peregrine Falcon, and Kestrel. Short-eared Owl is often here. Chinese Great Gray Shrike has occurred, so look carefully. By the end of October, Snow Buntings should be here. During migration this area has many shorebirds.

HINO RIVER

The Hino River flows into the ocean east of Yonago. Hwy. 9 crosses this river. The road on the east side of the river is best for birding. If you are traveling east, you will easily find this wide river and have plenty of time to make the turn to the left on the far side.

At the mouth of the river you should be able to see loons, grebes, sea ducks, and gulls. Between the highway and the mouth of the river there usually are other ducks and birds similar to those at the Hii River and the Iinashi River. This is a good place to find Gray-headed Bunting.

MT. DAISEN

Mt. Daisen has been discussed earlier. The Daisen Toll Road meets Hwy. 9 about 3 km. east of the Hino River. Allow plenty of time on Mt. Daisen in the spring. You will need a good map. There are plenty of hiking trails, and you can climb to the top if you have several hours. There are pasturelands on the lower slopes and mixed forests on the mountain. Japanese dwarf yew grows at the higher elevations.

Time:
I was here in winter for two full days, which was not enough. Three days would be the minimum, and that could not include more than a quick trip up the Daisen Toll Road and back. You must allow an hour to travel from Matsue to the birding sites on either end of the area. The Hii River and Hikona Reclaimed Land are worth a half day each even if you are hurrying. Some of the other places can be checked in one or two hours, but don't try to rush your visit. You will want time to enjoy the castle, shrines, museums, shopping, and exploring while you are here.

Food:
There are restaurants in Matsue and along the main highways. It will be better to start out with a packed lunch if you plan a whole day of birding. You can find coffee shops to warm up in, but you can waste a lot of time searching for a restaurant at lunchtime.

Accommodations:
There are plenty of places to stay in Matsue. It is here that I

found the place I consider a must for everyone except those who are immune to an appreciation of Japanese food, style, and tradition. The Minami-kan Ryokan is a lovely place where I felt I received the best value for money of all the places I stayed in Japan. I hope there are more places like this to be discovered, but the chances of a foreigner stumbling on one are slim.

Japanese travelers are turning away from the old style *ryokan* for Western hotels or *ryokan* which have adopted a lot of Western ways and decoration. Therefore, there may not be many places left like Minami-kan. I have stayed in some of the famous, elegant, traditional *ryokan* in Kyoto and in Kanazawa, but they were far more expensive than this one.

For ¥13,000 per person, my husband and I had a suite of three rooms with bath plus a small room at the front overlooking a beautiful traditional garden and Shinjiko. Every morning we saw Falcated Teal swimming in the lake only a few meters beyond our window. This *ryokan* is more than 100 years old, and the decor is completely authentic. Furthermore, the food was exquisite. I believe most of Minami-kan's business is from the restaurant. They also have branch restaurants in several cities, including Tokyo. The local specialties were perfectly prepared and beautifully served.

There are 14 rooms. The cost of room and two meals ranges from ¥12,000 to ¥18,000 per person. The price is constant throughout the year. There are a couple of large *ofuro*, or you can bathe in your room. I do not know if they will accept a group. Please, if you come here, put on your best Japanese manners and enjoy this place to the fullest for what it is. Accept what is offered and be appreciative so that this lovely place will always welcome foreign visitors.

Minami-kan is near the Shinjiko Bridge on the north side. It is hidden in the depths of the Kyomise Shopping Arcade. It is easy to find with the map in the JNTO Information Sheet MG-062. The telephone number is 0852-21-5131.

There is a Kokuminshukusha (government *minshuku*) by the lake at Jinsai-ko. The telephone number is 0853-43-2211. For Mt. Daisen, you could stay in Yonago or inquire locally about other places.

Maps and Information:
JNTO Information Sheet MG-062
Champion Maps, Vol. 3, Western Japan
Buyodo Map D-2

National Maps: 1:50,000 Matsue 松江

Yonago 米子

Imaichi (for Hii River) 今市

1:25,000 Daisen 伯耆大山

Useful Kanji:

Matsue	松江
Izumo	出雲
Izumo-Taisha Shrine	出雲大社
Hinomisaki	日御碕
Jinsai-ko	神西湖
Tabushiyama	旅伏山
Hii River	斐伊川
Mt. Makuragi	枕木山
Iinashi River	飯梨川
Hikona Reclaimed Land	彦名干拓地
Yonago	米子
Awashima Shrine	粟島神社
Hino River	日野川
Mt. Daisen	大山
Minami-kan Ryokan	南館旅館

ARASAKI CRANE RESERVE - IZUMI

Season: late November to mid-February
Specialties: six species of cranes, winter rarities

Izumi, in southwestern Kyushu, is an absolute must for any birder visiting Japan from the end of November through the middle of February. There may be no place else in the world where you can see so many species of cranes at once. Hooded Cranes make up the largest group, numbering around 5,000. There are approximately 1,000 White-naped Cranes. The other species are in small numbers. A few Common Cranes and a few Sandhill Cranes come every year. Sometimes there is a Siberian White Crane or a Demoiselle Crane. Some years all six have been there at the same time. Besides the cranes, there are many other birds to see in winter in the Izumi area, including some rare species.

Izumi

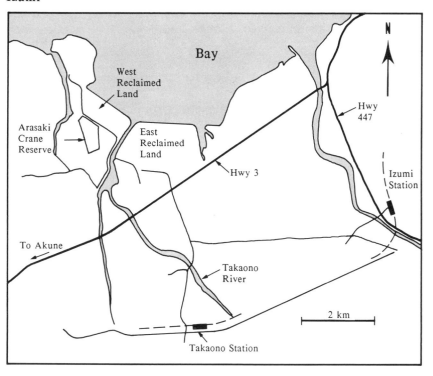

Transportation:
You have several options for getting to Izumi and getting around while there. A car is most convenient and will enable you to explore a much larger area and see more species. Finding the way is not difficult. It is possible to rent a car from a local agency in Izumi. (One possibility is Izumi Rent-a-Car, 09966-2-1332.) Or you can take a taxi from the station (about ¥1850) to the crane reserve and walk from there. It is far and cold.

If you are coming by public transportation all the way, consider an overnight train. You can leave Tokyo at 6:24 p.m., make one change at 10:52 p.m., and take a sleeping car to Izumi, arriving at 8:59 the next morning. Otherwise you can fly to Kagoshima (see details of connections under Miike) or to Kumamoto (connections with Tokyo, Osaka, Nagoya, and Okinawa), make your way to a train station, and come the rest of the way by train. Everything slows down at this point. It takes about an hour to get from Kagoshima Airport to Kagoshima Station and another hour and a half on the train to Izumi. From Kumamoto Airport it takes 50 minutes to get to Kumamoto Station and 1 hour, 40 minutes from there to Izumi.

If you fly into the area, it is best to rent a car at the airport and drive the rest of the way. Izumi is about 75 km. from Kagoshima Airport and 110 km. from Kumamoto Airport.

Directions:
By train from Tokyo, start on the Tokaido Shinkansen Hikari to Okayama. There you can change to a sleeping car on the JNR Limited Express Naha. Check the latest information with the JNR.

From the two airports, you will have to take a Limousine Bus to the train station. You can get a ticket there for Izumi. Check schedules before you start out.

By car from either airport, make your way to Izumi Station. Directions to the crane reserve and other birding sites will be given under Site and Birds starting from here. You will need a good map.

Site and Birds:
There is a large area to explore around Izumi, of which only a small part is the crane reserve. The cranes don't all stay on the

reserve all day, so you will have opportunities to get much closer to them in your car somewhere else. But the likelihood of your meeting a crane other than a Hooded or a White-naped off the reserve is slim.

The front side of the reserve has a carnival-like atmosphere. After you have looked at the cranes over the fence, you can move on away from this place and find excellent birding in much more pleasant surroundings.

I was here on a holiday weekend so saw the place at its worst. There is an observatory with pay telescopes on the second floor, a *minshuku*, several restaurants, and countless booths and stands where you can buy souvenirs and a wide variety of snacks. All this is crowded together next to a large parking lot. On the counter of one of these booths was a small dog in a cage the same size as the dog. A sign attached to the cage made an appeal to the reader to buy from the dog's master. The appeal was signed with the dog's pawprint. The crowds munch on octopus, dried fish, roasted ears of corn, and cotton candy as they line the fence looking at the cranes.

It is from this location that you are most likely to see the rare species, which usually stay in the middle of the sanctuary. It is here or at the *minshuku* run by Matano-san, who is also employed to take care of the sanctuary, that you will get information about the cranes and other birds in the area. You will get closest to the birds here when the food is put out early in the morning. Naturally this place appeals to photographers.

There used to be more crane habitat here. Development has changed that, so now the good habitat is limited to the reclaimed land around the reserve and the fields along the rivers. Even so, the number of cranes wintering here has increased dramatically in recent years. Since the farmers changed their methods and began planting winter crops, they have been doing battle with the cranes which move out of the sanctuary into the fields. Now the farmers put up scarecrows and wires with long strips of plastic hanging from them to scare the cranes. It isn't entirely effective. This competition between the farmers and the cranes is a source of great concern to those who want the cranes protected.

The large area of reclaimed land at Izumi attracts many birds in winter. There are also ducks and a few shorebirds around the rivermouths and Long-billed Ringed Plover and Greater Pied Kingfisher beside the rivers farther away from the ocean. A few patches of woods harbor still different species, such as Chinese Grosbeak and Japanese Grosbeak. Brown Dipper is up in the hills behind Izumi. There are many places and habitats to explore, but most of the birds will be on the reclaimed land and in the other fields.

Something rare or unusual turns up every winter. It could be a White Stork, one of the spoonbills, Oriental Ibis, Pied Harrier, Lesser Short-toed Lark, or Starling (this is terribly exciting for Japanese birdwatchers). You have a better chance of seeing Saunders's Gull, Red-throated Pipit, Pallas's Reed Bunting, Chinese Grosbeak, or a black-and-white Jackdaw (Daurian Jackdaw, *Corvus dauuricus*, not considered a separate species by the Japanese).

With your back to Izumi Station, go straight ahead on the main road, Hwy. 373. It angles this way and that, but shouldn't be hard to follow if you have a detailed map of Izumi. Shortly past the main part of town, the road curves to the right. From there it is straight for a long way. You will reach an intersection with a traffic light where it is possible to go straight, but the road ahead is much narrower. On the near left corner is a gasoline station. There is a Coca-Cola sign on the far left corner. Remember this corner because you will come back here later.

Since any birder will be eager to get to the cranes, trips in the opposite direction will be described later. Now, turn to your right at this corner. You will soon see a large orange sign on the right with "Co-op" written on it. Just before the Co-op sign, turn right onto a small street which goes past a school. There will be trees on your left in front of the school and trees and fields on your right. Look here for Chinese and Japanese Grosbeaks and other birds. Sometimes cranes are in the fields to the right beyond the school.

Go back to the Co-op corner and turn right. You will then be going in the same direction you were before you made this detour. Soon you will reach the intersection with Hwy. 3 (no sign). There is a sign showing Kagoshima 93 km. to the left and Kumamoto 109 km. to the right. Cross over the highway onto a much narrower road which leads into the east reclaimed land. Before you get into the open fields, you can turn left and drive along a twisting lane until you reach a pig farm and a small pond which is almost hidden behind thick vegetation. The pig farm is a good place for flocks of Gray Starlings, in which you might find a Starling if you care. The wet area is a good place to find Water Rail and Ruddy Crake as well as Black-crowned Night Heron, shorebirds, and ducks.

If you miss this turn to the pig farm, you can find it later. Next, go on into the fields in the east reclaimed land and see what you can find. When you are ready to leave, make your way to the west side and follow the road along the waterway. There will be ducks here. Work your way back to the south along the edge of the water until you reach a small bridge on your right. Cross that bridge and go again to your right. From here you can go forward until you see a sign for the crane reserve to the right. You can make your way from here to the main entrance. Otherwise you can drive along the west side of the waterway until you get to some houses, turn left, and come up on the side of the parking lot at the crane reserve. You may get confused in here, but you won't get far lost.

Now go back to the road along the west side of the waterway and go toward the ocean, turning to your left when the main road does. This road goes along the back side of the sanctuary. When you reach the point where this road curves to the right, toward the ocean again, you can take the small road to the left. There are some ponds on both sides of this road and a sign in Japanese saying to keep out of the sanctuary. You can walk along a dike with a wet, reedy area to your right and reeds and fields to your left. All of this territory that is open to you is excellent for birds. You should find Penduline Tits. This is the place to look for Pallas's Reed Buntings. Gray-headed Buntings are usually around.

Now go into the west reclaimed land between where you are and the ocean. This is a good area with many larks. Look for Short-toed and Lesser Short-toed, both rare. From here go to the rocky island on the northwest end. This is supposed to be a good place from which to look for Brown Booby and Japanese Murrelet out over the bay. I suspect that a better place might be near Akune where you have a view over the ocean. Don't overlook the waterway on the west end of the west reclaimed land while you are in the area.

There are other places to visit in the Izumi area away from the reclaimed land. Find your way back to Hwy. 3 and go to the east. About halfway between the east end of the east reclaimed land and the large rivermouth in the vicinity of the intersection of Hwy. 3 and Hwy. 447 (see map), turn left toward the ocean and look for Russet Sparrows which frequent the area. Then you can continue on to the rivermouth and check both sides for shorebirds and gulls.

Retrace part of your route on Hwy. 3 back to the place where you first crossed it going to the pig farm and the east reclaimed land. This time turn left (south), go past the Co-op sign, and make your way to the corner with the gasoline station and the Coca-Cola sign which you noted when coming from the station. Instead of turning to your left here and going back to the station, go straight until you reach the bridge over the Takaono River. Before you cross the bridge, turn left on the road going alongside the river. You cannot drive far, so park your car and walk along the river. You should find Long-billed Ringed Plover, Greater Pied Kingfisher, and Common Kingfisher.

Go back to the road, cross the bridge, then turn into the fields to your right. Search this area, especially the trees to the left, for Jackdaws. Flocks of Rooks and some Jackdaws are usually around here. This is where you are most likely to find a Daurian Jackdaw. It isn't easy, especially when they are in the trees. Give it plenty of time.

If you want to see a Brown Dipper, keep going in the same direction on this road until you cross a railroad track. Then turn to the left onto the main road which goes in front of Takaono Station and to the right onto the road which comes almost straight into the front of the station. Stay on this road and drive up into the hills to a dam. If you walk along the river below the dam, you should find some dippers.

Another excellent area to explore is along the river to the west of the Takaono River which also flows into the waterway dividing the east and west reclaimed land. (See a map.) Sometimes there are cranes in these fields. There is good habitat for other species, so don't neglect it.

The last place is farther away. Save it until you run out of something to do. Take Hwy. 3 to the southwest from Izumi to Akune. Here get off the highway and look around the port and the shoreline. You might find something different over here.

You are in southern Kyushu, but don't let that deceive you. It is often below freezing in winter. Sometimes there is snow. Be prepared for a strong, cold wind.

Time:
The time you come is important. Published reports vary as to when the cranes are here. It is possible to see some cranes in March, but they begin their migration by the middle of February. If you want to see all the species which are wintering at Arasaki, don't come later than that. All the cranes should arrive by December except for stragglers. If you can come in January or the beginning of February, you will have the best chance to see any rarities that have come. My last day here was the 13th of February. At that time the cranes were circling some, and Matano-san, the warden, believed they would begin to leave the following day.

If you want to see only cranes, this doesn't take long. If you want to enjoy fine birding and see a lot of species, allow at least two full days. Three days will not be boring.

Food:
You can get lunch or snacks at the crane reserve. There are restaurants in Izumi and scattered along the highway. I recommend a packed lunch with hot drinks or a stop to warm up in a coffee shop when it is convenient.

Accommodations:
Minshuku Tsurumi-Tei (09968-33944) is next to the fence at the crane sanctuary (easily recognized because the phone number is painted on the top). From some of the rooms and from the dining room, you can see the cranes, and you cannot see the parking lot and the clutter in the front. Tsurumi-Tei is associated with the WBSJ and is usually full of birders. It has a large capacity, so there is room for a group. You might find an English-speaking birder here who will give you information. The toilets are the non-flush variety. Toilet paper sometimes is supplied and sometimes isn't, so bring your own. All washing is at a long row of faucets with a supply of pans.

For those who prefer something different, Business Hotel Tsuru, also associated with the WBSJ, (09966-2-5353), Kakugyo Ryokan (09966-2-1538), and Hotel King (09966-2-1511) are all in Izumi.

Maps and Information:
Champion Maps, Vol. 4, Kyushu
Buyodo Map D-1

National Map: 1:50,000 Izumi 出水

Useful Kanji:

Izumi	出水
Arasaki	荒崎
Takaono River	高尾野川
Akune	阿久根

MIIKE YACHO NO MORI

Season: May - early June
Specialties: Ruddy Kingfisher, Fairy Pitta, Black Paradise
Flycatcher

Miike (Mi Pond) Yacho no Mori (Bird Woods) is just that, a rather dense forest surrounding a pond about 6 km. in circumference. It is in southern Kyushu within easy access of Kagoshima Airport. Fairy Pitta breeds here and is reasonably easy to find in late May and early June.

Transportation:
Miike is a little more than an hour by car from Kagoshima Airport. (Kagoshima is about an hour in the other direction from the airport.) Kagoshima Airport is served by ANA and TDA with flights to Tokyo (1 hour, 40 minutes), Osaka (1 hour, 5 minutes), Nagoya (1 hour, 20 minutes), Hiroshima (1 hour, 15 minutes), Amami Oshima (1 hour, 15 minutes), Okinawa (1 hour, 30 minutes), Fukuoka (40 minutes), and several smaller places less likely to be on your itinerary. Nippon Rent-a-Car has an agency directly across the street from Kagoshima Airport. Go to the counter in the terminal, and someone will take you to the office.

Directions:
From the rental car agency opposite the airport, turn right and go 6.7 km. on the road in front of the airport to Hwy. 223. Turn left on Hwy. 223, and stay on it all the way to Miike. When you get to Miike, you will be able to see the lake from the road. At the end of the lake there is a sign with "Wild Bird Forest" written in English. Turn left here and drive to the parking lot.

Alternately, if you wish to go to Ebino Kogen first, go about 23.2 km. on Hwy. 223 until you reach the turnoff which will take you to the toll road for Ebino Kogen. The signs are in Japanese. When you pass through the toll gate at the end, turn to the left. The Ebino Kogen Hotel will be about 6 km. ahead on your right.

Site and Birds:
From the parking lot at Miike, take the path straight ahead. Soon you will reach a path to the left going to the campground at the lakeshore. Ignore that path and keep going straight ahead. It is in this area just beyond the turnoff to the campground that you will

have your first chance of seeing the Fairy Pitta. Look and listen carefully here before you continue on. You could also find Ruddy Kingfisher and Black Paradise Flycatcher nearby. If you are not successful, keep going on the trails away from the lake. There are two more areas farther along where the Fairy Pitta might be.

Miike

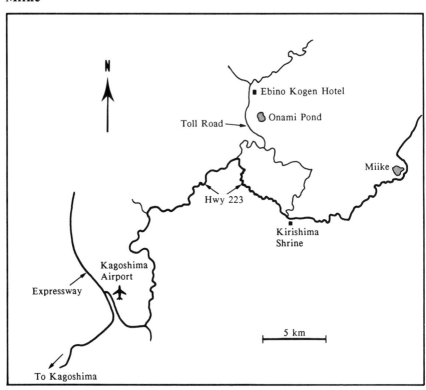

The forest is dense and dark, but beautiful. Later in the summer it can be almost birdless. There never are many birds, but the quality is high. In spring and early summer you should have a good chance of finding Ruddy Kingfisher, Fairy Pitta, Ashy Minivet, Narcissus Flycatcher, and Black Paradise Flycatcher. Little Grebe, Japanese Green Pigeon, Japanese Green Woodpecker, White-backed Woodpecker, Japanese Pygmy Woodpecker, Gray Wagtail, Bush Warbler, Long-tailed Tit, Coal Tit, Varied Tit, Great Tit, Nuthatch, Japanese White-eye, and Japanese Grosbeak are resident. Come as early as possible. After late morning the Fairy Pitta is extremely difficult to see.

Time:
It is easy to spend half a day hiking through this forest. After you find the Fairy Pitta, it isn't worth staying much longer if your time is limited. Certainly try to find Ruddy Kingfisher and Black Paradise Flycatcher, but except for these species you are likely to see little of interest. Scheduling is a problem because after coming this far, you want to allow all the time you need to find the pitta. It is too late in the day to count on finding it if you fly into Kagoshima in the morning and go straight to Miike. It usually works out best to get to Kagoshima one day and go to Ebino Kogen, leaving there early the next morning for Miike and taking a plane from Kagoshima that afternoon.

Food:
Bring it with you. On the southwest side of the lake, the opposite side from where you park, there are drink machines and snacks. You will be happier with a box lunch.

Accommodations:
Stay at Ebino Kogen, a plateau at 1200 meters in the Kirishima-Yaku National Park, less than an hour's drive from Miike. Ebino Kogen Hotel (09843-3-1155) is a good place in the center of the birding area. It costs approximately ¥7,000 per person including two meals. There is a less expensive place to stay across the road. Hayashida Onsen is in the area, but the birding is better at Ebino Kogen.

Note:
The area between Kagoshima Airport and Ebino Kogen and Miike is beautiful. Ebino Kogen is well known for interesting wildflowers, especially in May. There are a number of trails. The best one for birding is the one to Onami Pond, beginning behind the hotel. Both Copper and Common Pheasants, Japanese Green Woodpecker, White-backed Woodpecker, Japanese Pygmy Woodpecker, Bush Warbler, and five species of tits are resident. In summer you may find Common, Oriental, and Little Cuckoos and Japanese Robin.

Kirishima Shrine is between Ebino Kogen and Miike. You might find birds near the shrine. There is no need to walk too far from the shrine, because the birding gets worse the farther away you go. Broad-billed Roller has been reported here.

Maps and Information:
  Champion Maps, Vol. 4, Kyushu
  Buyodo Map D-1

Useful Kanji:
  Ebino Kogen   えびの高原
  Miike Yacho no Mori 御池野鳥の森
  Onami Pond   大浪池
  Kagoshima Airport   鹿児島空港

MT. ASO

Photographs of Aso National Park in central Kyushu are beautiful, and the account of it in *National Parks of Japan* by Sutherland and Britton makes it sound inviting. I was there when the weather was not clear, not unusual I understand, and found it disappointing. The main highway from Kumamoto to Aso is lined with an extraordinary collection of eyesores. Most of the structures are no less garish than the numerous *pachinko* parlors. On a Sunday, several gangs of motorcyclists and the usual stream of tour buses added to the unpleasantness of this drive. The local birders do not give Aso high marks for birds, though it is thought by some to be a good place to see Copper Pheasant, Yellow-throated Bunting, and Japanese Grosbeak. I don't think it is worth the trip solely for birds. If you go for the scenery, there are some places you should check.

If you are on Hwy. 57 coming from Kumamoto or the Kyushu Expressway, turn right when you get to Hwy. 325. This road takes you south of Mt. Aso to Takamori and is less congested with traffic and souvenir shops. Just before you reach Takamori, take Hwy. 265 to the left. At a T-junction, a highway sign shows Hwy. 265 to the right and the left. Takamori is to the right; Ichinomiya is to the left. All this is in *kanji*.

About 3 km. north of this junction, you will come to the Kyukamura Kokuminshukusha (09676-2-2111), a government-owned type of *minshuku*. It is large and looks fine from the outside. There are hiking trails leading from this area. It is away from the town in a pleasant location, convenient for birding. This is a favorite of the Japanese birders who live in Kyushu. Explore these trails and then drive around to search for more good places.

In summer, you might see Brown Hawk-Owl, Jungle Nightjar, Japanese Green Woodpecker, Ashy Minivet, Gray Thrush, Bush Warbler, Brown Flycatcher, Black Paradise Flycatcher, Great Tit, Japanese White-eye, Japanese Grosbeak, and Jay. In winter, look for Pale Thrush, Dusky Thrush, Yellow-throated Bunting, and Black-faced Bunting.

From here go back on Hwy. 325 in the direction from which you came, until you meet the toll road (¥1200) going across the park to the north. Take this road (to your right). It is about 30 km. to the other end.

Here take Hwy. 57 to the right (east) about 3.5 km. to Miyaji. Just north of the highway at Miyaji is Aso Shrine, where you should find Japanese Grosbeaks. Look all around Miyaji (on both sides of the highway) for stream beds near plantations of Japanese cedar. Some people have been successful in finding Copper Pheasants around here. Common Pheasants are also in the area.

Mt. Aso

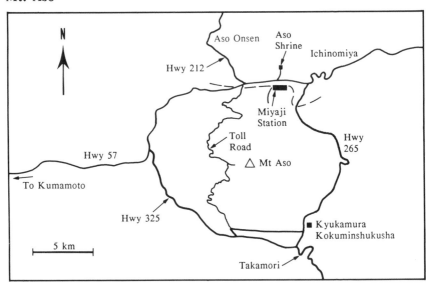

There are many places to stay at Aso Onsen, about 6 km. north of Hwy. 57 on Hwy. 212 (which meets Hwy. 57 near the north end of the toll road). There are many paddy fields along here where you may find Yellow-throated Bunting in winter. This is not an attractive town, but the view of Mt. Aso may be good from here on a clear day. On the basis of what I could see of the accommodations from the outside, I would choose Hotel Kadoman (09673-2-0615). It is large and better looking than the other hotels and seemed to be attracting bus groups. There may be some *minshuku* or small *ryokan* which were not evident. Inquire locally.

The local birders take Hwy. 265 north from Takamori to meet Hwy. 57 near Ichinomiya, bypassing the road over Mt. Aso.

Maybe there is better birding on that road, but if you miss seeing Mt. Aso, you've missed the whole point in coming. If you choose to stay at Takamori, you may have time to explore that road for some distance anyway.

Useful Kanji:

Takamori	高森
Ichinomiya	一の宮
Kyukamura Kokuminshukusha	南阿蘇国民休暇村
Miyaji	宮地
Aso Onsen	阿蘇温泉

ISAHAYA - ARIAKE BAY

Season: spring & fall migration, winter
Specialties: Spoonbill, Black-faced Spoonbill, Common Shelduck,
shorebirds, Saunders's Gull, Penduline Tit

Near Isahaya is an enormous tidal flat, an excellent place to see shorebirds during migration. There are many wintering species, including several which are unusual in Japan. Often there are some rarities as well. The tidal flat is viewed from a seawall which surrounds a large area of reclaimed land now under cultivation. It is an ideal spot for enjoyable birding, with much open space, a variety of habitat, and a beautiful view of Ariake Bay. It is convenient to Nagasaki Airport. Don't miss Isahaya if you are in this part of Japan.

Transportation:
Isahaya is within 30 minutes of Nagasaki Airport by car. Both TDA and ANA have flights here from Tokyo (1 hour, 55 minutes), Osaka (1 hour, 15 minutes), Nagoya (1 hour, 25 minutes), and Okinawa (1 hour, 25 minutes). NKA has flights from Kagoshima (35 minutes) and Tsushima (1 hour, 35 minutes). The birding place is about ten minutes by car from the center of town. Birding here is most convenient with a car. It is not difficult to find the way.

Directions:
Rental cars are available at Nagasaki Airport. I used Nippon Rent-a-Car, which gave me good service but which charged me an extra ¥500 for taking me from the counter at the airport to where they keep the cars across the causeway. (The airport is all alone on a spit of land in the bay.) I complained, but was told that was local policy. You don't want to walk, but they don't even tell you of this extraordinary practice until they have already performed the service. Because of the way things work in Japan, I wouldn't be surprised if all the car agencies at this location do the same thing. If it matters to you to have extra charges added to the published and already-agreed-upon rates, inquire carefully when you make your reservations.

From the causeway, go straight to the first traffic light, turn right, and you will shortly meet Hwy. 34. There turn to the right for Nagasaki. After a few kilometers you will begin seeing signs

Isahaya Area

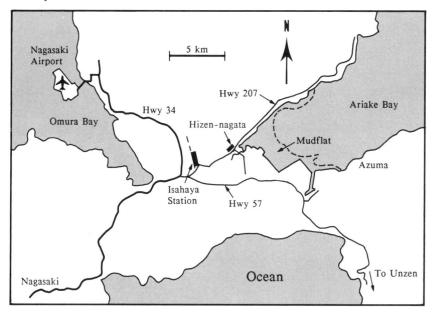

for Isahaya (all in *kanji*). Hwy. 34 goes to Nagasaki. You must turn off it (approximately 14.7 km. from the airport) to get to Isahaya. Follow your map and the *kanji* signs carefully. After you go through a tunnel, turn left to go to Isahaya Station. This is the center of the town and the best place from which to find your accommodations and the way to the birding place.

Because of the possibility of confusing the two roads which are Hwy. 57 (one is apparently the business route), directions to the reclaimed land and the tidal flat will start from the station. Once you find the tidal flat, it will be easy to move all around the area without losing your bearings.

With your back to Isahaya Station, go straight, cross the river, and turn right on the road immediately beyond the bridge. Go a short distance until you reach the next bridge over the river. This bridge is on your right when you get to the traffic signal. At the signal, turn left (do not cross the bridge). This road should be Hwy. 57 (business route). Measure your mileage from this point.

After you turn left on Hwy. 57, go straight until you reach an intersection where Hwy. 57 makes a turn to the right and Hwy. 207 goes almost straight ahead, angling slightly to the left. Take Hwy. 207, and continue on it until you have gone about 4.3 km. from the end of the bridge where you got on Hwy. 57. Shortly before you have gone the full distance, you will be able to see a blue bridge to your right. Turn right at the intersection 4.3 km. from your measuring point onto Hwy. 124. This road will take you across that blue bridge. At the intersection where you should turn off Hwy. 207, there is a post office on the far right-hand corner. This place is called Hizen-nagata, but there will probably be no sign you can read.

Turn left at the first road after you cross the blue bridge. Make your way to the edge of the reclaimed land and drive up on the seawall enclosing the rectangular section which sticks out by itself into the bay. It is from this seawall that you will have the best view of the tidal flat.

Ariake Bay at Isahaya

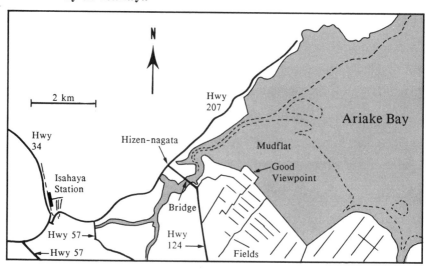

Site and Birds:
The best time for observing the tidal flat is about halfway between high and low tide. Before you go to Isahaya, make every effort to find out the tide schedule. During spring and fall migration, you could see anything here. In winter, I saw many

Snowy Plover, Black-bellied Plover, and Dunlin. There were some Curlew and a few odd shorebirds. There were at least 100 Common Shelducks quite close and probably many times that number farther out in the bay. You should see plenty of other ducks such as Mallard, Spot-billed Duck, Green-winged Teal, Pintail, Shoveler, Greater Scaup, Common Goldeneye, and Red-breasted Merganser.

Saunders's Gull is here occasionally in winter. This may be the most likely place to find it north of Okinawa. I had the good fortune to be here at the same time as a Black-faced Spoonbill. This species and Spoonbill sometimes occur in winter. While studying the area carefully through a telescope (which you will need), I thought I had been birding too much when I saw two flamingos. I later learned they were escapees and had been around for several weeks. You will probably see Great Crested Grebe, Eastern Reef Heron, and Gray Heron either here or nearby.

When you tire of the tidal flat, you can turn to the reclaimed land. There is an enormous stretch of open area with reeds, ditches, small waterways, cultivated fields, and many birds. The two days I was here I had the place all to myself except for a couple of farmers I could see working in the distance. It was one of the most pleasant birding trips I have had in Japan.

After you have carefully checked the fields inside this seawall, the whole flatland between the bay and the highway as far to the east as Azuma is worth exploring if you have time. You should see Skylark, Water Pipit, Dusky Thrush, Fan-tailed Warbler, Siberian Meadow Bunting, Rustic Bunting, Reed Bunting, Oriental Greenfinch, and Rook. Penduline Tits are here. You should find them if you look carefully. Don't fail to look carefully for Pallas's Reed Buntings. This is also a good place for birds of prey.

The checklist does not indicate abundance, but it lists plenty of good birds. Some of the migrant shorebirds included are Dotterel, Long-toed Stint, Baird's Sandpiper, Curlew Sandpiper, Great Knot, Spoon-billed Sandpiper, Ruff, Broad-billed Sandpiper, Spotted Greenshank, Terek Sandpiper, Slender-billed Curlew, and Little Whimbrel. Some of those could not have occurred more than once or twice, but it does show that this is a fine place. Some other interesting species on the list are Schrenck's Little Bittern, Purple Heron, Oriental Ibis, Ruddy Shelduck, Smew, Water Rail,

Ruddy Crake, Watercock, Indian Pratincole, and eight buntings.

You may see a Black-billed Magpie. If not, and it is important to you, drive up the coast on Hwy. 207. They are common in the Saga area, and some come farther south.

Note:
If you are driving to or from Fukuoka, you will pass through the Saga plain. The reclaimed land south of Saga at the north end of Ariake Bay is good for birds too. It is much more difficult there to find the way and get from one good place to another than it is around Isahaya. Also driving from Fukuoka is an extremely slow operation. There is much traffic, and the speed limits are low. After doing it both ways, I prefer to get to Isahaya as quickly as possible and spend all my time birding around there. Residents of Kyushu, however, will want to learn this area and devote some birding time to it.

Southwest of Isahaya is Mt. Unzen and Unzen Onsen, part of the Unzen - Amakusa National Park. The scenery is beautiful, but it is crowded with tourists and hotels. I went there for an annual meeting of the WBSJ and saw two birds, one Great Tit and one Siberian Meadow Bunting. I am sure there are more birds there, but I don't recommend it for a birding trip. If you are driving around Kyushu sightseeing, you should at least know that Unzen is nearby. From the east side of that peninsula at Shimabara you can get a ferry to Mizumi on the other side of the bay.

Time:
It will depend on the season and your time (as well as the tide schedule), but you will want at least one full day at Isahaya. During migration when the birds can vary every day, you may want another day or two to see what comes in.

Food:
There are restaurants in Isahaya, but nothing near the tidal flat and reclaimed land. Bring your lunch. It can be quite cold here in winter. You may welcome a thermos of hot tea or coffee.

Accommodations:
I stayed at the Business Hotel Janome, about a block from the Isahaya Station. It cost ¥3,000 for room only. Next time I will upgrade. I walked around the immediate area and saw several

small *ryokan* and *minshuku* which looked far superior to my hotel. The TIC provided the following names: Isahaya Kanko Hotel, 09572-2-3360, ¥7,000 - ¥20,000; Kanko Yachiyo Bekkan, 09572-3-1781, ¥5,500-¥8,000; and Senryu Hotel, 09572-2-0397, ¥6,000-¥8,000. I know nothing more about these places. There probably are others.

Maps and Information:
Champion Maps, Vol. 4, Kyushu
Buyodo Map D-1

National Map: 1:50,000 Isahaya 諫早

Useful Kanji:
Nagasaki	長崎
Isahaya City	諫早市
Isahaya Station	諫早駅
Hizen-nagata	肥前長田
Azuma	吾妻
Unzen	雲仙
Saga	佐賀

FUKUOKA AND HAKATA BAY

Season: migration, winter
Specialties: Great Crested Grebe, ducks, Oystercatcher, shorebirds

Fukuoka is the principal city of Kyushu. You might pass through here on the way to Tsushima, Okinawa, or some birding destination in Kyushu such as Arasaki Crane Reserve or Isahaya. If it is convenient, you should consider a stop to investigate Hakata Bay, the best place for birds in the area. If you have extra time in Fukuoka, you may want to visit Obori Park.

Transportation:
Fukuoka (Hakata Station) is 6 hours, 45 minutes from Tokyo on the Tokaido Shinkansen. There are many ways to reach Fukuoka by air. JAL has one flight from Sapporo (2 hours, 10 minutes) and one flight from Narita (1 hour, 40 minutes). TDA has flights from Sendai (1 hour, 40 minutes), Miyazaki (55 minutes), and Kagoshima (40 minutes). ANA has flights from Nagoya (1 hour, 10 minutes) and Komatsu (1 hour, 15 minutes). All three airlines have flights from Tokyo's Haneda Airport (1 hour, 30 minutes), and two have flights from Osaka (one hour) and Okinawa (1 hour, 30 minutes). NKA has seven flights a day to Tsushima.

The most convenient way to travel from Fukuoka Airport to the birding spots around Hakata Bay is by car. But the traffic congestion on the highway around the bay can be overwhelming, and it is difficult to find the way.

The two most important areas on Hakata Bay can be reached by train from Hakata Station. There also are buses, but this can be complicated.

Directions:
For Wajiro, take the JNR Kashiisen (Kashii Line) to Wajiro Station. Or drive to the northeast corner of the bay, first along Hwy. 3. Then when it turns inland, take the road which stays near the bay. There is also a toll road part of the way between Fukuoka and Wajiro. Be sure to get detailed directions, and try to find a good map.

For the Zuibaiji River and the area on the west side of the bay around Imazu, take the JNR Chikuhisen (Chikuhi Line) to

Imajuku Station. You can walk from here (about 30 minutes) or take a bus or taxi. By car, take Hwy. 202 to the west. At the end of the bay near Imajuku Station take the road which goes to the right along the west side of the bay.

Fukuoka Area

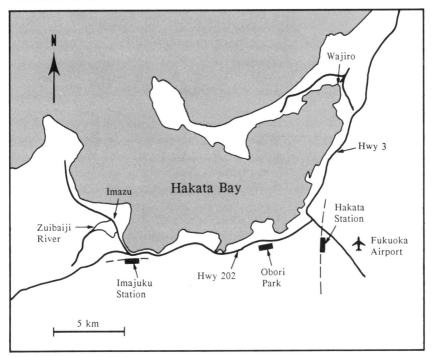

Site and Birds:
I was not destined to see Hakata Bay, so this account is based entirely on hearsay. I made four trips to Fukuoka for the purpose of investigating this area and, for four widely diverse reasons, failed all four times. The fourth time I cut a day from my schedule in southern Kyushu and made a desperate attempt with little time available, knowing I would not have another opportunity. I first tried to make my way from the Kyushu Expressway to Wajiro. When I got near the bay I got so hopelessly lost on a succession of highways, freeways, and toll roads, I gave up and headed for Imazu. I got near the port in Fukuoka with relative ease, eventually made my way to Hwy. 202 (I knew where I was, but the traffic was at a standstill), and then started the approximately 14-km. drive to meet the road which leads to the

Zuibaiji River. An hour and a half after I reached Fukuoka Port,
I determined I was traveling an average of 4 km. every half hour.
I gave up in disgust. This fiasco began in mid-morning of a
weekday. I am sure there must be a better way to do it. But don't
expect to drop in, rent a car, and in a few hours check out all the
birds around Hakata Bay before catching your plane.

The Imazu area seems to be where you can see the most birds.
More than 160 species have been recorded here. The best place is
a tidal flat where the Zuibaiji River flows into Hakata Bay. As
you go down the road along the west side of the bay, you should
find this on your left, 2 or 3 km. from Hwy. 202.

This is an excellent area for shorebirds during the spring and fall
migrations. There seems to be a difference of opinion just when
the peak periods are. It should be worth a visit any time from late
March to mid-May or in August and September. In winter you
should see loons, grebes, ducks (possibly including Falcated Teal),
and birds of prey. There are, of course, herons and gulls. The
surrounding reedbeds and fields are good for the usual species.
Look especially for Penduline Tit. It is hard to find, but it does
occur here. Don't fail to check the gulls. Saunders's Gull has been
seen on occasion. In the winter of 1984, a Slender-billed Gull, the
first for Japan, came for a long visit.

Check the bay on this side from every point where you can get a
good view. In winter there should be loons, grebes, and sea ducks.
Great Crested Grebes winter here in large numbers.

The Wajiro area also has Great Crested Grebes, but it is best
known for the few Oystercatchers that are here between
September and April. It has many ducks and shorebirds. Small
flocks of Common Shelduck occur occasionally. Since this is a
popular holiday spot during spring and autumn, sometimes too
many people spoil the birdwatching. If you are in a car, it should
be worth a trip to the end of the peninsula, checking birds in the
bay and in the ocean. The best three places are Shiohama, the
RKV facility, and the Karatsu River.

Obori Park (Obori Koen) is close to the center of Fukuoka. It is
most convenient to take the subway to Obori Koen Station. The
best season is from the end of November to early March. There
usually are several species of ducks, including Pochard, on the

pond. Spot-billed Duck is resident. Near the pond you might see Japanese Green Pigeon, Japanese Pygmy Woodpecker, Great Tit, Siberian Meadow Bunting, and Oriental Greenfinch. In winter you have a chance of seeing Daurian Redstart.

Time:
From my experience, already recounted, it would seem you would need the better part of a day for birding around Hakata Bay. In order to do both sides of the bay in one day, you would need your own transportation, an empty road, and a clear understanding of where you are going.

Food:
You shouldn't ever be far away from food, but taking it with you is best.

Accommodations:
Fukuoka is a large city with many hotels of all grades. I know of no accommodations near the birding sites.

Maps and Information:
Champion Maps, Vol. 4, Kyushu
Buyodo Map D-1

National Maps: 1:50,000 Fukuoka 福岡

Ube 宇部

Useful Kanji:

Fukuoka	福岡
Hakata Bay	博多湾
JNR Chikuhisen	国鉄筑肥線
Imajuku Station	今宿駅
Imazu	今津
Zuibaiji River	瑞梅寺川
JNR Kashiisen	国鉄香椎線
Wajiro	和白

TSUSHIMA

Season: spring migration
Specialties: rare migrants, Chinese Pond Heron, Chinese Egret,
Pied Harrier, Black-capped Kingfisher, Forest
Wagtail, Yellow Wagtail, Richard's Pipit, buntings

Tsushima is a large island (actually two islands connected by a bridge) in the Sea of Japan, about halfway between Kyushu and Korea. It has few human visitors, but especially in spring, it is a way station for migrant birds. Many species which stop here are seldom seen anywhere else in Japan, except perhaps on Hegura-jima. The islands are mountainous and picturesque. The villages still retain their traditional character. This is an excellent place to experience the excitement of migration without the transportation hazards of Hegura-jima. And there is more to see and do here if the birding is poor. Tsushima does not attract nearly as many migrants in the fall.

Transportation:
There are seven flights daily to Tsushima on NKA from Fukuoka (¥15,000) and two from Nagasaki (¥19,000). The time varies from about 35 minutes to 45 minutes depending on the type of aircraft. The price of the ticket is slightly more for a faster plane.

It takes about five hours to reach Tsushima by ferry. There are two ferry trips each day from Fukuoka (Hakata) to Izuhara and one each day from Kokura to Hitakatsu. The cost is between ¥3,000 and ¥4,000.

It saves time and is much more convenient to rent a car when you arrive on the island. Arrange this in advance.

Directions:
Although the islands cover a lot of territory, due to the mountains, the best birding is limited to two places. The Sago area, where you will spend most of your time, is on the northwest tip of the north island. Izuhara, where the ferry from Fukuoka (Hakata) arrives, is on the southern island. Allow about three hours to drive from there to Sago. The airport is a few kilometers north of Izuhara.

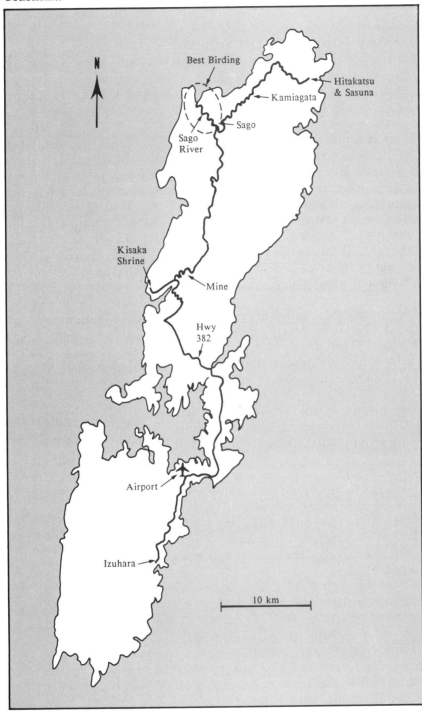

Best Birding

Hitakatsu & Sasuna

Kamiagata

Sago

Sago River

Kisaka Shrine

Mine

Hwy 382

Airport

Izuhara

10 km

The ferry from Kokura goes to Hitakatsu, much nearer where you want to go. Kokura is on the Shinkansen line (as is Hakata). If you are traveling by train, it is convenient. If you fly into Fukuoka, you must get to Hakata Station and then go to Kokura (25 minutes). You can work out the way that suits you best.

There is a map of Tsushima on the back of the Buyodo map D-1, but it doesn't have Tsushima written in Roman letters. Izuhara is in Roman letters, so you will eventually find it. If you arrive at Izuhara or at the airport, you will want to go north on Hwy. 382. Sago, your ultimate destination, on this map is at the intersection to the southwest of Kamiagata where a small road with no color branches off the highway to the northwest. The whole area along that road, from the highway to the ocean, is where you will look for birds. (There is a map of Tsushima on page five of the Champion Maps, Vol. 4.)

The other place you will want to go is Kisaka Shrine and bird forest (Yacho no Mori) on the southwestern side of the northern island. To get there, turn off Hwy. 382 south of Mine where a small road goes to the southwest just north of a blue body of water on your map. Go to the end of the road.

The telephone numbers for rental car agencies at the airport are 09206-2-4161 and 2-2406, at Izuhara 09205-2-5000, and at Hitakatsu (Sasuna) 09208-6-2310.

Site and Birds:
The Sago River valley is probably attractive to migrants because it may be the largest expanse of protected flatland on the island. There isn't much of it, but many birds are in this valley on a good day during spring migration. There are paddy fields, some scattered woods, the river, and some small water courses to examine.

Start from the highway and look at everything. You will soon get to know this valley well. Go down all the roads on both sides of the river. There is a trail through the woods behind the campground on the west side of the rivermouth. This is a good place for forest birds. A Japanese Night Heron was here at least once. Follow the road on the east side of the rivermouth until it ends. There are some paddy fields hidden in here and some good woods on both sides. When I was here, several Forest Wagtails were in the woods just before these fields. You can walk into the woods. In fact, you can go wherever you want through any of these fields, but be careful not to walk on the farmers' crops.

Sago Area

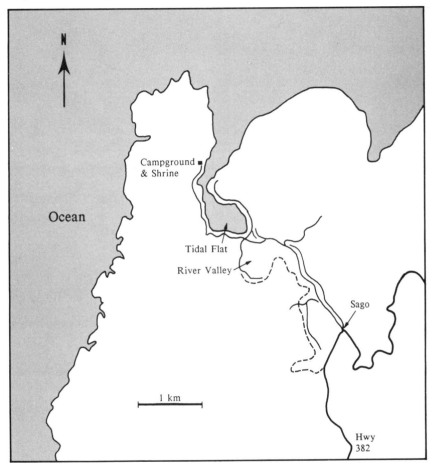

Japanese birders come here during the Golden Week holiday, which begins about the 29th of April. They insist that Tsushima has an extremely short season for good birding in the spring, but some of us skeptics think the migration may last longer than the Japanese holiday period. The majority of the data available comes from that week, so there is no way to know for sure what the trends are throughout the normal spring migration. I suspect it should be safe to go between the middle of April and the middle of May. A friend went in late May and saw nothing. Other than that, I have no information.

Sago is alive with birders during Golden Week. That has advantages and disadvantages. In this location, the birders don't appear to be disturbing the birds and causing them to leave. During that week, news of the latest sightings is constantly passed from group to group, so you are not likely to overlook anything. But all the accommodations are packed full. If you don't make your reservations months in advance, you may have to stay some distance from Sago. And, of course, travel during any Japanese holiday period is an ordeal. You might prefer to risk missing a bird in order to see this peaceful valley in its normal state and enjoy watching the birds without so many people around.

The ferry trip over is not particularly productive. You should see Streaked Shearwater and Northern Phalarope in great numbers. You may also see Red-throated Loon, Temminck's Cormorant, Pelagic Cormorant, and some gulls and terns. A Middendorff's Grasshopper Warbler landed on the ferry during my voyage, but that doesn't count.

Tsushima is interesting because it is impossible to know what you will see. And depending on the weather conditions, the birds can change significantly from one day to the next. Some of the rare species have occurred often enough that people now expect to see them in the Sago area every year even though sometimes only a single bird is observed in a season.

There are many migrant shorebirds in the fine shorebird habitat in the paddy fields and at the rivermouth. Among those reported are Mongolian Plover, Gray-headed Lapwing, Rufous-necked Stint, Long-toed Stint, Sharp-tailed Sandpiper, Great Knot, Spotted Redshank, Greenshank, Green Sandpiper, Wood Sandpiper, Gray-tailed Tattler, Terek Sandpiper, Black-tailed Godwit, Curlew, and Australian Curlew. Other birds you should look for during this season are Chinese Pond Heron, Chinese Egret, Purple Heron, Gray-faced Buzzard-Eagle, Pied Harrier (this one comes in the middle of April), Indian Pratincole, Black-capped Kingfisher, Short-toed Lark, Forest Wagtail, Yellow Wagtail, Richard's Pipit, Red-throated Pipit, Penduline Tit, Brambling, and Chinese Grosbeak.

This is the place to see buntings. I saw Siberian Meadow Bunting, Tristram's Bunting, Gray-headed Bunting, Little Bunting, Yellow-browed Bunting, Rustic Bunting, Yellow-breasted Bunting, Chestnut Bunting, Japanese Yellow Bunting, and Black-faced Bunting. Other buntings on the Tsushima list are Japanese Reed Bunting, Yellow-throated Bunting, Gray Bunting, and Reed Bunting.

Japanese Night Heron stays for the summer. This bird is one of the most difficult to see in Japan. Look carefully for it at Kisaka at the shrine and in the bird forest as well as behind the campground at the mouth of the Sago River. Among the summer visitors are Schrenck's Little Bittern, Green-backed Heron, Ruddy Crake, Little Ringed Plover, Japanese Green Pigeon, Horsfield's Hawk-Cuckoo, Scops Owl, Brown Hawk-Owl, Ruddy Kingfisher, Broad-billed Roller, Fairy Pitta (but no one can find it), Thick-billed Shrike, Pale-legged Willow Warbler, Crowned Willow Warbler, Narcissus Flycatcher, Blue-and-White Flycatcher, and Black Paradise Flycatcher. The Fairy Pitta used to be in a mountainous area away from Sago. We checked the place and found poor habitat. It is unlikely that the pitta has occurred there in recent years.

Although it is considered by the Japanese to be the same species as the Common Pheasant (Japanese Green Pheasant), the pheasant on Tsushima is the Ring-necked Pheasant. It is common (and introduced). Other residents of interest include Eastern Reef Heron, Hodgson's Hawk-Eagle, Common Quail, Bamboo Partridge, Japanese Wood Pigeon, Collared Scops Owl, Greater Pied Kingfisher, Blue Rockthrush, and Short-tailed Bush Warbler. Many ducks and birds of prey, as well as assorted passerines, winter on Tsushima.

A trip to this island is an adventure. From the cultural standpoint, you will see much that is different from the main islands. Most of the people earn their living from fishing, but you will notice *shiitake* mushroom cultivation in forests as you drive down the highway. Stop and have a close look. The method is interesting. And as far as birding is concerned, you can't help but have a good time. It may rain (be prepared for the possibility of heavy rain), but that's not always bad during migration. You don't need specific instructions for finding the one good bush where the birds are. There is a lot of excellent habitat for you to explore and make your own discoveries.

Time:

I stayed on the island seven days during spring migration and never tired of it. The problem is to decide how much time you can afford. Not counting the day you arrive or the day you leave, two full days would be a minimum during spring migration. You go to a lot of trouble to get here, and the fun is in waiting for a change in the weather to see what comes next. Don't cut it too short. You will enjoy this place. You might not enjoy Hegura-jima.

Food:

Get a packed lunch. We had to stay outside of Sago, so we brought a packed breakfast too or bought snacks. If you stay in Sago, you can go back for a quick breakfast. There are a couple of grocery stores around, but I found the available snacks limited to soft, fluffy, almost sweetish bread, only slightly more dense than cotton candy. Health food addicts would collapse if they saw what we lunched on sometimes. It is better to get a packed lunch of *nigiri* where you stay. You can find cold drinks at a grocery store.

Accommodations:

Sugawa Ryokan (09208-4-5175) is the one in Sago where you should try to stay. Aoyagi Ryokan (09208-3-0316) and Minshuku Inatome (09208-3-0743) are near Kisaka, but that is too far away to stay for birding in Sago. If you cannot get in Sugawa Ryokan, get help in finding the nearest available place.

Maps and Information:

    Champion Maps, Vol. 4, Kyushu
    Buyodo Map D-1
    National Maps: 1:25,000 Sago 佐護

                      Mine 三根

Useful Kanji:

Tsushima 対馬

Izuhara 厳原

Hitakatsu 比田勝

Sago 佐護

Kisaka Jinja (shrine) 木板神社

Kisaka Yacho no Mori (bird forest) 木板野鳥の森

Sasuna 佐須奈

Mine 三根

AMAMI OSHIMA

Season: all year
Specialties: Cinnamon Bittern, Amami Woodcock, Black-naped
Tern, Japanese Wood Pigeon, Red-capped Green
Pigeon, Pacific Swallow, Ryukyu Robin, Lidth's Jay

Amami Oshima is an island between Kyushu and Okinawa which
has three endemic species: Amami Woodcock, Ryukyu Robin, and
Lidth's Jay. It is the northernmost place to see some of the typical
Ryukyu species such as Cinnamon Bittern, Black-naped Tern,
Red-capped Green Pigeon, and Pacific Swallow. Ryukyu Scops
Owl, considered to be a separate species by some (but not the
Japanese), can be included on that list. In addition, there are a
number of subspecies on this island which are distinct in
appearance from those on the main islands.

Transportation:
There are direct flights to Amami Oshima on both ANA and TDA
from Kagoshima (1 hour, 15 minutes), on ANA from Okinawa (1
hour, 10 minutes), and on TDA from Osaka (1 hour, 25 minutes).
Round-trip fare from Kagoshima is about ¥26,000. You will need
a rent car on the island, although it is not impossible to get to
most places by a combination of bus and taxi.

Directions:
I recommend that you limit your birding here to the north end of
the island. It is most convenient to stay in Naze, the main city.
Directions to the birding sites will be given under Site and Birds
starting from the intersection in Naze where Hwy. 58 makes a left
turn, leaving the harbor and turning inland. This is about 29 km.
from the rental car agency at the airport.

A good map will be valuable provided you can find one. I haven't
so far. The detailed national maps were prepared so long ago that
they do not show most of the roads you will be using. A new
airport is being built to the north of the old airport. If you arrive
after it is operating (1988), remember these directions are from
the old airport.

As far as I can tell, there is only one rental car agency on Amami
Oshima. Before I left for my first trip, I could learn nothing about
renting cars on the island. When I got there, I discovered that the

local agent is a man who, when a plane arrives, stands in the parking lot next to an old green car with a sign on top. I now have two phone numbers, but no matter which I call, I end up dealing with the man beside the green car. The phone numbers are 09976-3-0240 and 2-1710.

The rates are high. The cheapest car is ¥13,000 for 24 hours. The rate decreases for additional days. Beware of the man beside the green car. His idea is to charge by the calendar day rather than by 24-hour periods. The whole operation is quite different from what you will experience on the main islands. You can bargain with him. You will not win anything, but you may succeed in getting the published rate rather than the higher one he wants to charge. The 24-hour day problem is always serious. When I came again with Japanese companions, the same thing happened, resulting in a 30-minute argument before we ever started off. This sort of confrontation is most un-Japanese. He speaks no English, so you will be in for an interesting experience unless he changes his ways. But don't give in.

The man will drive you in the green car to his office in a garage just down the road. From here continue in the same direction on that road for about 7.5 km. Turn left at the intersection with Hwy. 58. There is a sign indicating Naze 25 km. At 19.8 km. from the garage, note where you are. This is where you turn right for the Honchatoge Pass, described later.

Birding from this highway is impossible. It twists and turns, is crowded, and has no place to pull off. Be careful. But you may see Lidth's Jay flying across the road when you drive through the wooded area in the mountains. You will see more, so don't take any unnecessary risks.

Follow Hwy. 58 all the way into Naze. When you are getting near, you will come to a tunnel. You have the choice of going through it or around it. Go through. The road goes beside the harbor for some distance after you reach the town and then makes a sharp left turn just before you get to the Naze Prince Hotel. The hotel will be on your right and easy to see. Where the highway turns is 28.9 km. from where you started. I realize this doesn't agree with the "Naze - 25 km." sign you saw earlier. Whatever the cause of the discrepancy, the Naze Prince is obvious. (The name of this hotel may now be Naze Kanko. If the Prince sign is gone, look for

Kanko. The hotel, even without a sign, is a good landmark.)

Amami Oshima

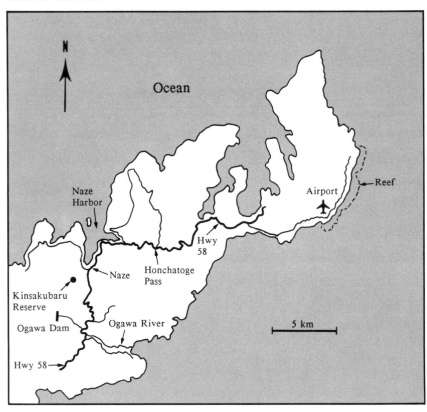

Site and Birds:
The most important thing you should know about Amami Oshima is that the snake *habu* is common and deadly. This snake occurs from here to Iriomote, but the ones on this island are the most poisonous of all. The *habu* is difficult to guard against because it often hangs from trees or other vegetation and drops on people. You must stay well away from vegetation, always in the middle of the road, while birding on this island. If you are driving down a narrow road with vegetation on each side, you must not open the doors and step out. You are likely to step right on a *habu* since they are fond of the sides of roads. Be sure to keep your windows closed.

I understand well the sometimes overwhelming desire of birders to get into the brush, but on Amami, don't. I visited a professor doing research on these snakes on Amami, and I am now convinced of the seriousness of a bite. There is no antidote. Wear boots at all times, and most of all, be extremely careful.

Amami Oshima is worth a visit at any time of year to see the three endemics. Lidth's Jay can be seen with the same degree of ease throughout the year. The Amami Woodcock is easier to see in July and August, but possible all year. The best time for seeing the Ryukyu Robin is from October through June. There are more species in winter, but summer is just as likely to bring rare birds as is winter. Winter is wet, and summer is hot. It can be even wetter during the rainy season, mid-May through the end of June.

In winter, Woodcock is present along with Amami Woodcock, so you must be careful with identification. In this season, Gray-faced Buzzard-Eagle is common. In summer, Roseate and Black-naped Terns breed on a rock in Naze harbor, and Ruddy Kingfisher and Black Paradise Flycatcher are easy to see. Cinnamon Bittern, Green-backed Heron, Japanese Lesser Sparrow Hawk, Japanese Wood Pigeon, Red-capped Green Pigeon, Ryukyu Scops Owl, White-backed Woodpecker (this subspecies has only a few white spots on its back), Pacific Swallow, and Ashy Minivet are resident.

Rufous Turtle Dove, Japanese Pygmy Woodpecker, Ashy Minivet, and Brown-eared Bulbul are all darker than those on the main islands. The Varied Tit looks like a mixture of the two subspecies pictured in the field guide.

On my first visit, two of the local experts showed me their favorite birding spots, all of which were on the north end of the island. On my second visit, with Japanese companions, we covered the whole island. I am convinced that the locals know best. Unless you want to go sightseeing, spend your time in the good habitat in the north. It takes a lot of time to get to the south, and there is nothing there you can't see more of easier in the north.

Your success with the three most important birds on this island will depend on your birding style. You have to find the Amami Woodcock with a light at night or shortly before dawn. You should hear Ryukyu Robin, but it is never easy to see. It is more difficult here than on Okinawa. If you are at the right place just before it gets light, you will have a good chance of seeing it. The efficient way to do this is to arrive at Kinsakubaru Reserve before first light. In one area you should find both Amami Woodcock and Ryukyu Robin. At the same time in the same place you should see Ryukyu Scops Owl.

Lidth's Jay is all over the place, but it can be missed entirely. To be sure of seeing this bird, you must have patience and not look for it from a moving automobile. When you get in Lidth's Jay habitat, get out of the car, walk around a bit, and wait awhile. They can sit still and keep quiet. You will be surprised how well such large, colorful, and noisy birds can blend into the foliage and stay hidden.

KINSAKUBARU RESERVE

Kinsakubaru Reserve and the good habitat you pass through getting there from Naze is my number one choice for good birding. From the place where Hwy. 58 turns inland near the Naze Prince Hotel, go straight instead of turning with the highway. Follow the main road as it leads to the west side of the harbor. The road curves to the right at some blinking lights, then curves back to the left a bit. After a Mobil station on the right, the road straightens out. Go through a signal light and then under a pedestrian overpass. You will come to a signboard over the road showing three choices. A sharp right turn leads to the port, a small road goes straight ahead, and the main road curves to the right in between the two.

Take the small road straight ahead which almost immediately goes to the right and slightly uphill. There are traffic lights and much congestion at this spot, but you should see the big Sanyo sign in front of you. Your small road goes in front of that Sanyo sign. This road was being repaired when I was there, so it may become easier to negotiate. Anyway, you want to be to the left and above the main road. (Kinsakubaru Reserve is approximately 13 km. from this Sanyo sign, so you may want to measure from here.)

Your road curves back to the left and soon branches. You can go uphill or downhill. Go uphill (the left fork). The road is now surfaced. From here you can begin looking for birds, although it gets better the farther you go. When you reach a T-junction, you have the choice of two roads to the right, uphill or downhill, and a road and a driveway to the left. Take the road to the left. At this junction there is a large signboard with a map showing the reserve where you are headed.

Lidth's Jays are sometimes in the trees along this road. There are few stopping places, but look if you can. You will pass a driving range, a junkyard, and eventually on your right a tall smokestack and the local garbage incinerator. Just beyond the incinerator, the main road turns to the left. (This is about 5.2 km. from the Sanyo sign.) Leave the main road and go straight on the unsurfaced road.

About 2 km. from here, if you watch carefully, you will see a rough road leading off to the right. Don't turn in, but leave your car on the side of the road. Walk down that road at least as far as the curve. You will have a good view across a valley. This is an excellent place to find a White-backed Woodpecker as well as Lidth's Jays. In summer many Black Paradise Flycatchers are here. The rare Red Turtle Dove also chose this location when it stayed for the summer recently.

Return to your car and continue along the unsurfaced road. Shortly you will see a sign for Ukin 33 km. straight and Sato 4 km. to the right. Next comes the sign for Ukin 31 km. straight and Chinaze 6 km. to the right. Keep going toward Ukin. The reserve is about 5 km. from your last stop. The first sign beside the road for the reserve is not out where you can see it easily, so pay attention. You will go left at a fork and quickly come to a large signboard similiar to the one you encountered shortly after leaving Naze. It is best to park near this signboard and walk down the road as far as you care to.

Before dawn you should find several Amami Woodcocks in the road near this sign (or perhaps even before you get to it). They will generally freeze in your headlights. You will be better off if you have a big flashlight with you. The Ryukyu Robins stay in the jungle downhill to your left. Sometimes, just at dawn, they are out in the road or along the edge. You might see these birds later, but you will be taking a great risk to pass up the time before dawn.

This is a good birding area at more conventional hours too. You will probably want to find your way up here the first time in daylight. It is a good plan to get to the reserve before daylight, spend as much time as you want, and then bird carefully along the road back, arriving in Naze for a late breakfast. A better plan is to take your breakfast with you.

If you have a good map or are courageous, there is another way back to Naze for your daytime expedition. Return to the sign pointing to Sato and take that road. It will take you through an attractive area with some different vegetation. You can eventually work your way to the coast and back east to Naze.

OGAWA DAM AND RIVERMOUTH

Go back to the intersection near the Naze Prince Hotel where Hwy. 58 turns inland. This time take Hwy. 58 going away from the harbor. After you get out of town, the road goes up into the mountains. Here again is good Lidth's Jay habitat, but the road is crowded and dangerous with no place to stop. After you have gone about 7.6 km. from the intersection near the Naze Prince, you can turn off to the right to Ogawa Dam. A narrow road goes to the left here, but the sign says it is dangerous and cars are not permitted. There is good habitat along the road leading to the dam. You can get out and walk near the river. Pacific Swallows are often flying around the dam.

When you finish birding along the road to the dam, go back to the highway, ignore the narrow road going the other way, cross over the bridge, and continue on Hwy. 58. After a short distance, the highway goes to the right, but you should stay on the road which goes along the river valley toward the mouth of the river. To your left will be a large area of paddy fields on both sides of the river. Make your way down there where you can drive or walk along the dikes to look for birds. Check this area carefully, all the way to the ocean. This is excellent territory in winter and should not be missed on a visit to Amami Oshima. I have not been here in summer, but have a look then too.

NAZE HARBOR

If you come in summer, it will be too hot in the middle of the day for productive birding. This is a good time to go to Naze harbor to see the Roseate and Black-naped Terns which nest on the small rock at the end of the harbor. Find a seawall out toward the entrance to the harbor. If you sit out there, you can get excellent photographs of terns flying past.

HONCHATOGE

Go back on Hwy. 58 in the direction of the airport to the turn at the top of the mountain which you noticed on your way into town the first time. This turn is approximatly 10 km. from the now well-known intersection where Hwy. 58 turns inland from the harbor. On the right side of the highway near the summit is a large white dome. It is easy to be looking the wrong way and miss it. On the left side is a tall structure with a chute coming from it. There is a sign in Japanese which ends with K.K. A drink machine is on the corner just before the structure with the chute. Turn left at the drink machine.

After this intersection, Hwy. 58 immediately begins to go downhill. This will help you tell if you have missed your turn. A bit farther downhill is a Tatsugo T sign on the left. If you see this, turn around and go back.

It is possible to stay on this road at Honchatoge Pass all the way down from the mountain to the flatland almost at the ocean. From there you can follow the road back to your left and eventually into Naze. I have done this only once, at night in the rain looking for Amami Woodcock, so I am unable to describe the habitat. When the road reaches the flatland, it goes through some paddy fields where we found Short-eared Owl.

I went part way along this road in daylight on another trip to Amami. The area near Hwy. 58 is becoming more developed, but there are still some good places for birds. A farmer in this vicinity feeds Lidth's Jays, so you should be able to find them. We spent little time here, but still saw Ruddy Kingfisher. The habitat is not as good as at Kinsakubaru Reserve, but it is still worth exploring. This used to be a good place to look for Ryukyu Robin.

REEF

The reef north of the airport is a good place to look for Eastern Reef Heron, a rare Black-faced Spoonbill which sometimes comes, ducks, and shorebirds. The new airport may destroy this area.

To get here continue on the road which goes by the rental car garage to the entrance to the airport. Go 4.7 km. beyond the airport turnoff to a small town. You will see a post office on the left. Look for a small school on a corner on the right. Look carefully; it isn't immediately obvious that this is a school. Turn right at this corner to make your way to the ocean and a place where there is a good view of the reef. This is a good place to end your birdwatching on Amami before catching your plane. Bring a picnic lunch if you are catching an afternoon flight.

Time:
Two nights is a minimum here. You could manage if you arrived one afternoon in time for some late birding, had all the following day for birding, and left in the afternoon on the day after that. In winter when it isn't so hot, you might enjoy more time. It also can rain, so you may need more time. But this will give you a good chance to see the endemics and the other species you need if you don't plan to visit the islands farther south.

Food:
There are restaurants in Naze. In winter you will want a packed lunch so you will not have to interrupt your birding. In summer, if you can afford the time, you might want to give up birding in the middle of the day and cool off in a restaurant. I still prefer eating where I have a chance of seeing birds.

Accommodations:
The two best hotels in Naze are the Naze Prince (room charge ¥12,000 for twin, telephone 09975-2-6151) which is on the main road at the harbor and the Amami Grand Hotel (room charge ¥10,000 for twin, telephone 09975-2-6411) which is above the town, overlooking the harbor. Both are easy to find. The Emerald Hotel, in the center of Naze, (room charge ¥5,000 single, telephone 09975-3-7111) is a business hotel, which is clean and adequate. I have also stayed at the Central Hotel, which is only ¥3,700 for a single room. The Emerald is the better value for that type hotel.

Maps and Information:

National Maps: 1:200,000 Amami Oshima   奄美大島

1:50,000 Akagina   赤木名

Useful Kanji:

Kinsakubaru Reserve	金作原自然観察林
Ogawa Dam	大川ダム
Honchatoge	本茶峠
Naze	名瀬

OKINAWA

Season: all year
Specialties: Okinawa Rail, Saunders's Gull, Pryer's Woodpecker,
*   Ryukyu Robin*

Okinawa has two endemics, many shorebirds, several species
which don't occur on the main islands, and enough rarities to keep
it interesting. You will have a reasonable chance of seeing Pryer's
Woodpecker, but don't expect the Okinawa Rail. Birdwatchers who
have searched for it understand well how it could have remained
undiscovered until 1981.

Transportation:
There are many flights every day to Naha, Okinawa. JAL and
ANA have four flights each from Tokyo (2½ hours), three from
Osaka (2 hours, 5 minutes), and two from Fukuoka (1½ hours). In
addition, ANA has two flights from Nagoya and one each from
Sendai, Kumamoto, Nagasaki, Kagoshima, and Miyazaki. Round-
trip fare from Tokyo is ¥67,400. You will need a car outside
Naha.

Directions:
Rental cars are available at the airport. Although there is a great
deal of traffic congestion in the south, with a good map you will
find driving here much easier than in any other place of
comparable size in Japan. Most roads on Okinawa are marked in
English. Many people here speak English, so you won't be in
terrible trouble if you get lost. When you get to the north of the
island, you will have more difficulty communicating. Finding the
way isn't a problem, but making yourself understood in hotels and
restaurants may be. Detailed directions to birding sites are in the
next section.

Site and Birds:
The destruction of good bird habitat on Okinawa continues at a
fast pace. The forests have been cut until the Pryer's Woodpecker
is endangered. The tops of hills are cleared and planted in
pineapple. The resulting erosion has covered coral reefs with red
earth and destroyed them. It is also filling the tiny ponds and
narrow streams at the foot of these hills with red mud. This is the
habitat of the Okinawa Rail. There is not enough known at
present about the Okinawa Rail to evaluate accurately the harm

this is doing, but one famous Okinawa Rail was discovered stuck in this red mud.

Okinawa

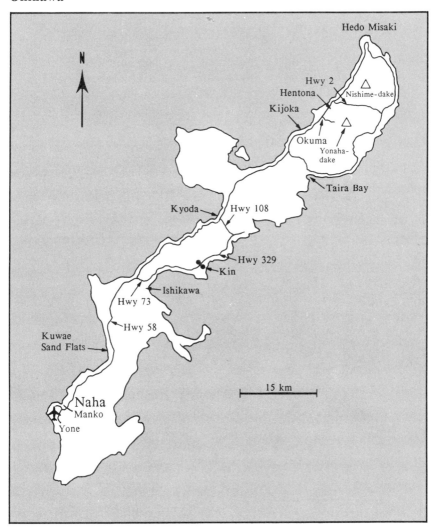

The government is actively promoting development of all kinds on the island. It seems to be especially pushing land reclamation projects, inviting industry to locate in coastal areas. Development of a port to relieve the port at Naha is currently taking place on the site of what was the second-best shorebird habitat on

Okinawa. All efforts of the local birdwatchers failed to deter this. With so much of the natural environment already destroyed, it is depressing to see no slowing down of this tendency to turn the whole country into concrete.

THE MANKO AND YONE

The Manko and Yone are excellent areas for shorebirds, just next to and near the airport at Naha. The largest concentration of birds is here from mid-October until mid-March, but it is good from August to May. Actually, it is so convenient to the airport, you should at least look here at any time of the year. In the summer you can see the resident Pacific Swallow even if nothing else of great interest is around. Most people go to the Manko, but there are always a few extra species at Yone. If you can, check both places. In winter, expect at least 15 species of shorebirds.

The Manko

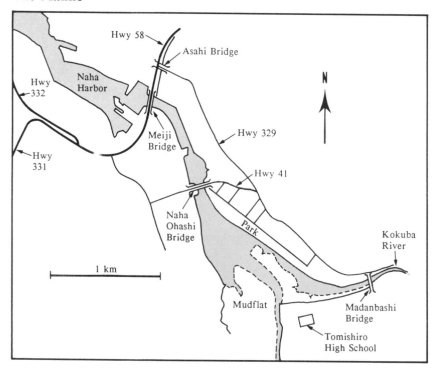

These two spots are the best places to look for rarities. You can count on seeing something unusual. Except for Saunders's Gull, however, nothing is reliable. Your best chance for seeing a Saunders's Gull in Japan is probably right here. For the last several winters this bird has almost always been here from December through February. During my visit to the Manko in a driving rain in mid-February, I saw Spoonbill, Black-faced Spoonbill, Canvasback, and Saunders's Gull. Other rarities which have occurred include Purple Heron, Watercock, Dotterel, Spoon-billed Sandpiper, Broad-billed Sandpiper, Asiatic Dowitcher, and Spotted Greenshank.

Some less rare birds which you are more likely to see are Greater Sand Plover, Terek Sandpiper, Black-tailed Godwit, and Bar-tailed Godwit. You can expect Little Ringed Plover, Mongolian Plover, Rufous-necked Stint, Redshank, Greenshank, Curlew, and Australian Curlew. There are ducks in winter.

It is easy to get to the Manko. If you are driving from the airport, go toward Naha. About 3 km. from the airport terminal building you will cross the Meiji Bridge. Naha Harbor will be to your left, the Kokuba River to your right. The main part of the mudflat will be farther to your right, beyond the next bridge, the Naha Ohashi (Naha Bridge). If you have the Japan Guide Map Co. Okinawa map, this is all clear on the Naha map. You must cross the Meiji Bridge and make a right turn at the next place you can (over the Asahi Bridge). You will pass the bus terminal on your left. At the fork, go to the right. This is Hwy. 329.

After you have gone 1.6 km. from where you made a right turn over the Asahi Bridge, you can turn right onto Hwy. 41 or continue on Hwy. 329. If you choose Hwy. 41, turn left before you get to the bridge, and you will reach the park beside the Manko. If you go straight on Hwy. 329, you can easily make a right turn on a side street and reach the park. After you finish along this side, make your way to the Madanbashi (bridge) and take the road to the right on the other side in front of the Tomishiro High School. On sunny days and in the morning, the best places to watch shorebirds are from the end of this road and from the park. It is best to bird this area from at least two sites.

You can get here easily by taxi from the airport if you have no other need for a car on Okinawa. The easiest way is to tell the taxi driver to take you to Tomishiro High School. Then walk back across the Madanbashi, along the park, across the Naha Ohashi, and south on the other side until you reach the end. With a map, you might be able to make the driver understand other places you want to go if you prefer not to walk.

To get to Yone, go south on Hwy. 331 for 4.1 km. from where Hwy. 332 meets Hwy. 331 (the turnoff to the airport). You will see an A&W Root Beer place on your right, 0.4 km. before you reach the place where you should make a right turn. This road will take you to Senaga Island, but turn left before the shrine and look for birds on the rocky flats and at the pond beyond them. Then go back to the road to Senaga Island and check the birds on both sides of the causeway. By taxi, tell the driver to take you to Senaga-jima.

Except for these places, the best birding is in the north. On the way, there are some places to stop and look. But plan to stay in the north and spend most of your birding time there.

KUWAE SAND FLATS

The Kuwae sand flats are worth a stop on your way north if you have plenty of time. The area is best at low or changing tides from August to April or May. You should see Snowy, Mongolian, Greater Sand, Lesser Golden, and Black-bellied Plovers, Greenshank, Gray-tailed Tattler, and Australian Curlew. During migration you might see both godwits and Curlew. This is not an important place, but it never hurts to look. And you don't have to go out of your way to do it.

This is a highly congested area with especially heavy traffic during the evening rush hour (4:00-7:00 p.m.). It is easy to miss the stopping places, so measure carefully. The starting point will again be the intersection of Highways 332 and 331 at the entrance to the airport. Go north on Hwy. 58. At 17.1 km., Hwy. 130 will go to your right. Notice this, but continue on Hwy. 58. Soon after this at 17.9 km., 18.2 km., and 18.9 km., there are small dirt roads or parking areas from which you can view the sand flats.

KIN RIVER AND PADDY FIELDS

The Kin River and especially the neighboring paddy fields should not be missed. It is a quiet and pleasant area where you can get close looks at birds in the paddies. More than 20 species of shorebirds have been seen here. You will have a good chance of seeing something rare or at least interesting. Morning is the best time, but any time of day is ok.

It is a good place to look for Long-toed Stint, Temminck's Stint, Broad-billed Sandpiper, and Spotted Redshank. Rare birds for Okinawa such as Baillon's Crake, Pectoral Sandpiper, and Stonechat have come here. Best of all, it is a popular location with snipe and pipits. It's a fine place to study these species since you can get so close to them. Pechora Pipits come in January and February. Birding is excellent here during spring and fall migration.

It is a good idea to drive around first to see where the birds are and then walk. Try to stay off the paddy dikes unless you are faced with a real emergency, such as a Pechora Pipit you can't see from anywhere else. Before you leave, check the river, where there is one of the biggest patches of mangroves on the island. Common Kingfisher is resident. Japanese Lesser Sparrow Hawk often calls from the mangroves at night.

To get to the Kin paddies, continue north on Hwy. 58 from the Kuwae sand flats. The kilometers given still start from the entrance to the airport. At 20.1 km. you will pass Gate 1 for Kadena Air Force Base. At 24.0 km. there is a ramp to the right to Chibana. Ignore that and follow the sign for Nago to the left. You will enter a traffic circle at 24.4 km. and should leave it at 24.6 km. At 24.7 km. a sign above the road indicates Nago 42 km. and Onna 19 km. ahead. After you have negotiated this traffic circle, you should still be on Hwy. 58.

At 35.0 km. and 35.2 km. there are signs pointing left to Nakadomari and right to Nago. You will soon go over an overpass. Immediately on the other side of it (35.9 km.) turn right toward Ishikawa and the Okinawa Expressway. At 36.5 km. you will be at the end of this ramp and on Hwy. 73. You will pass the entrance to the expressway at 39.1 km. and reach Hwy. 329, where you should turn left at 39.5 km. Here there is a sign indicating Yaka to the left and Okinawa City to the right. At 40.0 km. (on Hwy. 329) a sign shows Nago 38 km. and Kin 11 km. straight ahead.

You will pass Gates 1 and 2 to Camp Hansen at 50.3 km. and 51.9 km. At 52.1 km. turn off the highway to the right (this point will be 0.0 km. for the next measurements to the north), go 0.85 km. and turn left on a small road, and you will reach the Kin paddies 1.0 km. from the highway.

KIN RESERVOIR

Kin Reservoir is across the highway, so stop in there before you leave the area. Go back the way you came and cross Hwy. 329. At 0.7 km. from the highway, you will cross over the Okinawa Expressway, and at 1.1 km. a dirt road goes to the left toward Kin Reservoir. There is a gate at the entrance to the road, but it is usually open. You can drive in to a parking area at 1.3 km. The road is rough, so it is best to park here and walk to the reservoir at 1.8 km.

Morning is the best time. You will see passerines along the path and, from October to March, some ducks on the reservoir. When the water is down, look for White-breasted Waterhen. Japanese Lesser Sparrow Hawk is here, but it is more often heard than seen. Ryukyu Scops Owl (*Otus elegans*) and Collared Scops Owl have been recorded in February and March. They probably are here all year.

KYODA

At Kyoda there is a colony of Pacific Swallows under the overpasses where Highways 108 and 58 meet. In summer, look there in the shallow bay for flocks of terns. You might see Common (subspecies *longipennis*), Roseate, and Black-naped.

From the point on Hwy. 329 where you turned off to Kin paddies and to Kin Reservoir (now 0.0 km.) go north on Hwy. 329 for 10.3 km. and turn left on Hwy. 108. Cross the island on this road, and you will meet Hwy. 58 at 15.5 km. This is where you look for the birds. The Okinawa Expressway meets Hwy. 58 at 15.9 km. For the rest of the way, kilometers will be measured from here.

KIJOKA

Kijoka is the next area to visit. The paddies are good for shorebirds as well as for Cinnamon Bittern and Green-backed

Heron. This is also a good place for interesting passerines. Bluethroat and Little Bunting have been here. Above the paddies, both roads going up into the hills are worth checking. Japanese Wood Pigeon and Ryukyu Robin are resident. The robin is always easiest to see at dawn. Look for Gray Bunting in winter. Collared Scops Owl and Brown Hawk-Owl are resident. This is a good area for Ruddy Kingfisher from late April.

Hentona Area

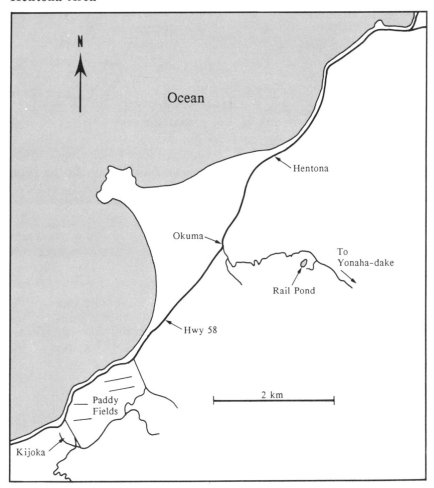

From where the expressway meets Hwy. 58, you must make your way through Nago. There are large signs, so you shouldn't have any trouble. Measuring from the end of the expressway, at 4.4 km. there is a sign for Nago City to the right. Do not take this road. At 5.7 km. Hwy. 58 makes a right turn. Stay on the highway. At 6.0 km. there is a sign for Motobu to the left on Hwy. 116. Don't turn there either. Continue on Hwy. 58. At 11.8 km. a road to the right goes to Tano-dake, at 12.9 km. there is a sign for Hentona 23 km. and Ogimi 16 km. straight ahead, at 23.0 km. you will cross a red bridge, and at 30.6 km. you should turn off to the right to Kijoka. See the accompanying map.

OKUMA AREA

The only widely-known site for the Okinawa Rail comes next. Any birder who makes it this far will want to try to see this bird. You must consider it one of the great moments of your birding career if you actually get even a glimpse of it. This location is easy to find. Although it is accessible without special permission, it is a good idea to go in groups of no more than two or three persons. This should not disturb the local people, and it will give you a better chance to see the bird.

Despite the unlikely appearance of the place, this is where many people who have seen the rail have found it. I sat here long cold hours on two successive days and saw nothing. On the following day when I went somewhere else, two people sat side by side and again kept watch for hours. One saw the bird stick its head out of the weeds for a split second, but the person sitting next to him missed it. Many people have devoted considerably more than three days to this task and have failed to see the bird. Another of the lucky ones sat here for seven days before it appeared.

The habits of the Okinawa Rail remain a mystery, but it makes appearances more often in the early morning and at dusk. It seems to spend most of its time in thick sedges in marshy areas around small ponds or narrow streams in protected areas. It seldom shows itself for more than a few seconds at the edge of the water, although one was seen running across a road and another swimming across a pond.

I saw this bird through the generosity of researchers from the WBSJ who allowed me to accompany them. We sat hidden and absolutely quiet all day and finally saw it for only a moment. Even so, I was extremely lucky. They had access to a special place, but still would sit for days on end and see nothing. All this is to let you know what you are up against so you won't make a trip all the way to Okinawa expecting to see this bird.

To get to the rail place, go back to the turnoff for Kijoka at 30.6 km. and continue north on Hwy. 58. At 33.6 km. there is a Caltex gasoline station on the right, at 34.5 km. the road to the left goes to Okuma Beach, and at 34.9 km. there is a traffic light where you should turn to the right. This is Okuma village. From here it is 2.5 km. to the rail site. After you make the right turn from the highway, make another right turn almost immediately. You will pass a school on your right. Take the road which curves around to the left and goes uphill, ultimately to Yonaha-dake (Mt. Yonaha).

This road is being improved, probably for the benefit of the lumbering industry in the area. When I visited this place there was much construction and confusion. But 2.5 km. from the highway you should see some concrete pillars on the right with a cow shed behind them and a small road going steeply downhill. Go down this little road. The pond is in a depression to the right and is not easily seen from the road. After the steep downhill part, there is a flat area on the right where you can park. If you walk across this flat area, you can look down on the pond. This is probably the best vantage point.

Be prepared for a long wait. In winter you can get cold sitting here. You must be absolutely still and quiet. This will be easier if you can bring or find something to sit on other than the cold, wet ground. A thermos of hot tea or coffee will help your feelings as will something to eat, if you can manage without rattling the wrappings.

When I was here the road construction prevented it, but you should be able to get up Yonaha-dake now. It might be worthwhile if you have enough time. It used to be possible to drive along this road for about 20 minutes from Okuma village to a small parking area and then walk an hour to the top. This is (or was) good habitat for Pryer's Woodpecker. The areas where the trees have not been cut should be good for all the species which prefer the higher elevations. These include the Japanese Wood Pigeon, Red-capped Green Pigeon, and Ryukyu Robin. If you walk up here, stay on the forest road. The footpath is dangerous, especially because of *habu* (see Amami Oshima).

NORTHERN CROSS-ISLAND ROAD

The Northern Cross-Island Road winds through the hills and has a number of small side roads leading from it where you can walk. This road goes through what formerly was good habitat for Pryer's Woodpecker. The area is being developed and the forests cut. If you have time to check this, you might find something interesting on one of the side roads.

To get here, go back to Hwy. 58 where you turned off at Okuma village to get to the rail site and Yonaha-dake (34.9 km.). Continue on Hwy 58, going through Hentona and then through a tunnel at 40.2 km. At 41.0 km. the Northern Cross-Island Road (Hwy. 2) goes to the right.

NISHIME-DAKE

Nishime-dake (Mt. Nishime) has the most accessible primary forest on the island. This is the best place to see Pryer's Woodpecker, but you must be here before dawn to have a reasonable chance for it. At that hour, the Ryukyu Robin should be easy. Ryukyu Robins seem to have an affinity for road edges at dawn. After that they disappear into the thicket. Pryer's Woodpecker is never easy. The bird is here, but in this case your skill may be more important than your luck in determining whether or not you see it.

Other birds likely in this area are Japanese Wood Pigeon, Red-capped Green Pigeon, Scops Owl (Ryukyu Scops, *Otus elegans*), Japanese Pygmy Woodpecker, Ashy Minivet, and Bush Warbler. From April on through summer, this is a good place for Ruddy Kingfisher, Narcissus Flycatcher, and Black Paradise Flycatcher.

To get here, continue north on Hwy. 58. At 46.3 km. turn right on the road behind the cement factory, ignoring the big road in front of the cement factory. From this turn, go 5.7 km. The pavement should end about here, but this could change. Anyway, this is the place where the forest is best and where you are most likely to find the woodpecker. Wander about, but don't get off the road. The slopes are steep and crumbly, but a more important reason is that *habu* are in this area.

HEDO-MISAKI

Hedo-misaki (Cape Hedo) is at the northern tip of the island. From the cement factory, continue north on Hwy. 58 for approximately 7 km. There are never many birds here, but it is a good place to check for strays. Migration is the best time. Check the ground between the parking lot and the end of the cape. Near the parking lot are some clumps of casuarinas which should be investigated thoroughly. South of the cape, there are roads through the cane fields where you can drive or walk.

This is a good place for birds of prey. Daurian Redstart, Stonechat, Ijima's Willow Warbler, Brown Flycatcher, Little Bunting (all rare for Okinawa) have turned up here. Look for thrushes and finches in winter.

Now you are on your own to explore. From the cape, you can drive on around the eastern coast checking good habitat along the main road and all the side roads. There are some good places, though nothing as dependable as what has already been described. There is little point in extending your serious exploration on the east side any farther south than about Taira Bay.

A bird which has not been mentioned, but which should not be overlooked, is Barred Buttonquail. Look beside the road next to cane fields anywhere on the island. Beware of *habu* at all times. You could walk in cut fields where there is only stubble, but wear sturdy boots. Stay out of deep vegetation of any kind.

Time:
It is difficult to be helpful here. One fact which may be useful is that in very early morning before the traffic gets congested, it takes 3½ hours to drive from Naha City to Hentona, just north of Okuma. This is by the direct route, Hwy. 58 all the way, with no stopping. Your timing on Okinawa will depend on your goals. It is a long way to come to rush through. Two nights on the north end of the island would be a minimum.

Food:
In the south there are restaurants everywhere. They thin out considerably as you go north. There is a place occasionally where

you can buy cold drinks or snacks. It will be most convenient to take a packed lunch or buy supplies at a grocery store before you get far north.

Accommodations:
The island is full of hotels of all sorts, but few are convenient to the best birding areas. If you plan to be at good sites before the sun comes up, nearness can be a more important factor than comfort.

The Miyashiro Hotel (098042-2337 and 5320) in Hentona (km. 36.1) is acceptable. The Yoneko Minshuku (098042-5433) is in Okuma. No one speaks English.

Maps and Information:
  Champion Maps, Vol. 4, Kyushu
  Japan Guide Map Co. Ltd., Handy Map of Okinawa

  National Map: 1:50,000 Hentona 辺土名

If you come while Doug McWhirter is still a resident, he will be happy to talk with you about birds on Okinawa. His home telephone number is 0989-38-1111 ext. 39070.

Useful Kanji:
  The Manko   漫湖
  Tomishiro High School   豊見城高校
  Senaga-jima   瀬長島
  Kijoka   喜如嘉
  Okuma   奥間
  Yonaha-dake   与那覇岳
  Nishime-dake   西銘岳

ISHIGAKI AND IRIOMOTE ISLANDS

Season: November - March, May - July
Specialties: Malay Night Heron, Purple Heron, Crested Serpent-
Eagle, Barred Buttonquail, Banded Crake, Black-
naped Tern, Bridled Tern, Emerald Dove, Red-capped
Green Pigeon, Chinese Bulbul, Gray-backed Myna

These two islands are described together because if you go, you
should visit both of them. They belong to the Yaeyama Islands
group at the southern end of the Ryukyu Islands, near the Tropic
of Cancer and Taiwan. So far, they still retain their coral reefs
and much fine habitat for birds. The birdlife is quite different
from that on the main islands. More species are here in winter,
including a large number of wintering shorebirds, but summer
brings several species of breeding terns, Ruddy Kingfisher, and
Black Paradise Flycatcher. The culture is distinctive. This is an
enjoyable and important birding area which, despite the distance,
should be seriously considered as a destination for all birders
visiting Japan.

Transportation:
There are about eleven flights every day on Southwest Air Lines
from Naha (Okinawa) to Ishigaki Island. A round-trip ticket costs
¥26,500. The Tokyo - Okinawa round-trip fare is ¥67,400. Since
most birders will go as far south as Kyushu anyway and will have
the benefit of all flights on one fare calculation, the added cost of
going to Ishigaki will have to be figured individually.

The flight from Okinawa takes 55 minutes. A direct flight from
Tokyo to Okinawa takes 2 hours, 50 minutes.

Rental cars are available at Ishigaki Airport. There are boats to
Iriomote Island in the morning and in mid-afternoon (about one
hour). Cars can be rented on Iriomote at the ports. There are some
buses on these islands, but birding with a car is much more
efficient and enjoyable.

Directions:
Where to go on these islands will be discussed under Site and
Birds. If you intend to start on Iriomote Island, you can get a taxi
from the airport to the port at Ishigaki. It isn't far. But make
arrangements for a car for your return. It is possible to deal with

some rental car agencies through various shops around the port, but it may not be evident to you. Here, also, you will have a language problem.

The building where you buy your ferry ticket is on the side of the port, to the left of a cream-colored building with a clock at the top. In the winter there are two boats which make two trips daily to Ohara Port on Iriomote. They are the Tropical Queen (¥2,000) and the Hirugi (¥1,330). You get what you pay for. In winter, boats leave at 8:40 a.m. and 9:00 a.m. and at 3:00 p.m. and 3:25 p.m. In summer, boats go also to Funaura Port. There are probably more choices. Check the current schedule. The telephone number for the ferry office is 09808-2-5010.

There are three rental car companies at Ohara and one at Funaura. For groups, the Azuma Bus Co. (09808-2-2054) on Ishigaki and Tobukutsu on Iriomote handle bus charters. In summer, especially, you should make reservations for cars and for accommodations.

Site and Birds:
Approximately 100 species of birds winter here, but there are only about 40 breeding species in summer. Winter tends to be wet with the minimum temperature around 10°C. Summer is dry with respect to rain, but has high humidity and temperatures to 32°C. The area is famous for butterflies, but most are here in spring and fall. You will see the most birds from November through March, but you may be bothered by rain. May is the best month to see the breeding birds, except for the seabirds. June and July are better for them. In any season, you must be careful of *habu*. (See Amami Oshima.)

Among the resident birds which you could see anytime are Brown Booby, Cinnamon Bittern, Malay Night Heron, Eastern Reef Heron, Purple Heron, Japanese Lesser Sparrow Hawk, Crested Serpent-Eagle, Barred Buttonquail, Banded Crake, Ruddy Crake, White-breasted Waterhen, Watercock, Japanese Wood Pigeon, Emerald Dove, Red-capped Green Pigeon, Scops Owl (some consider the Ryukyu Scops Owl a distinct species), Ashy Minivet (also possibly distinct), and Chinese Bulbul. The Jungle Crow (*Corvus macrorhynchos osai*) is much smaller than the subspecies on the main islands.

The birds you can see here only in summer are Bulwer's Petrel,

Streaked Shearwater, Roseate Tern, Black-naped Tern, Bridled Tern, Sooty Tern, Little Tern, Brown Noddy, Ruddy Kingfisher, and Black Paradise Flycatcher. Don't count Bulwer's Petrel, Sooty Tern, and Brown Noddy until you see them. You will have a chance, but a slim one, of seeing them from the boat between Ishigaki and Iriomote. Roseate and Black-naped nest on rocks near Cape Tamatori on the northeast side of Ishigaki. They are easy to see. Little Tern nests on reclaimed land in Ishigaki harbor. Bridled Tern nests farther away, but does come in to the reef. You have a fair chance of seeing it. There is a colony of Sooty Terns on a rock north of Taketomi Island, which is between Ishigaki and Iriomote. I have not been there, so I don't know what your chances are for that one. (Taketomi is noted for its weaving, which is demonstrated for visitors. It is probably worth a visit to learn more about the local culture.)

This is a fine place for shorebirds, with excellent habitat on Ishigaki. There is good shorebird habitat on Iriomote, but more of it on Ishigaki. Besides the transients, many winter here. That list includes Little Ringed Plover, Mongolian Plover, Lesser Golden Plover, Black-bellied Plover, Ruddy Turnstone, Rufous-necked Stint, Dunlin, Redshank, Greenshank, Green Sandpiper, Wood Sandpiper, Gray-tailed Tattler, Common Sandpiper, Terek Sandpiper, Black-tailed Godwit, Curlew, Whimbrel, and Common Snipe. I have seen a few of these here in the summer, though they aren't on the list for that season. There is a place to look for Bittern on Iriomote. At least one Chinese Egret has wintered on Ishigaki in recent years. Gray-faced Buzzard-Eagle is abundant in winter. Yellow, Gray, and White Wagtails are easy to see in winter, along with Red-throated Pipit, Brown Shrike, Brown Thrush, Pale Thrush, Dusky Thrush (including subspecies *naumanni*), and Brambling. Silky Starling is a rare winter visitor. Gray-backed Myna regularly winters here, but in small numbers. It is difficult to find.

Purple Heron, Crested Serpent-Eagle, and Chinese Bulbul are in greater numbers and much easier to see on Iriomote than on Ishigaki. Except for those species, the birds are about the same on both islands. But some are easier to find on one island than on the other. There is more flatland on Ishigaki.

ISHIGAKI ISLAND

Ishigaki has a larger population and is more developed than
Iriomote. But after you have traveled on the main islands of
Japan, you will think it is almost deserted. It still has good habitat
and many birds.

Ishigaki Island

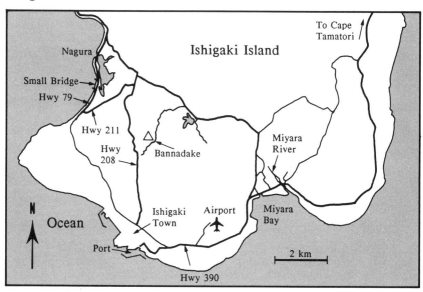

At the moment a controversy is raging over a plan to construct a
new airport on Ishigaki at Shiraho, the only place on Ishigaki
where the coral is thriving. The mayor wants to increase tourism
significantly on this island and believes an airport which can
handle airbuses is the answer. The airport has been authorized by
the Transport Ministry, and the site has been purchased. The plan
is to demolish Karetake, a nearby hill, and use its rock to build a
runway 3 km. long on top of the coral. Although construction is
due to begin immediately, environmentalists and others have
begun a campaign to oppose the airport. There is at least a chance
that this additional development on Ishigaki will be delayed for a
while.

You will need a detailed map for getting around Ishigaki and for locating more easily the sites marked on the accompanying map. You will enjoy exploring on your own, but the most important areas are indicated. The southernmost part of the island is best for birds.

From the airport, take Hwy. 390 to the east toward the Miyara River. At the top of Miyara Bay, before you reach the river, you should see a small Caltex gasoline station on the left. Turn left at that corner and look on your left for a pond where eel are raised. There is a narrow stream next to this. Many tiny fish gather where the water comes from the pond into the stream. Walk along here to look for Cinnamon Bittern, Green-backed Heron, and other birds.

Near this place, but to the right, you will see a large, green, two-story building with a tower and a blue building next to it. There are also two tall smokestacks in the vicinity. Drive all around here. If Silky Starlings are to be found, it will probably be in this area. Somewhere nearby you should find a large manure dump. (The location changes from year to year.) This is sometimes covered with birds, usually shorebirds and wagtails, including Yellow Wagtail. The starlings are often near the manure dump.

Go slightly north toward the river and find the cow pens. There are many birds in here. It is wooded with a lot of low vegetation. Look for Malay Night Heron. There is an easier place to find it on Iriomote, but don't pass up any opportunities to look for it. You can walk through this woods over to the river's edge.

Go back to Hwy. 390 and cross the Miyara River. Turn left when you reach the road where a tree and a stone marker are in the middle of the intersection. Go down this road until you come to an intersection where you can see eight tall red towers to your left. Turn right and go to the next big intersection. There go left. This road goes through an open area of small woods, paddy fields, and watercourses. Spoonbill does not occur every year, but this is the best place to look for it.

The next place is a bit confusing, but important. You want to go to Bannadake (Banna Protected Forest). The Japan Guide Map Co. map of Okinawa has a mark and "Botanical Garden" at this point. (Okinawa Island and everything south is part of Okinawa Prefecture.) The national map of Ishigaki shows a lake about 5 km. directly north of Hwy. 390 if you measure from Hwy. 390 just to the west of the airport. The main road on the north side of that lake is what you are looking for.

When you get in that vicinity, you will find on the south side of the road a sign between two narrow roads. One road goes uphill. Take the other. This will lead you to an unsurfaced road. When you get to where you can't go any farther, park your car and find the trails which lead through a lovely, dense forest. You can walk beside a stream and enjoy the interesting vegetation. My recollection of this does not exactly match the map. The two roads are not shown. On the national map, the road to the west of the lake and dam is the one you want. It goes to the southwest from the main road.

Malay Night Heron lives here too. In summer, Ruddy Kingfisher and Black Paradise Flycatcher are common. This is a good place to look for Banded Crake and Emerald Dove. If you can't find them in here, explore as much of the forest on this particular hill as you can gain access to. They do live on this hill.

An old couple who live on this hill feed Emerald Doves. For five years a Ruddy Kingfisher came to stay with them every summer. It ate live cockroaches out of their hands. All their friends and relatives worked hard to catch roaches for the kingfisher. This bird behaved much like a pet dog. It would come in the house, walk across the floor to where they usually sat watching TV, and beg for roaches. The whole story is preposterous. But I have visited these people a couple of times and seen numerous photographs of the Ruddy Kingfisher indeed walking across their *tatami* floor and begging for roaches. It was sad when, after five seasons, the Ruddy Kingfisher failed to return. You can understand that it isn't appropriate for foreign visitors to intrude on these lovely old people, especially without speaking their language. There is no longer a kingfisher to see. And the Emerald Doves are on the hill, thanks to their attention. You should be able to find them.

Scops Owl is here. I saw a nest near the road which leads to the southeast from the lake (see the map). And by walking (in high boots and taking great care for *habu*) through a field with short stubble southeast of the lake, I flushed and got excellent views of Barred Buttonquail.

Back to the road on the north side of that lake, go west until you reach Hwy. 208. Turn right and go to the ocean, north of the large lagoon at Nagura. When you reach the ocean, turn back to the left (south) on Hwy. 79. This is excellent habitat. If you are going south, shortly before you reach the small bridge at the south end of the lagoon, there is a path to your left into the mangroves. It is hard to find, so stop your car and look for it on foot if necessary. In a few meters you will be through the trees and out onto the edge of the lagoon. With boots you can walk some distance, passing patches of mangroves. There usually are birds all over the place. You should see herons, ducks, shorebirds, gulls, terns, and assorted passerines. This is the place favored by the Chinese Egret. Sometimes Black-faced Spoonbill occurs.

Then continue down Hwy. 79 until Hwy. 211 leads off to the northeast. Turn left here and look for birds all the way until the road meets Hwy. 208. This is an excellent area for Ruddy Crake and Watercock. In fact, all of this corner of the island is good territory. Don't pass up the paddy fields immediately to the northwest of Ishigaki town.

If you come in summer, drive north up the east coast on Hwy. 390 to Cape Tamatori. From the lookout point, with a telescope you can see Roseate and Black-naped Terns on the rocks beyond the cape. Then go back to the south along the highway until you find an unsurfaced track to the left which you can drive down. You should reach a wide place where you can park. Then walk to the beach. You can get a much better look at the terns from here.

The beach directly south of the airport and the beach on the east side of Ishigaki near a rivermouth about 4 km. north of the southeastern tip of the island are good birding spots. In winter Gray-backed Myna is usually in Ishigaki town. Look on all the wires. You are on your own from here. You should have pleasant and productive birding on Ishigaki. If your time is limited, remember that the locals agree that the southern part of the island is best.

IRIOMOTE ISLAND

Only about one-third of Iriomote Island belongs to the Iriomote National Park. Foreigners who visit Iriomote are usually surprised to find so much development. They probably assume that most of this island is included in the park and don't realize that Japan does not restrict development in national parks to the extent that they expect. The main industries on Iriomote are pineapple growing and tourism. Much of the island remains untouched, but one can't help but wonder how long it will remain so.

Iriomote Island

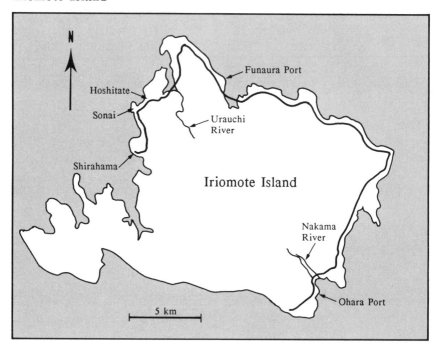

This is also the home of the famous Iriomote Wildcat, which has been designated as a Special Natural Living Monument. It can be hoped that interest in this creature will ultimately lead to the preservation of the island. This small cat (there are only a few) is nocturnal. You would have to take extraordinary steps to see one.

From Ohara Port, first take the main road to the left (southwest). The hard surface soon ends, and the road may be too muddy for your car. In that case, walk. It isn't far to the beach. This area is good all the way, with a mixture of woods and fields. When you go back toward Ohara, follow the road closest to the water's edge. The area here between the main road and the ocean is excellent for birds, as are the rice paddies to the north of the road immediately west of Ohara village.

Back in Ohara a good place to see Chinese Bulbul and Dusky Thrush (subspecies *naumanni*) is in the vicinity of the school. Then follow the road up the west side of the Nakama River. This is the largest mangrove swamp on the island and is a place to look for Malay Night Heron. Oriental Ibis also has occurred here. Return to the main road (there is only one on Iriomote), cross the bridge over the Nakama River, and take the road to the left parallel to the east side of the river. Investigate these fields before going farther around the island.

As you continue, you can birdwatch from the road. You should easily see Crested Serpent-Eagle and Purple Heron. Stop when you cross all rivers and swampy places and check them carefully. If you have a 1:25,000 map, you will be able to find all the trails and small roads that will take you off the main one.

Be sure to notice when you get to the wide rivermouth just before Funaura. This is an excellent area for shorebirds. On the other side of the northernmost tip of the island where you cross the Urauchi River, there is an area which also should be examined carefully. If you want to take the boat trip up the Urauchi River, turn to the left on the small road on the east side of the river. I saw nothing but Crested Serpent-Eagles when I went, but it is a pleasant enough trip if you have plenty of time.

On the far side of this lagoon there is a path leading to the right (toward the ocean) with trees on one side and mangroves on the other. You can walk for some distance along here. This is where the Bittern winters.

From here, the next road leading off to the right from the main road will take you into Hoshitate village, a delightful place. This is where you should be able to find the Malay Night Heron. It wanders around the village. When you drive off the main road, you will soon come to a gasoline station on your right. Park across from it and take the path beside it (on the left) and continue on behind the gasoline station until you reach the paddy fields behind the village.

Malay Night Heron and Banded Crake could be anywhere in here around the houses and in the vegetation. At dawn and at dusk the Malay Night Heron comes out around the edges of this paddy field. If you want to be sure to see it, the time of day is important. I have been in this village several times when I had no control over when we came or how we looked for this bird. We saw nothing. But a friend reported to me that he saw lots of them at sunrise and sunset. The one time I was here about sunset, the heron was standing on an oil can in front of the gasoline station.

The paddy fields are good for other birds too. And you should walk up the hill behind them (to the right) to the shrine. You will be wise to walk all over this village, especially along the shore just to the north. In the vegetation to your right is another good place to look for the Banded Crake. This bird is extremely difficult to find, so look carefully.

Hoshitate village is made up almost entirely of houses of the traditional style. It is an ideal place to study the architecture and observe life much as it has always been. Some wonderful weaving is done here, but it isn't for tourists to see. You will have a chance, however, of seeing women working outdoors with their dyes.

Just over the next bridge from Hoshitate is Sonai, where there are at least two places to stay. There is also good habitat for White-breasted Waterhen across the road. This is the most convenient place to stay for birding. It enables you to be at Hoshitate village at the proper hours, and it is near other good habitat.

About 1.5 km. south of Sonai as you continue on the main road, you will be able to turn off the road to the left and drive between some paddy fields. This is an excellent area. In summer you will have a good chance of seeing Ruddy Kingfisher near the road. The road ends just beyond here at Shirohama port. You must retrace your route to get back to the ferry.

Time:
If you take the early boat to Iriomote, spend the night at Sonai, and return on the boat late the following afternoon, it should be enough time. That gives you two chances to find the Malay Night Heron. This is where you should make sure you find it if it is important to you. For a leisurely trip, another day would not be too much.

Sonai Area

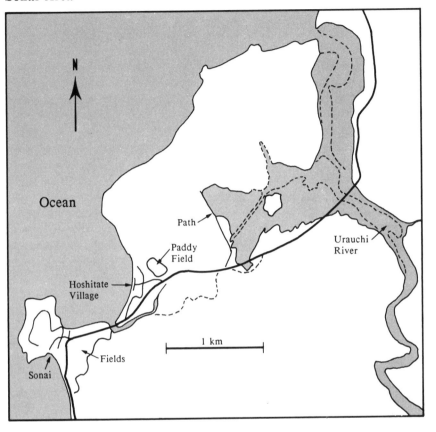

You should allow more time for birding on Ishigaki because there is more to see and more territory to cover. It certainly requires two full days. A third day or at least the better part of it would be good. If you go in summer, you can cut down some on the time for both islands.

Food:
There are restaurants in Ishigaki town and one on Hwy. 208 shortly before it joins Hwy. 79 north of Nagura Lagoon. A packed lunch will allow more birding time.

On Iriomote it is almost imperative to take a packed lunch from your hotel or *minshuku*. There are few restaurants, even fewer open in the winter, and they are difficult to recognize. Just across the bridge over the Nakama River from Ohara Port is a small restaurant called Yasumiya. This is the one good place I know of to get lunch. Order *tofu champu*, the local specialty. It is a mixture of *tofu* and vegetables. You are sure to like it.

Accommodations:
The cheaper accommodations on these islands (I've sampled five) tend to be a bit grimmer than similar places farther north. Probably the climate is to blame. Usually they are not air-conditioned, there is mildew about, insects are common, and, for some reason which I don't understand, most do not provide a sheet for the *futon*. Bring mosquito coils, bug spray if you can afford the space in your luggage, and rubber thong sandals for emergencies.

Ishigaki has several modern hotels which I have seen only from the outside. More are being built, so ask for the latest information if this is what you want. Distances are not significant, so with a car, you need not choose your accommodation on the basis of location. Hotel Sun Coast, near the airport, looks like a good hotel. The telephone number is 09808-2-6171.

In Ishigaki town I have stayed at a *minshuku* on the street behind the side of the port. I definitely do not recommend it. I also stayed at Ryokan Tairyokan (09808-2-7810). This had a Western-style bed, toilet, and shower in each room. It has room for only eight people. Each room has an air conditioner which will operate for ¥100/hour. It takes enough coins for only four hours at a time, but you will wake up when it goes off. Tairyokan costs ¥3,000 per person with breakfast only. It is in the town, and many restaurants are nearby.

Minshuku Toyokawa-so (09808-2-1739), affiliated with the WBSJ, is north of Nagura Lagoon up on a small hill overlooking the bay. The road from the highway leading up to the *minshuku* passes some good birding habitat. The owner pointed out a Japanese Lesser Sparrow Hawk nest. Around some ponds on one side were some Black Paradise Flycatchers. The owner also showed us a Scops Owl nearby. This *minshuku* is not air-conditioned, so you will need mosquito coils and bug spray. The people were friendly, and they have an *ofuro*.

Another associated with the WBSJ is Minshuku Ishigakijima
(09808-2-6066). The price is ¥4,000.

On Iriomote in Sonai village there is Minshuku Hoshizunaso
(098096-2250) and Hotel Iriomote Island (09808-5-6225). The
minshuku is acceptable; the hotel looks better from the outside.
There are others on that end of the island. There are two
minshuku associated with the WBSJ on the west side of Iriomote.
They are Minshuku Kiyomi-so (09808-5-6251) and Minshiku
Sumiyoshi-so (09808-5-6439). Both charge ¥3,500 per person with
two meals.

Maps and Information:
Japan Guide Map Co. Ltd., Handy Map of Okinawa

National Maps: 1:50,000 Ishigaki 石垣島

1:25,000 Iriomote Ohara 西表大原

Mihara 美原

Funaura 船浦

Useful Kanji:
Ishigaki	石垣島
Miyara River	宮良川
Bannadake	バンナ岳
Nagura	名蔵
Ohara	大原
Nakama River	仲間川
Yasumiya	やすみや
Funaura	船浦
Urauchi River	浦内川
Hoshitate	干立（星立）
Sonai	祖納

APPENDIX I: REFERENCES AND RESOURCES

The Japan National Travel Organization (JNTO) provides excellent material free of charge. You should be able to have the publications listed below sent to you before you leave for Japan. Ask for any other specific items you need which are mentioned under the site guides. If you can't get them by mail, you can pick them up along with other helpful information at the Tourist Information Center (TIC) in Tokyo.

> The Tourist's Handbook
> Condensed Railway Timetable
> Your Guide to Japan
> Maps:
> > Tourist Map of Japan
> > Tourist Map of Tokyo
> > Map of Tokyo & Vicinity
> > Osaka and Vicinity
> > Tourist Map of Kyoto-Nara
> Hotels in Japan
> Japan Ryokan Guide
> Reasonable Accommodations in Japan

You can write to the JNTO at the following addresses:

> Japan National Travel Organization
> 10-1, Yurakucho 2-chome
> Chiyoda-ku
> Tokyo 100

> Rockefeller Plaza
> 630 Fifth Ave.
> New York, N.Y.   10111

> 167 Regent Street
> London W1

In addition, there are also offices in Canada, Australia, Hong Kong, Thailand, France, Switzerland, Germany, Mexico, Brazil, and in five other cities in the United States.

In Tokyo, visit the

> Tourist Information Center
> 6-6, Yurakucho 1-chome
> Tokyo
> Tel. 03-502-1461

The location is clearly marked on the Tourist Map of Tokyo.

To purchase English-language books in Tokyo, try the bookshops in the major hotels (especially the Imperial and the Okura) or

> Maruzen Co., Ltd.
> 3-10, Nihonbashi 2-chome
> Chuo-ku
> Tokyo 103

> Jena Co., Ltd.
> 6-1, Ginza 5-chome
> Chuo-ku
> Tokyo 104

> Kinokunia
> 3-17-7, Shinjuku
> Shinjuku-ku
> Tokyo 160

Ordering books and maps from Tokyo will present a problem. It will require time and patience, and you may or may not succeed. Japanese bookstores are not accustomed to filling mail orders overseas and some don't appear particularly interested in offering this service. If you don't get an immediate response, try another store. Many Japanese businesses ignore letters written in English even when they have staff members who can deal with them.

In any case, you must first write to find out if they will send what you want, the price, and the shipping cost. Then you must send full payment in advance in yen before your order will be sent. Depending on where you live, you may be able to send a payment in foreign currency at a much lower cost through your post office than through your bank.

The only maps you should attempt to buy before you arrive in Japan are the four volumes of Champion Maps published by the Buyodo Company. Maruzen does not sell these maps and will not get them, but it would be worth trying to order any books you need from Maruzen since they have a large stock of English-language books on Japan. Sources for the Champion Maps are

Taiseido Book Center
1-22-4, Jinnan
Shibuya-ku
Tokyo 150
Attn: Map Department

Books Sanseido
1-1, Jinbo-cho
Kanda
Chiyoda-ku
Tokyo 101

Kinokunia in Shinjuku sells these maps, but they say they have no system for filling mail orders. They recommend placing orders with their overseas branches in Los Angeles, San Francisco, or New York.

The Hokkaido Map and Colour Guide, mentioned in the site guides, is entirely in Japanese, but it is useful for giving an overall view of Hokkaido. If you want to purchase it, you will need to explain that it is the Union Road Map #1, Hokkaido. "Hokkaido" and "Map & Colour Guide" are written in English on the cover, but the actual title is Union Road Map #1, Hokkaido.

In Japanese this is ユニオンロードマップ
(Union Rodo Mappu)

If you run into difficulty making people understand what you want when you are trying to purchase any of the national maps referred to, show them these characters:

(chikeizu) 地形図   (chiseizu) 地勢図

Both words mean topographical map.

Books which will be helpful to have before you go to Japan include

A *Field Guide to the Birds of Japan*, published by the Wild Bird Society of Japan and Kodansha International Ltd., 1982.

Richie, Donald. *A Taste of Japan.* Tokyo: Kodansha International Ltd., 1985.

Marcus, Russell and Plimpton, Jack. *The Guide to Japanese Food and Restaurants.* Tokyo: Shufunotomo Co., Ltd., 1984.

Nagasawa, Kimiko and Condon, Camy. *Eating Cheap in Japan.* Tokyo: Shufunotomo Co., Ltd.

Kodansha International publications are distributed in the United States, the United Kingdom, and Australia by Harper & Row. If you fail to get the books published by Shufunotomo Co. from a bookstore, try writing the publisher at

Shufunotomo Co., Ltd.
6, Kanda Surugadai 1-chome
Chiyoda-ku
Tokyo 101

Other books which will be helpful but are not necessary to have in advance include

Mizutani, Osamu and Mizutani, Nobuko. *Travelers' Japanese.* Tokyo: The Japan Times, Ltd. (This is in the bookstores or it can be ordered from The Japan Times, Ltd., 5-4, Shibaura 4-chome, Minato-ku, Tokyo 108).

De Mente, Boye. *Reading Your Way Around Japan.* Tokyo: Lotus Press Ltd., 1981. (Distributed in the United States by Phoenix Books, 6505 N. 43rd Place, Paradise Valley, Arizona 85253).

APPENDIX II: ESSENTIAL KANJI

north 北
south 南
east 東
west 西

exit 出口
entrance 入口

town 町
city 市

airport 空港
train station 駅
express (train) 急行
Limited Express 特急

stop 止まれ
parking lot 駐車場
bypass バイパス

prohibited 禁

koban (police box) 交番

post office 郵便局
symbol for post office 〒

open for business 営業中

hotel	ホテル
ryokan	旅館
minshuku	民宿
toilet	御手洗 or 化粧室
men	男 or 男子 or 紳士
women	女 女子 婦人
ofuro (bath)	風呂

(for drinks in vending machines)

    hot あたたかい 熱 or 温

    cold つめたい 冷

    with milk and sugar   ミルク　さとう入り

    without milk and sugar ブラック

APPENDIX III: TARGET BIRDS

Selecting target birds for Japan is highly subjective. It will be wise to go through the field guide with great care and prepare your own list of target birds. This list contains endemics and endemic breeders as well as some which may be easier to see in Japan than in the other places where they occur. Eastern Siberia is beyond the reach of most birders. Limitations on travel in China will make finding particular birds there sometimes difficult. Some birds which occur outside of Japan only in these areas or in some cases in Korea are included, but no fast rule was used to determine the birds on this list. Many of the birds in Japan are found outside Japan only in Siberia, China, Korea, Taiwan, and the Philippines. It is best to decide for yourself which ones should be given top priority for your trip to Japan.

Short-tailed Albatross
Matsudaira's Storm Petrel
Temminck's Cormorant
Japanese Night Heron
Steller's Sea-Eagle
Copper Pheasant
Japanese Crane
Hooded Crane
White-naped Crane
Okinawa Rail
Amami Woodcock
Latham's Snipe
Slaty-backed Gull
Black-tailed Gull
Saunders's Gull
Spectacled Guillemot
Japanese Murrelet
Japanese Wood Pigeon
Blakiston's Fish-Owl
Japanese Green Woodpecker
Pryer's Woodpecker
Japanese Wagtail
Japanese Waxwing
Japanese Accentor
Japanese Robin
Ryukyu Robin
Gray Thrush

Brown Thrush
Izu Islands Thrush
Japanese Marsh Warbler
Ijima's Willow Warbler
Bonin Islands Honeyeater
Japanese Reed Bunting
Japanese Yellow Bunting
Gray Bunting
Japanese Grosbeak
Red-cheeked Myna
Lidth's Jay

In addition, the birds below qualify for this list. They are not included in the field guide as distinct species, but they are considered as such by other authorities.

Green Pheasant	*Phasianus versicolor*
Ryukyu Scops Owl	*Otus elegans*
Black-backed Wagtail	*Moticilla lugens*
Ryukyu Minivet	*Pericrocotus tegimae*

The quail in Japan, shown in the field guide as *Coturnix coturnix*, Common Quail, is, according to many authorities, *Coturnix japonica*, Japanese Quail. The field guide shows *Charadrius asiaticus*, Caspian Plover. Other authorities believe the bird which occurs in Japan is *Charadrius veredus*, Oriental Plover.

INDEX OF BIRDS